The Actor's Survival Guide

The Actor's Survival Guide

HOW TO MAKE YOUR WAY
IN HOLLYWOOD

Jon S. Robbins

continuum

NEW YORK • LONDON

2008

The Continuum International Publishing Group Inc
80 Maiden Lane, New York, NY 10038

The Continuum International Publishing Group Ltd
The Tower Building, 11 York Road, London SE1 7NX

www.continuumbooks.com

Printed in the United States of America

Library of Congress Cataloging-in-Publication Data

Robbins, Jon S.
    The Actor's survival guide : how to make your way in Hollywood / by Jon S. Robbins.
        p. cm.
    Includes bibliographical references and index.
    ISBN–13: 978–0–8264–2834–9 (pbk. : alk. paper)
    ISBN–10: 0–8264–2834–7 (pbk. : alk. paper)
    1. Motion picture acting—Vocational guidance—California—Los Angeles. I. Title.

PN1995.9.P75R62 2007
791.4302'8'2379494—dc22

2007034393

To Donald
Thank you for taking me on this journey

Contents

Acknowledgments

I would like to thank Gordon Thomson, Jacque Lynn Colton, Sajen Corona, and Tang Nyugen for their time and cooperation; Ronald and Donald Welch for their support and advice; Seattle SAG Executive Director Dena Beatty for her consultation; Professor Andrew Buchman of The Evergreen State College for his editing expertise; and the many, many working actors who contributed advice and information to this effort.

Preface

LIKE MOST EDUCATORS, I have heard that inglorious taunt, "Those who can, do. Those who can't, teach." I have been offended by its implication that college professors, verily all teachers, teach not out of a commitment to education but out of financial necessity. Perhaps overly sensitive to this allegation or perhaps just practicing good pedagogy, I often salted my college acting classes with personal anecdotes of my years as a professional actor, now some twenty years ago. In doing so I emphasized the professional discipline of auditions and performance, not just as good ethics but also as a practical strategy for success. Not surprisingly, each year those anecdotes grew staler and less resonant.

In one spring quarter's advanced acting class, a rather direct student challenged my sage advice by posing a question: "If you haven't worked professionally in twenty years, how do we know you know what you're talking about?" I responded characteristically, puffed up in a professorial pique, but then paused as a tiny voice in my head conceded, "Point taken!" That student was right. I lacked credibility. The entertainment industry had undoubtedly changed in the previous twenty years, and the probability existed that I didn't know what I was talking about but only thought I did—a bad habit among college professors. I could see only one solution—a sabbatical from academia and a return to the life of a professional actor. Just like any other wannabe professional actor, newly graduated and minted, I would move to Hollywood, follow my learned, academic, professorial advice, and see just how far it got me.

And so I did. With not much more than a chest of clothes (okay, maybe two), a computer, and an inflatable bed, I moved to Hollywood and resurrected my long dormant career. I held one distinct advantage in having maintained my membership in the Screen Actors Guild, whose lapse would have been an obstacle that could have taken years to overcome. I found a talent agent with relative ease and began submitting for studio and network projects almost immediately. During the course of that year, I auditioned for sixty projects and booked twenty-four, consisting of four commercials (one national), three episodics, one national reality program, three music videos, four films, four plays, and two print jobs. Financially, I only broke even for the year, a better than average year for most SAG members. Sadly, less than 1 percent of SAG members make a yearly living wage, and the vast majority of those who call themselves actors in Los Angeles are nonunion. Building a career takes many years of systematic marketing strategies and more than a few obstacles to overcome.

Time had indeed moved beyond a 1970s Hollywood world of showcases, answering services, and black and white headshots. Casting workshops, cell phones, and digital marketing services have taken their place, requiring vastly different skill sets in marketing, business, and technology. And the clichéd theatrical talent agent from the 1900s who knocks on every casting director's door has long been replaced by a twenty-first century, technologically connected jobber who barters an actor's digital wares in cyberspace.

The playing field has changed as well. Just as live theater gave way to film and film gave way to television, television must now give way to a host of digital platforms such as iPods and cell phones. Music videos, podcasts, reality programming, and cable networks such as MTV, the Fox network, and HBO have permanently transformed the industry, creating new paradigms that fall far outside of commercial network dominion and union oversight. Surprisingly, though, the film industry has changed little in the past twenty years other than in technology. But the studios have evolved into a vastly different landscape of computerized technology and global marketing by parental megacorporations with global resources at their disposal. An actor's success depends upon his or her ability to navigate this evolving marketplace. Much had changed, and a few surprises awaited me.

Surprise number 1. Actors have much more control over their careers than in the past. Twenty years ago an actor had little access to casting breakdowns unless this was shared by one's talent agent. The trade papers published only a few casting notices, mostly nonunion and sometimes of questionable validity. Actors relied solely upon talent agents for their submissions and rarely had much input. Today a variety of legitimate electronic casting services offer actors Internet access to casting breakdowns that likewise assist their talent agents in making submissions.

Surprise number 2. The actors unions have grown considerably weaker over the past twenty years. As a longtime union member, I remember several costly and contentious strikes that culminated in a strongly united union of professional artists and technicians who negotiated fair compensation and work conditions for the thousands of working professionals in the film and television industry. The unions had respect and strength.

Today unions have lost that edge, and, while they remain a primary factor in scripted projects, nontraditional programming such as reality shows and music videos have served to splinter the unions' dominance. More disquieting, nonunion projects now represent an increasing percentage of the professional work in Hollywood. Some genres, such as reality programming and music videos, nearly always film as nonunion projects unless they involve a high-profile musician or actor. Regional commercials primarily film as nonunion projects, and cable networks have no contractual prohibition against purchasing nonunion projects for their prime-time programming. Actors are on their own in these situations. As a result, union actors face the conundrum of turning down nonunion jobs and rarely working, or accepting them, which risks union sanctions and, in effect, contributes to the problem. To their credit, the unions still fight the good fight, and new leadership has changed their direction.

Surprise number 3. Compensation has not kept up with inflation. Yes, superstars can make over $20 million for a film or negotiate multimillion-dollar television contracts, but they represent the top 1 percent of all professional actors. Most actors, even those with years of credits and recognizable names, often work for scale, which was $759.00 per day as of July 1, 2007—not bad, if one works every day. But more often than not, bookings come sporadically—a two- or three-day shoot once in a while, then maybe nothing for months, sometimes years. In the meantime an actor needs money for pictures, postage, workshops, and a dozen other business costs. Hollywood has now truly become a global marketplace among all professional fields within the entertainment industry, and actors especially face a fiercely competitive and crowded talent pool.

Surprise number 4. No one should be surprised to learn that a class system exists in Hollywood. We often hear of the "A list" actors, bankable actors whose name alone ensures the financial success of a project, and the "B list" actors, whose faces we may recognize but whose names we probably do not. But I learned that the middle class of the acting community had grown extensively, making it even more difficult for an actor of the proletariat to move up the ladder.

Why is this? Now with over fifty years of television programming, thousands of actors have experienced their day in the sun. The sheer volume of shows having come and gone in these years has created a subculture of "C list" celebrities, actors who were once regulars, recurring characters, or cohosts on a past television show and as such have recognizable names in the industry, if not to the public. Next, the siblings of Hollywood celebrities form the "D list." These progeny of Hollywood royalty have the magical power to move to the head of the line and finesse access to casting offices, often at the expense of the rest of us "E list" actors.

Surprise number 5. Theatre is alive and well in Los Angeles, a fact that surprised me since my past involvement with live theatre in L.A. had reflected a town more single-mindedly focused on film and television than the stage. I experienced actors with no work discipline or ethics, directors with no stage savvy, and producers only concerned with money and not art. And why should this have surprised me? People came to Hollywood for the film and television industry, not the stage. Hollywood drew a wide spectrum of wannabes, from conservatory-trained stage actors to last year's high school prom queens and football heroes with little theatre experience, all with one concern in common—the film and television industry. For most of those actors, the stage served only to showcase for talent agents, casting directors, and producers. Few Equity houses existed, and professional theatre consisted mostly of road shows cast in New York and a few Equity Waiver theatres doting the urban matrix of Greater Los Angeles.

But times have changed. Serious theatre abounds, with many resident companies and Equity houses having grown out of the artistic successes of those fledgling Equity Waiver theatres. And the many writers' and actors' workshops have given rise to a rather serious center of American theatre. Occasionally an extraordinary production emerges as Broadway bound. All in all, the theatre scene in Los Angeles still yields a minefield of unfulfilled dreams mixed with good intentions, but it can also be exciting and full of artistic potential if one knows where to look and when to get involved and, more importantly, when not to.

Surprise number 6. Years ago, all actors needed to work in Hollywood was a black and white photo and a resume. Eventually, actors needed a "reel," a collection of taped or filmed excerpts from their work. But today, actors need sophisticated marketing tools such as personal websites and DVDs of their clips.

During my sabbatical year, as a struggling actor I learned that success in today's marketplace requires considerable marketing skills and technological savvy. For the actor, technology has provided more control over one's career and marketing decisions. But college acting programs don't teach marketing skills, any more than medical programs teach doctors the business skills needed to set up a private practice or a medical partnership. Many college-trained actors spend years training for the moment they become a player in the industry, only to fail, unprepared for the reality of the business. Actors in Hollywood must consider themselves a commodity, no different from the newest electronic gadget or household convenience, and they must approach the launching of a career no differently from starting any other small business. A business plan is a necessity. Start-up costs, an operational base, a technologically efficient workstation, funding sources, a marketing plan—all these represent major decisions that take planning and advice. This book attempts to prepare the serious film and television actor for the *business* of Hollywood that few college programs teach and that would take Hollywood newcomers years to learn and master on their own.

The chapters have been organized sequentially, from planning, to establishing a base of operations, to tackling career obstacles. Much of the research I conducted on the Internet, using Web sites available to anyone. Each chapter begins with an "Actor's Forum," providing interview excerpts from four different professional working actors in Hollywood of different ages, genders, ethnicities, and perspectives.

Tang Nyugen—A young, Asian actor, trained in martial arts, recently seen as a recurring character on *American Dreams* and as a guest actor on *The West Wing, The Shield, Monk,* and *CSI—Las Vegas.*

Jacque Lynn Colton—A veteran character actor of hundreds of commercials. Her film credits include *Gremlins 2, Mr. Mom,* and *Heartbreak Hotel,* as well as television appearances on *Hart to Hart, Three's Company,* and *Charles in Charge.*

Gordon Thomson—A veteran dramatic television star most famous for his role as Adam Carrington on Aaron Spelling's *Dynasty.* Television audiences may also remember him from appearances on *Passions, The Young and the Restless,* and countless other soap operas. He was most recently seen in the film *Little Miss Sunshine.*

Sajen Corona—A young, Latin comedic actor and writer, most recently seen in the film *Gettin' It* and as the subject of a documentary, *Chasing the Dream,* produced and directed by A. J. Shepard.

I have also compiled some useful sources of information for each chapter, including Web links, telephone numbers, and street locations, and have placed them in a "Resource Box" at the head of each chapter. I also share personal anecdotes, which are in boxes labeled, "In the Box." This phrase refers to the actual moment in which actors place their professional integrity on the line, whether in an audition or performance. Those failures and successes become true learning moments for an actor.

This book's goal is to provide advice to beginning actors from the perspective of those who actually act for a living, not those who just talk about it. Throughout I have tried to emphasize the business decisions necessary to sustain oneself for the three to five years or longer needed to become established in Hollywood. Newcomers will still find Hollywood a minefield within a maze. But I have tried to provide a guide, a road map through the pitfalls and wrong turns that derail too many promising careers and frustrate even the most dedicated actors. I point out the scams and frauds that con artists use to prey upon the glitter of fame and fortune in an artist's eyes with no other intention than to separate them from their money. I debunk some myths, issue a few warnings about strategies to avoid, and try to point toward more sustainable, low-cost alternatives for actors with slim budgets.

This book, though, was not written to supplant or replace the training, discipline, and experience students acquire in formal acting programs, in college or other places. This book will not teach the reader how to act and will certainly not guarantee success. No book can substitute for the hard work, solid training, and dedication to technique and craft one needs to learn before others will take one's career seriously. The bios of most successful serious film and television actors reveal college degrees, comprehensive stage training, and resumes that reflect hard work and dues paying to the acting craft.

In retrospect, my return to the acting profession not only revitalized my commitment to education but also made me a much better teacher. I now have a more realistic understanding of the obstacles students will encounter if they, too, follow their own Hollywood dreams. As my sabbatical year drew to a close and I prepared for my imminent return to academia, part of me resisted, struggling once again to hold on to that artistic dream that all actors must possess. For one fleeting moment it would not have taken much to convince me to give up my academic career and permanently return to that carnival ride. But in the end, while I did have days of applause and success, I had many more discouraging days, reminding me once again that the entertainment industry is, after all, just a business. The work I do in academia offers me vastly greater rewards. My return to academia revealed to me the startling truth that I had chosen educational involvement over show business success not because I couldn't "do," but because I had made a commitment to education. Perhaps all college professors should be required to periodically leave the cocoon of academia and experience the business side of their chosen profession, if only for a year, to learn or update skills and perhaps rediscover why they became educators in the first place. It is certainly comforting when confronted with the "Those who can't do" insult, to know that I can!

Actors Forum

When I first moved to Los Angeles, I lived in Orange County with my uncle. It was a way of getting myself out here and to get my basics estab-lished, have a car, have some money, a flexible job. I didn't have any auditions because LA was a good hour drive away, so I didn't pursue it much. But then I moved up to Burbank about a year later.

Tang Nguyen

When I was in college, I read books about how to succeed in New York. They told you to wear white gloves and high-heeled shoes. It was kind of ridiculous. In New York I was totally lost. I didn't have a proper picture and resume. I came out to LA as the fifth lead in the national company of a Broadway show with a list of people to call who worked in the business. I had a couple of national commercials running and I was able to get an agent immediately. If you have anybody who will stake you in LA, so you don't have to degrade yourself and don't have to kill yourself to keep a roof over your head, then count yourself lucky, and if you're saving up money to do it, then give yourself a big nest egg so that you don't have to scrounge around to live.

Jacque Lynn Colton

I lived and worked in Canada until 1980. The restrictions placed on Canadians as actors in the States are ferocious. I was offered the part of Dorian Gray in a two-hour film directed by Glen Jordan. We met, I read, and I was forced to say no because I didn't have a green card or an H-1 visa. Be as familiar with the industry as much as you can. Use the Web. It's a fabulous tool. Log on to as many informational sites as you can—casting sites, agent sites, manager sites. Take courses if you can find one. Protect yourself. You need armor of every sort—emotional, spiritual, and financial. Make friends or come with somebody. Have a plan when you get here.

Gordon Thomson

I was born and raised in Culver City, the movie capital of the world. I've lived here all my life. I always knew as a child this was something I wanted to do, but my dad steered me away from it during high school and unfortunately I chased his dream, which was basically to start a business, do real estate, or sell cars. I mean, I was selling cars before I started in this business. I was doing well, making $7,000 a month, which isn't bad for a guy without a college degree. But I remember after 9/11, I decided that I would chase my dream, not his.

Sajen Corona

1

Moving to Los Angeles
"Simple Is as Simple Does"

I learned this, at least, by my experiment; that if one advances confidently in the direction of his dreams, and endeavors to live the life which he has imagined, he will meet with a success unexpected in common hours.

Henry David Thoreau, *Walden*

Los Angeles Resource Websites

From the official Web site for the Housing Department of the City of Los Angeles
"Rent News of Interest to Landlords and Tenants in 2006"
http://www.lacity.org/lahd/rentnews2006.pdf

Los Angeles map on Windows Live Local
http://local.live.com/

Los Angeles City Beat
http://www.lacitybeat.com/

@ LA—The Southern California Directory and Search Engine for Greater Los Angeles, Orange County, and the Inland Empire
http://www.at-la.com/

So you've decided to move to Los Angeles. You've trained for it and worked for it with classes in acting, movement, improvisation, and stage combat. You're ready. You have the chops. No one can talk you out of it and no one should; otherwise, you risk becoming what Thoreau identified as "men who lead lives of quiet desperation." And if you truly have the fire in your belly, then nothing will change your mind. But you do need to know that you will be one of thousands of wannabe professional actors who each year move to Los Angeles to follow that dream, and nine out of ten of them give up within the first year.

Dreamers fail for many reasons. Lack of planning ranks high among them. Los Angeles has grown to a megalopolis of over 11 million people, stretched over 100 square miles of suburban jungle. Dorothy Parker called it "seventy-two suburbs in search of a city." Raymond Chandler called it "a big, hard-boiled city with no more personality than a paper cup." You will probably come up with your own epithet, but before you can call it "home," you will need to do some serious planning, which can begin with these dos and don'ts.

WHAT SHOULD I DO BEFORE I MOVE?

Do Some Research

Follow the informational highway while preparing for your journey. Learn as much about the city as possible on the Internet. The City of Los Angeles and the many independent municipalities that exist within the greater Los Angeles area all maintain Web sites that will provide renter's rights information. The Los Angeles City Department of Transportation provides online virtual maps that display traffic flow on the city's infrastructure: major boulevards and freeway systems organized by neighborhoods and topography. The County Transportation Authority's Web site gives comprehensive mass transit maps and information. Other Web sites can provide cultural and business information for just about any neighborhood in Los Angeles.

Prepare Two Contrasting Monologues

An actor should have two monologues prepared at all times, even though they are not requested often. While professional theatre directors still initially screen actors through prepared monologues, it is highly unlikely that anyone in film and television casting will ever ask to see your monologue. But talent agents do ask to see a prepared scene before deciding whether or not to represent an actor, and it is for them that an actor will commit two scenes to memorization. One should be comic and the other dramatic. They don't necessarily need to be from stage scripts. As this is the film and television industry, a cutting from a film or television script is permissible. Film scripts are easily downloaded online. Work on these scenes with a coach until they are consistent, honest, and representational of your talent.

In the Box

Years ago my weekly jogging schedule down a narrow Hollywood Hills street often coincided with the jogging schedule of television star Ed Asner of *The Mary Tyler Moore Show* fame. I once gathered the nerve to ask the Emmy-winning actor why he thought he had finally succeeded after so many years of trying. Between gasps of air he told me that the entertainment business was nothing more than a merry-go-round. "Everybody eventually gets their chance at the gold ring," he explained. "The secret is to stay on the merry-go-round long enough to get your shot at it!"

Formulate a Business Plan

Business insiders caution that professional actors take an average of three to five years to establish themselves in Hollywood. One tempts failure if one is not able to sustain oneself while struggling to establish a career. Like any small business, you need a business plan, a strategy for establishing a physical workstation, a funding stream, and access for your product to the market. Like any start-up company, take time and carefully consider your resources. This planning may mean the difference between success and failure! Your business plan should include the following:

A funding stream. A consistent and adequate source of income from a flexible employment situation represents the ideal. One should not be faced with choosing between an audition or a job, unless it really is a lousy job! Develop as many marketable skills as possible: clerical, technological, servile, anything that you can rely upon for a steady source of income.

Location. Find a temporary place to land when you arrive, such as a relative or friend's home, or a cheap hotel room. Once you have established a funding stream, then find a suitable and affordable location to establish a home/office. Only then will you know how much you can afford to pay. Are you single or do you have a family? Rent for a one-bedroom apartment ranges from $1,000 to $2,000 a month, with two-bedrooms easily twice that amount (*Los Angeles Apartments & Rentals Rent Survey, 2007*). Housing will be your biggest expense but should not cost more than a third of your monthly family income.

Accessibility. Mastering the physical obstacles of transportation over approximately 100 square miles of urban landscape remains the most difficult challenge in Los Angeles. Custom built for the automobile, the city now counts the automobile as its nemesis. But savvy drivers know precisely where and when to travel to avoid gridlock. Others rely upon the piecemeal puzzle of busses, subways, and light rail that has defaulted as Los Angeles's public transportation system.

Save Lots of Money

Moving to Los Angeles will take considerable financial resources. So carefully count your shekels before determining a plan of action. Los Angeles sucks the life out of a nest egg and can be either affordable or overwhelming in direct proportion to how complicated one makes it. One sagacious maxim to follow: The more one brings, the more expensive it is to live. The fewer needs one has, the more likely it is that one will live comfortably without compromising career goals. Stated Thoreau, "Our life is frittered away by detail. . . . Simplicity, simplicity, simplicity!"

Develop an Employable Skill

If you have already lived the life of a starving artist in college, then you are eminently qualified for the actor's lifestyle in Los Angeles, having most likely learned at least one menial service profession in your life, such as server, chef, retail clerk, bartender, or office assistant. As such, you will easily find employment, as this city verily crawls with the nouveau riche, who need such services. Those jobs, always in demand, may not pay as well as professional positions, but they do provide one very important requirement—flexibility.

Whatever work you pursue to accommodate your artistic vent, it must provide adjustable hours and adaptable responsibilities, something that professional and managerial positions rarely do. So if you have thus far lived a life of leisure and privilege, I strongly suggest that you gain some working class skills quickly, unless you have the resources to finance that lifestyle indefinitely. Once established, you will find more lucrative alternatives through networking or entrepreneurship, but make certain that you have at least one easily marketable skill before moving to Los Angeles.

Contact Relatives and Friends in Los Angeles

Securing a landing pad in Los Angeles helps immensely. It takes time to acclimate to the city, find employment, and establish a career, as does finding a suitable living space. Motels in Los Angeles are pricey. Hostels less so. Apartments may require three months' rent in advance, equal to several thousand dollars. Craigslist (http://losangeles.craigslist.org/) has sublet listings, as many residents are bicoastal, bouncing between two locations and in need of someone to sublet a space for the limited time they will be gone, which is perfect for someone moving fresh to Los Angeles. If someone does offer temporary housing, think seriously about taking the offer. This can provide some breathing room while you become acclimated to the city and secure employment. But remember that temporary housing means just that—temporary!

So gather your resources while you can. If you have friends or relatives already living in the Los Angeles area, let them know your plans to move there. Some will be helpful, others may not be. But always let them make the offer of assistance first. Otherwise, good intentions can turn into a lost friendship or a distant relative. Still, moving, especially on limited resources, takes planning, and one will find any help much appreciated, especially meals, lodging, advice, and directions.

Finish Your Education

A BFA or an MFA degree in acting won't help in finding professional work in Los Angeles. Producers and casting directors couldn't care less. But the training provides preparation and discipline for a professional life. The more training and experience obtained, the more versatile—and thus, the more castable—the actor. So complete those course requirements, finish those lab hours, and write those papers. While you're at it, take those juggling lessons, learn how to fence, explore martial arts classes, or get up on a horse and go riding. Focus on developing marketable employment skills as well. Success will to some extent depend upon your skill inventory. There are still times when the actor who gets the part is the one who fits the costume.

Have Photos Taken

How many hopeful actors spend money on photos, move to Los Angeles, and find a talent agent or manager who makes them spend more money on new photos? Should you save money and wait? No. An actor needs photos to land a talent agent or manager. Have photos taken, but don't spend a lot of money on them. No matter how great a reputation the local photographer might have, Hollywood talent agents and managers have a keener sense of what works and what Los Angeles casting directors look for. An actor must be packaged and marketed much like any other product. Once an actor is established with an agency, his or her old photos will be replaced by something more industry minded.

In the Box

When I moved to Los Angeles from Pittsburgh, I always planned it as a permanent move regardless of my career outcome. But I could only bring what possessions my Chevy van could hold. I donated books to the local library and held a yard sale to liquidate furniture and other possessions. The rest sought refuge in my sister's basement until some future visit. Over the years as I returned to visit, each time I left with suitcases stuffed with books and memorabilia. Fifteen years later I received five mysterious boxes from my sister. They contained my HO gauge train set, some old books, and assorted high school memorabilia. It was a walk down memory lane, but it made me remember how broke I was when I first arrived in Los Angeles, how many times I had to move, and how thankful I was that I had brought so little with me.

WHAT SHOULDN'T I DO BEFORE I MOVE?

Don't Bring All Your Worldly Possessions

Once again, this can be complicated or simple. Wives, husbands, and children you can do nothing about. Pets, large pieces of furniture, and four years of college books you can. Now is the best time to clean house. Sell, store, or give away anything you don't need. Pets force hard decisions. Cats and small dogs acclimate to small spaces but will still limit housing options. Most landlords will consider a small pet but rarely a big dog. Try to find ways to simplify your life, and then, depending upon your accumulated possessions, plan on moving in stages.

Stop and ask yourself, as did Thoreau, what the necessities are of your life. Thoreau identified "food, shelter, clothing, and fuel." To that list I might add a dependable car, a fairly sophisticated computer, and an inflatable bed. Those items are all one really needs in Los Angeles. Everything else—furniture, electronics, and personal memorabilia—can follow once you are established.

Don't Burn Bridges

Leaving behind friends and family presents an enormous challenge. One never knows which seeds we sow today will reap an abundant harvest tomorrow. College cohorts, business colleagues, friends, and even family all serve to feed the destiny of the entertainment industry. Work begets work, and that small-town director or college classmate or business associate or next-door writing collaborator may someday succeed where you have failed, and drag you kicking and screaming with them to success. Always make a graceful exit from wherever your roots have been laid, but always allow for an imminent return. Plan for a back door, an escape hatch, a plan B, a safety net, just in case you find yourself singing, "Oh, why oh, why oh, did I leave Ohio?"

Actors Forum

My first impression was that physically Hollywood looked pretty dirty. But I did see this as a place of opportunity. At that point I didn't have an agent. I had a very low paying job. I had car payments and insurance payments. It was really tough the first couple of years. But until you have the basics down it's really hard to move forward.

Tang Nguyen

When I arrived in LA, I stayed with one of the girls from the chorus out in West LA. We had to drive in to the Music Center. I had lived in New York and hadn't driven for almost 11 years, and never on an LA freeway where the normal speed is 60 miles an hour. She said to me, "Here are the car keys." So I get in the car and go on the freeway. She gave me directions written on some notebook paper. I thought I was going to die! It was the worst initiation to drive on the freeway. But I made it. I called a friend I had done a television show with once. She said, "I can help you. If you want to look successful you should go as far west as you can. It looks like you're really successful if you're living in an apartment on the Westside. I wasn't raised that way, to impress people. I found an apartment Mid-Wilshire, which meant I could drive to the Music Center in a very short period of time.

Jacque Lynn Colton

I loathed Los Angeles. I still do. I don't like virtually unchanging seasons. I'm Canadian and I love the seasons changing. It's a healthy thing to experience as a human being. I like seeing flowers die and leaves die and fall, snow come and roots freeze and thaw. And they bloom again. I like having gardens in my life and, yes, there's greenery and there's gardens here, but there's too much goddamn sun and not enough variety. It's very hard to get around by car. You must have a car in Los Angeles. You must also have a Thomas Guide. That's essential. And you must have a lot of resilience.

Gordon Thomson

There's one thing about this city that people need to know. You can't consider San Bernardino as Los Angeles. You can't consider Riverside as Los Angeles, not Corona, not even Upland. When you say Los Angeles, you are saying area codes 818, 323, 301, and 213. That is Los Angeles. Yeah, maybe South Bay, but the epicenter is the Westside and Hollywood.

Sajen Corona

2
Living in Los Angeles

While popular culture might lead one to believe that Los Angeles consists only of the shiny office towers, . . . the blighted streets of South Los Angeles, the endless suburban tracts of the San Fernando Valley, and the gated estates of the Hollywood Hills and Bel-Air, its neighborhoods display a degree of diversity well befitting the second-largest city in the United States. Many Los Angeles neighborhoods . . . are fairly close-knit, culturally distinctive communities.
Wikipedia, "Districts and Neighborhoods of Los Angeles"

Community Web Sites

Wikipedia, "Los Angeles County"
http://en.wikipedia.org/wiki/Los_Angeles_County%2C_California

Beachwood Canyon Neighborhood Association
http://www.beachwoodcanyon.org/

West Los Angeles Crime Statistics
http://www.lapdonline.org/assets/pdf/wlaprof.pdf

Mt. Olympus News
http://www.topix.net/city/los-angeles-ca-mount-olympus

Los Angeles Street Map
http://www.aaccessmaps.com/show/map/lametro

Grass Roots Venice Neighborhood Council
http://www.grvnc.org/

The Venice Forum
http://www.veniceforum.org/

NoHo Arts District Community Page
http://www.nohoartsdistrict.com/community1/

Los Feliz Neighborhood Site
http://www.netpursuits.com/losfeliz/

Welcome to Los Angeles, all four thousand smog plagued miles of it! Served by five airports, three harbors, a web of freeways, and a mix of heavy and light rail systems, the world's seventeenth-largest economy provides the world with aerospace technology, manufacturing, telecommunications, tourist attractions, and entertainment, some of it unintentional. Annual rainfall averages 15.11 inches, but occasional years of two inches or less eventually give way to years of more than 30 inches, when hillsides move and freeways turn into concrete rivers. A balmy average temperature of 66 degrees can swell to 110 or fall to below freezing, all within a few days (*Los Angeles Almanac*, "Temperature Normals and Records"). The most populous U.S. county and second-largest U.S. city are also demographically the most diverse. The city is home to over 224 identifiable languages, city emergency services respond to "more than 150 languages," and the Los Angeles Unified School District recognizes approximately 90 (Los Angeles Fire Department, "LAFD News"). Los Angeles also hosts the largest populations of Armenians, Bulgarians, Ethiopians, Filipinos, Guatemalans, Salvadorans, Nicaraguans, Hungarians, Koreans, Mexicans, Pacific Islanders, Russians, and Thais in the country.

Greater Los Angeles can be many things to many people. Ten million residents share a semitropical climate, virtually endless sunshine, and a penchant for quirkiness. They also share torrential rains, wildfires, mudslides, and earthquakes. Yes, earthquakes happen, mostly little 3.2 shakers, Mother Nature's way of reminding that she's still in charge. After the Northridge Earthquake in 1994, long-time resident Bette Midler promptly packed up and moved to New York City. She could do that because she's Bette Midler. A struggling actor can't do so without starting over, so you had better make peace with the earth's occasional betrayals before settling into this geologically unsettled region.

Though somewhat confusing, the moniker of "Los Angeles" refers to the county, the city, and the 88 other municipalities that collectively constitute the mythos of this region, making for a patchwork of conflicting jurisdictions. Therefore, it is important to plan exactly where you want to live and work. West

Hollywood maintains strict rent control regulations. But living one block in another direction places one under LA city jurisdiction with almost no regulation. Taxi drivers licensed in the county can't pick up fares in the city, and vice versa. A permit to work in the county may not be valid in Beverly Hills. It will help to learn a little about both the county and the city that bear the name Los Angeles.

LOS ANGELES COUNTY

Home to almost ten million people, Los Angeles County has the distinction of being the most populous county in the United States—and the most chopped up. The county consists of many odd unincorporated sections, some of them badlands, others mountainous or of strategic importance for transportation right of ways.

Governed by an elected five-member Board of Supervisors, the county assumes responsibility for implementing many of the state's requirements in the areas of transportation (LA Metro), justice (Los Angeles Superior Court), and public assistance (Department of Social Services), as well as providing a strategic health and safety redundancy in the form of the Sheriff's Department and the Fire Department. Los Angeles County/USC Medical Center, the nation's largest teaching hospital, provides "accessible, affordable, and culturally sensitive" emergency, acute, HIV, and psychiatric care among many other public services. It cannot be stressed too much how important it is for a struggling actor to know of such publicly funded services and resources at his or her disposal. The time may come when welfare is better than no care, and the county's safety net can provide much-needed temporary assistance (LADHS, "Spirit of LAC").

LOS ANGELES CITY

The city is divided into districts, many of which have formed advisory neighborhood councils. These councils have helped mold city policy, most notably the suspension of a recent increase in water rates. The city is served by an extensive public library system, two airports, and a harbor. Streets are patrolled by the Los Angeles Police Department (LAPD).

Los Angeles can be divided into eight regions: Downtown, Greater Hollywood, Mid-Wilshire, West Los Angeles, South Los Angeles, East Los Angeles, the San Fernando Valley, and the Harbor District. The Harbor District was created solely to give Los Angeles its own harbor, and while people do live there, its distance from the creative heart makes it unattractive for artists. Downtown can be very artist friendly, but only if one has the money. Within these regions reside hundreds of neighborhoods named after annexed farm towns or incorporated municipalities founded to escape the big government of the city in their shadow.

88 SMALL TOWNS IN SEARCH OF A CITY

Successful actors have emerged from every corner of Los Angeles, but there are some communities and neighborhoods in particular that offer an actor-friendly combination of affordable housing, a supportive environment, and proximity to the entertainment industry. The industry remains relatively close-knit, forming a kind of parallelogram that is bordered by the San Diego Freeway (405) to the west, the Golden State Freeway (5) to the east, the Ventura Freeway (137) to the north, and the Santa Monica Freeway to the south, with the Hollywood Freeway (101) slicing it into two triangles (see appendix A, figure 1). Within this geometric quadrant one will find all the major studios and 90 percent of casting and talent agents, not to mention seemingly limitless support businesses. Within that parallelogram one finds many artist-friendly neighborhoods or communities that exist as either entertainment industry centers, such as Hollywood, Studio City, or Culver City, or that have a reputation for harboring and nurturing artist types such as visual artists who are not considered part of the entertainment industry. But at its heart, Los Angeles is truly a collection of small towns populated by transplants from other small towns across America. For actors to survive, they must simply find the "small town" that fits their needs and provides sustainability. Here, organized topographically, are a few to consider (see appendix A, figure 2).

THE HILLS—HOLLYWOOD OR BEVERLY?

The Santa Monica Mountains cover 250 square miles, rising out of the Pacific Ocean to a height of over three thousand feet. Geographically, they divide Los Angeles in half from Los Feliz to the Pacific Palisades. And while there are other "hills" in Los Angeles, such as the Whittier Hills and the Baldwin Hills, the Hollywood Hills section of the Santa Monica Mountains tends to be more central to the activity of the entertainment industry. At its eastern end is Griffith Park, at 4,210 acres one of the largest urban parks in North America and home of the Greek Theater. Slightly to the west one encounters the sprawling Universal City studio and theme park, Citywalk and Amphitheater complex, and then finally the ever popular Hollywood Bowl. From there to the Palisades westward, cantilevered homes, mansions, chateaus, estates, and condominiums cling to the narrow hillsides upon both sides in subdivisions that have names such as Mt. Olympus, Whitley Heights, Lookout Mountain, Beverly Glen, Beverly Crest, and Bel-Air Estates. Among them are nestled small apartments, guesthouses, converted garages, and anything imaginable for rent within the constraints of the county safety code. Artists make popular roommates, housemates, or renters, especially if they can provide a needed service in return, such as gardening, housekeeping, or babysitting.

Living in the Hills remains very popular despite brush fires, mudslides, and earthquakes. The simplest errand requires a thirty-minute drive. Outdoor pets fall prey to coyotes, and treacherous roads and scarce parking add to the inconvenience. But spectacular views and exclusive addresses make it all worthwhile to those who can afford it.

THE CANYONS—BEACHWOOD OR LAUREL?

Long, winding roads up and down these hills follow deep canyons where communities have evolved as distinct as the history they preserve. Names such as Nichol's Canyon, Benedict Canyon, Franklin Canyon, and Mandeville Canyon enshroud numerous artist enclaves where small grocery stores and cafes create distinct communities served by bulletin boards, neighborhood watch programs, and Web sites. Moving from east to west one finds the following canyons.

Developed in 1923, Beachwood Canyon was the "Hollywoodland" that the famous sign promoted. Only part of the sign survives, as does the stone gateway and guard tower, but much of old Hollywood survives as well. One can still take trail rides up to the Hollywood sign or meet colorful industry folk in the quaint markets and cafes at its base. To the south lies the heart of Hollywood.

Ever since folk singer Joni Mitchell sang of "The Ladies of the Canyon" in the 1960s, Laurel Canyon has been synonymous with the music industry and the counterculture. Rock pioneers such as Frank Zappa, the Byrds, and Buffalo Springfield lived and played here, and their bohemian spirit still endures. But Laurel Canyon's legendary history began much earlier, with silent film star cowboy Tom Mix, golden-age stars such as Errol Flynn, and the legendary magician Harry Houdini. The ruins of their homes are still visible. The canyon is a major transit corridor between the San Fernando Valley and Hollywood, but commuters have been deprived of this alternative to congested freeways since 2004 when part of the road partially washed away. The unstable hillside above the canyon suggests that the road, now reduced to one lane, will not be reinstated any time soon.

Known principally as the home of the TreePeople, an ecological, nonprofit organization offering sustainable solutions to urban ecosystem problems, Coldwater Canyon lacks the distinctive aura of the other canyons, but what it lacks in personality, it gains in convenience. It provides yet another quick alternative connection between the San Fernando Valley and the Westside of Los Angeles. Still further west, Beverly Glen Boulevard connects Sherman Oaks with Beverly Hills and shares its border with Bel-Air. At its summit cafes and restaurants have long been intimately tied to the entertainment industry, now with four notable restaurants and Glen Centre, a hillside shopping center. Though mostly upscale residential areas, where one finds money, one also often finds overfinanced homeowners in need of a renter to subsidize their mortgage.

THE BEACHES—SANTA MONICA OR VENICE?

A generation of moviegoers has worshiped the Los Angeles beach scene vicariously through a plethora of bikini and surfing films. Despite a laid-back culture and the lure of fresh air and sunny beach days, in general the beach communities' distance from the entertainment industry centers and their higher cost of living make them less viable alternatives for a struggling actor new to the city.

Malibu Beach's $102,000 median income celebrity hideaway renders it an unlikely choice for a struggling actor. Just south lies the city of Santa Monica, with the crumbling bluffs of Palisades Park and the carnival at Santa Monica Pier all too familiar to middle America as a backdrop for countless films and television shows. Today a vibrant tourist economy and a booming pub and artisan culture have translated to a significant increase in jobs for actors. A substantial artist community does exist, as well as a highly educated one (see appendix B, table 6). Affordable housing was easier to find before the city's tough rent control law was partially overturned in 1999. Today decades of left-leaning politics have led to a responsive, consumer-oriented city policy, but the city is also plagued by a lenient homeless policy and rampant gentrification (City of Santa Monica, "About Santa Monica"). Increased demand in housing has driven rents higher. But the legendary "Blue Bus" line connects to LA Metro, offering the only viable alternative to the often gridlocked Santa Monica Freeway to Hollywood.

The boardwalk defines the beach community of Venice, an oceanfront promenade notorious for street performers, tennis courts, a skate dancing plaza, numerous volleyball courts, a bike trail, hundreds of businesses, and outrageous behavior. Spiritualists, artists, performers, and musicians of all ilk reside happily in this bohemian community with the exotic name that really does have canals. Unfortunately, Venice also has gangs, making it dangerous after dark. As a district of Los Angeles, the city's failure to stem violent crime has created residential divisions and a cry for incorporation as a city in its own right. Whatever the outcome, Venice offers artists a safe haven, a free family clinic, eclectic artistic outlets such as art galleries, nightclubs, and trendy apparel shops, and affordable housing (depending on proximity to the ocean), but also long distances from the business end of Hollywood and narrow dense streets that add to traffic congestion and time delays.

Marina del Rey, an unincorporated county development, exists for one reason and one reason only—the Marina, the world's largest manmade recreational harbor. Its pricey condos and apartments offer occasional housing opportunities for subrentals, but the Marina is more likely to be a source of employment than housing, with its many high value restaurants and nightspots.

Playa del Rey, a bedroom community just south of the Culver City studios, lost its surfing luster of the sixties with the harsh realities of the last Los Angeles International Airport expansion. Sound abatement has not prevented the desertion of all but those living farthest north toward Culver Boulevard with easy access to Culver's City's studios.

Farther south lie Hermosa Beach, Redondo Beach, and Manhattan Beach, all charming beach communities though somewhat too removed from Hollywood and the other entertainment industry centers.

THE VALLEY—NOHO OR BURBANK?

Miles of strip malls, apartment complexes, and high-priced housing subdivisions have replaced the acres of orange groves that once covered this expansive valley. Angelinos speak casually of "The Valley," often referring collectively to the San Fernando, San Gabriel, and Simi Valleys as one. They are not, as residents will point out. Home to many major film, television, and recording studios and production companies, such as CBS Studio Center, NBC-Universal, ABC/Walt Disney, and Warner Brothers, the Valley has also earned its nickname of "San Pornando," as it is also home to a multibillion-dollar pornography industry. Warmer than the Basin—the central region of Los Angeles—in the summer and colder in the winter, rents tend to be cheaper but jobs not as exotic or lucrative. Many people live in the Valley and work in the Basin, adding to rush hour congestion on most connecting throughways, such as the Hollywood Freeway, Cahuenga Pass, and Laurel Canyon (see appendix A, figure 3).

Studio City grew from the Mack Sennett silent film studio in the 1920s into a company town and a major support center for the film and television industry. CBS Studio Center still produces a steady stream of television network programming, and Ventura Boulevard still offers a mom and pop atmosphere of hometown shops where crime remains relatively low. Residents have historically been gay friendly, less affected, and predominately white in a Valley that is now 50 percent Hispanic. Ventura Boulevard parallels the Ventura Freeway, which connects Studio City to a vast web of freeways. All in all, Studio City offers actors generally affordable housing, easy access to the Hollywood area, and a small-town atmosphere.

To the west, Sherman Oaks grew as an upscale suburban alternative neighborhood to Studio City, with high-fashion boutiques, trendy restaurants, and artist studios. Ranch-style houses, condos, and luxury apartments line the wider streets of this more affluent community. Better schools, better apartments, and safer streets, though, also often mean higher rents.

Directly north of Studio City sprawl North Hollywood and Valley Village, an eclectic mix of arts, religion, and strip malls. Struggling artists, orthodox Jews, Buddhists, Bahá'ís, and Latino, Middle Eastern, and Asian immigrants all coexist in this vast apartment outgrowth. The NoHo Artists District represents North Hollywood's jewel, a once blighted area now flourishing with art galleries, theatre spaces, film screenings, music, dance, and the Academy of Television Arts & Sciences at its center. Coffee houses, clubs, cafes, and recording and postproduction facilities soon followed. Boasts the Universal City/North Hollywood Chamber of Commerce, "Anything that an artist, or arts-patron, of any genre could need is within our ever-expanding boundaries. We even have the Metro system for easy transportation" (Universal City/North Hollywood Chamber of Commerce, "Noho Arts District"). As the northern hub of the Red Line subway system, North Hollywood offers easy access to Universal City Studios and Theme Park, Hollywood, Mid-Wilshire, Downtown, and Union Station, the train depot. The multitude of apartment complexes promises affordable housing options for most budgets. A very family friendly neighborhood, North Hollywood has the highest percentage of children of any neighborhood in the city, a plus for some, a minus for others (see appendix B, table 3).

Bordered by two studios, Warner Brothers and Universal, Toluka Lake once existed solely as a safe haven for film stars who wanted a short commute to the studios. But a six-acre lake and a private golf club didn't hurt. Few stars inhabit this community now, but its tree-lined streets still run through reclusive, albeit pricey, neighborhoods. West Toluca Lake and Toluca Woods just to the north, bordering North Hollywood, offer more reasonable rental rates. No real business district exists here, but Riverside Drive boasts a few restaurants and the Falcon Theater. These neighborhoods are within walking distance of five major studios, but cheaper rents can be found farther northeast in the cities of Burbank and Glendale.

The aviation and entertainment industries, both searching for more wide-open spaces, created Burbank. Lockheed Aircraft and Warner Brothers were the first, followed by Disney and Columbia. Lockheed no longer resides here, but the company left its legacy, the Burbank airport, recently renamed the Bob Hope Airport. But Warner and Disney still call Burbank home, as do ABC, the Cartoon Network, NBC, Dick Clark Productions, and Nickelodeon. With CBS Studio Center to the west and Universal Studios to the south, it is not surprising that many major casting offices surround this configuration of studios, as do many talent agents and actors resources. Rents are reasonable, and Burbank provides easy access to Hollywood with the Cahuenga Pass, one of the best-kept secrets in Los Angeles. Even at rush hour it's possible to drive from Burbank to Hollywood in less than thirty minutes (City of Burbank, "History of Burbank"). For many of its mostly foreign-born residents, Glendale represents the "American Dream." Statistically, Glendale represents a study in contradiction. Originally a white suburban enclave, Glendale has evolved from its religiously intolerant past to one of ethnic and religious diversity. Predominately white, ethnically Glendale leans heavily Armenian, 40 percent according to 2000 census statistics, with only 33 percent of its "Caucasian" residents considered Anglo. Demographically, Glendale splits into two geographic areas, its southern half more densely populated and poorer in per capita income than its more affluent northern half (City of Glendale, "Census Information"). Atwater Village, directly to the south, offers a more middle class environment still within a suburban context (see appendix B, table 1). Though Glendale is home to three well respected theatres—the Alex Theater, A Noise Within, and Glendale Centre Theatre—its main attraction for actors is their equal proximity to Downtown, Hollywood, and the Valley while retaining their suburban environment and its many foreign languages.

THE BASIN—WEST HOLLYWOOD OR SILVERLAKE?

The central city of Los Angeles exists in what is geographically a depository of centuries of mud and silt from the Santa Monica Mountains, known to Angelenos as "the Basin." The once small pueblo where now downtown Los Angeles exists grew in all directions and quickly gained notoriety as the home of the film industry.

The Hollywood of the Hollywood Canteen and the Brown Derby disappeared long ago, replaced by streets of broken dreams and besieged by runaways, prostitutes, and drug addicts. Add a higher than average crime rate and Hollywood no longer looks so inviting. Hollywood, though, remains the nominal center of the entertainment industry, a fact that has been acknowledged by the frequent major theatrical premieres at historic Hollywood theatres and the designation of the newly constructed Kodak Theater as the home of the Academy Awards. Most of the major studios have relocated to West LA and the Valley, but Paramount, Sunset/Gower, and Raleigh Studios, as well as ABC-TV Center, still reside here, as do many casting and talent agents, photographers, and other actor-related services.

Hollywood is not a city in itself but is a district of the city of Los Angeles, and many eclectic neighborhoods have evolved in this fabled area. Rents remain relatively affordable, although what passes as a certified residence often boggles the mind. The Hollywood Freeway slices through its center, providing easy access north to the Valley or parts south and west through the Cahuenga Pass. Besides providing a transportation corridor to the Valley, many affordable apartments and rentals can be found along Hollywood's side streets.

Los Feliz borders Hollywood on the east and extends north into the Valley, sandwiched between the Hollywood Freeway (Hwy. 101) and the Golden State Freeway (I-5). Pronounced "Los Fee-lez," this often mispronounced Spanish named neighborhood once was the most chic and artsy neighborhood of Los Angeles, although it is now more infamous as the site of the first of the Manson murders. Still, older Spanish bungalows, duplexes, and apartments line the many boulevards that converge through this pass or lead into the Hollywood Hills and Griffith Park, where some of Los Angeles's most expensive and architecturally unique homes exist. For the struggling actor, though, easy freeway access, quaint and affordable housing, and a plethora of nearby restaurants, bars, clubs, theatres, and various support industries that employ struggling artists makes Los Feliz an ideal residential area.

Originally retained by the county as an emergency right of way, West Hollywood once had only warehouses and seedy bars lining its streets. Gays seeking refuge from the homophobic LAPD, seniors seeking affordable housing, and Russian Jewish immigrants discovered this tolerant island trapped between Hollywood and Beverly Hills. Trendy bars and restaurants followed, and in 1984 West Hollywood won cityhood and gained notoriety as America's first "gay city." Today West Hollywood is 44 percent gay and lesbian, 21 percent senior citizen, and 8 percent Russian immigrant, though, according to city statistics, the average resident is a Caucasian, heterosexual male, aged 35–44, who lives alone in a rented apartment, has at least a four-year college degree, and makes between $50,000 and $100,000 a year (City of West Hollywood, *Highlights of West Hollywood*, 6–7).

Though not a family friendly city, West Hollywood has become a model of progressive innovation, embracing the needs of disabled residents, HIV sufferers, senior citizens, and renters (see appendix B, tables 3 and 4). The city's many famous clubs, bars, and restaurants on and around the Sunset Strip attract the rich and the famous and employ legions of struggling actors. But its popularity quickly led to gridlocked boulevards and hopeless parking options. Rents tend to be on the high side as one progresses toward the "West Side," but creative living arrangements exist and deals can still be found. The city council has most recently battled gentrification by requiring that any new development in the city must include a certain square footage of affordable housing. West Hollywood's main deficit, however, is its lack of accessibility to major freeways.

Bordering Hollywood to the southeast, Silver Lake harbors a manmade reservoir named not after the water's color but for a city bureaucrat, Herman Silver. His namesake has become an ethnically and culturally diverse artistic collective ranging from alternative rock to leather fetishes to community activism. Though primarily populated by Hispanic/Latino residents, Silver Lake received an influx of gays in the 1980s that led to a volatile situation. Residents eventually found common ground and a resolution to the conflict in the form of a community music festival, the Sunset Junction Street Fair. It presented an eclectic roster of music styles that reflected the musical culture of its residents. It attracted visitors from all over the city and forged a groundbreaking community alliance that still thrives today and has spawned an art collective and a film festival. Silver Lake's winding, hilly streets offer endless residential options, although its artistic bent may be its undoing in the form of gentrification, as many upwardly mobile residents have been attracted by its artistic reputation.

Beverly Hills, Bel-Air, and Brentwood represent the consummate Los Angeles affluent lifestyle, with the highest median household incomes in the area (see appendix B, table 2). Given their reputation, these communities may well be too elitist and too expensive for a struggling actor. Although this is largely true, the rich need services such as nannies, pool men, chauffeurs, trainers, secretaries, assistants, and gardeners, and they may offer to provide housing in return. Any option that provides flexibility should be considered.

As one might tell from its name, Beverly Hills Adjacent is more known for what it is not than for what it is. It is not West Hollywood to its north, it is not Beverly Hills to its west and south, and it is not the Fairfax District to its east. As such, it lacks the charm but not the higher rents and costs of living.

The Fairfax District's Jewish community, which once supported twelve synagogues, has now largely moved west to the Pico/Robertson Boulevard area of Beverlywood, leaving behind a tourist economy centered around quaint old Jewish businesses, the open air stalls of the Farmer's Market, CBS Studio Center, and The Grove, a chic new outdoor mall. The community still retains a mix of Jewish residents and seniors, but the artsy scene on Melrose Avenue has also attracted a much younger and creative element. Housing tends to be more affordable than in West Hollywood, but like West Hollywood, it lacks easy access to the freeway system.

The Beverly Hills of the silent film era, Hancock Park has wide streets and large mansions that feature some of Los Angeles's most interesting architecture. More affordable Larchmont Village sits to the north. Somewhat quaint, it appeals to the arts community and provides proximity to Hollywood in a more suburban atmosphere and with cheaper rents. Windsor Square, one of the oldest neighborhoods of the city, sports old barnlike homes with broad lawns and well-tended gardens, often with rooms to rent. Nearby, running east to west, from the beach to downtown, Wilshire's concrete corridor of high-rise offices and apartment complexes from South Carthay to Wilshire Center became known as the Miracle Mile because of its rapid development. Finally, along the Fairfax corridor sprawls Park La Brea, a corporate development of high-rise apartments, townhouses, and duplexes.

While Los Angeles contains many ethnic support communities, such as Chinatown, Little Tokyo, Filipinotown, Little Armenia, Thai Town, and Little Ethiopia, to name a few, Koreatown offers a possible alternative location as a result of a recent revitalization program that has attracted affordable housing and a vital nightlife. In addition, Koreatown's access to the subway and the free-way system makes it an attractive option for all struggling actors regardless of race. But because a high percentage of the population is below the poverty level, its high crime rate and overcrowded schools may not make it a viable option for struggling actors with families (see appendix B, tables 5 and 7).

Home to the University of California, Los Angeles (UCLA), Westwood is very much a college town. For some that may be a comfortable environment while for others not so much. Whether a student or not, in Westwood one has to be prepared to live with hopelessly crowded side streets, a parking nightmare, and loud, boisterous parties, all typical features of a vibrant college community. On the other hand, those very same students may also be looking for a roommate.

To the south, West Los Angeles offers a "Westside" address, freeway access, and proximity to the entertainment industry but without the frat party atmosphere.

Rancho Park is home to 20th Century Fox Studios and the Hillcrest Country Club, its tree-lined medians and nineteenth century streetlights offering less for a struggling actor than the Beverlywood neighborhood to its east. Both are cen-ters of Jewish life where temples, hospitals, and senior centers all become one. But Rancho Park offers no real business district, while Beverlywood's Pico Boulevard (east/west) and Robertson Boulevard (north/south) have a well de-veloped mix of cultural and general retail businesses, not to mention quicker access to Interstate-10.

Culver City follows Washington Boulevard from mid-city nearly to the ocean and forms the final corner of the entertainment industry parallelogram. Along its wide boulevard still proudly stands MGM Studios. Built in the 1920s, MGM shares a great history with Culver City, including the making of films such as *The Wizard of Oz* and *Gone with the Wind*. Now also home to Sony Pictures Studios and Culver Studios, Culver City stands on par with Studio City, Burbank, or even Hollywood as an industry center. Culver City's busy industry economy and its close proximity to the beaches and the Marina offer almost limitless employment options. The freeway system runs through the city in all four directions. Unfortunately, millions of others live here too, and so Culver City has arguably the worst traffic and gridlocked freeways in the area. LA Metro has just begun construction of a light rail public transportation system connect-ing to Downtown with expected completion in 2008.

Housing tends to be pricey, but the surrounding Los Angeles city neigh-borhoods such as Palms continue to be affordable. Approximately 70 percent apartments, this once crime-ridden neighborhood has been more recently discovered by young professionals and college students. Census demographics indicate a very diverse population, consisting mostly of Middle Eastern, South Asian, and Brazilian immigrants.

Of course, there are hundreds of other neighborhoods and communities in the Greater Los Angeles region. A free room might trump all other concerns unless its distance from work and the entertainment industry centers precludes having a life. Whatever your priority, carefully consider the concerns of accessibility, affordability, and support, and closely research your neighborhood preferences before signing a lease and committing what will seem like a life's savings to a future landlord.

Actors Forum

Originally when I first moved here my first priority was to get a job. So I worked doing odd jobs. I was a bus boy at an Olive Garden. I delivered medication for a pharmaceutical company. I worked at a hotel. I did personal assisting work for a family in the entertainment industry. They were very flexible. I initially came on board as someone to help around the house, feed the dogs, watch and pick up their kids. They were in the industry, so they knew how it works. I didn't have a car, so when I got my car, it got me into even more debt, so I had to maintain the job just to pay that. The secret of survival, I think, is networking with really supportive people and finding people who see your vision and will support you.

Tang Nguyen

You need to get into a lifestyle that you can afford where you're not going from paycheck to paycheck, because when the rich times come, when the paycheck comes, you need to put it away. You invest it. You save it because you'll need it later. That was what saved me. I never had to go from paycheck to paycheck. I always had savings. But when I came out here, I didn't have a penny.

Jacque Lynn Colton

Don't be alone when you come here. I wasn't alone. I had a wonderful common law wife, also an actor, and she and I had a very mutually supportive relationship. Being good looking is not really an asset, but it meant I could work for the Sears catalog and do catalog modeling that paid the rent frequently. I could sing and move a bit, so I was able to do industrial shows. Versatility is useful to have. I think it helps you if you can learn to read music. If you have a voice, learn how to use it. I could shuffle, hop, step, ball change. I could do a time step. I worked with gypsies, and they taught me. Get as well equipped as you can in as many areas as you can, because if you can read music and you've got a decent voice, you may get lucky and do a set in a studio for a commercial. If you have a voice that is soothing, or if you have a cartoony voice, hone that. Voice-overs can be a great source of income.

Gordon Thomson

Rejection is the hardest part of this business for me. You're going to get rejected not once, not twice, not a hundred times, but a thousand times. Personally as an actor, I'll break down crying or just go into the closet and cry. If you haven't broken down crying in this business, you're not chasing your dream. . . . Forget the hours of preparation—what about the hour and a half you spent in traffic and the parking ticket you got while waiting? . . . And when the girls come out here, they bring their boyfriends with them. So I remember this one lady came to acting class and brought her husband with her. There was this one scene, a military guy during the Kuwait war in this town where he's basically drinking and talking to this stripper. The military guy goes, "Show me what you got baby," and I'm looking at this girl who brought her husband. At the end of the class, I walked up to Amy, the acting coach, and said, "You'll never see them again." She said, "Of course not."

Sajen Corona

3

Surviving in Los Angeles
Employment, Housing, and Transportation

*It is almost as if you were frantically constructing another world while the
world that you live in dissolves beneath your feet, and that your survival
depends on completing this construction at least one second before the old
habitation collapses.*

Tennessee Williams, *Camino Real*

Employment, Housing, and Transportation Information Sources

The Zami Los Angeles Yellow Pages—Employment Agencies
http://losangeles.zami.com/Employment_Agencies

California Department of Consumer Affairs—Boards, Bureaus and
Committees
www.dca.ca.gov/about_dca/profession.shtml

Contractors State License Board
http://www.cslb.ca.gov/

California State Board of Barbering and Cosmetology
http://www.barbercosmo.ca.gov/

Contractors License Examination Study Guides
http://www.cslb.ca.gov/studyguides/default.asp

Guide to California Residential Tenants' and Landlords' Rights and
Responsibilities
http://www.dca.ca.gov/publications/landlordbook/index.shtml

California's Renters Resources
http://ohmyapt.apartmentratings.com/california-tenants-law.html

Los Angeles County Department of Consumer Affairs—Information for Renters
http://consumer-affairs.co.la.ca.us/mnRenters.htm

Los Angeles City Department of Housing
http://www.lacity.org/lahd/

Los Angeles City Traffic Conditions—LADOT
http://trafficinfo.lacity.org/

Los Angeles County Metropolitan Transportation Authority
http://www.mta.net/default.asp

Wherever you decide to settle, it's not likely to be permanent. Friends or family will quickly grow weary of your career quest. Not making relocation a top priority will alienate friends and strain family relations. Many decisions await, such as developing a dependable revenue stream, a permanent base of operations, and a transportation strategy. Your business plan should now be implemented.

IMPLEMENTING YOUR BUSINESS PLAN

With sustainability still the initial goal, housing and transportation costs must be determined by your monthly income, or lack thereof in some cases. Employment must be the initial goal. That nest egg won't last long, and bankruptcy has ended more than one promising career. Formulate a budget and stick to it. Housing should cost no more than one-third of your monthly income or you risk financial default. But until you actually have an income, knowing what is affordable is a gamble at best.

Sample Budget

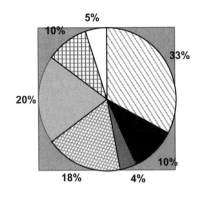

- Housing
- Food
- Utilities
- Transportation
- Career Costs
- Health
- Misc.

EMPLOYMENT

Who hires struggling actors in Los Angeles?

Finding a job in Los Angeles is easy. Keeping the job will be hard. Most employers want dependable full-time employees who are available from nine to five, Monday through Friday. Actors are not now and will never be. But what actors lack, they more than amply compensate for in areas of personality and skill. Here are a few businesses that by their nature hire struggling actors (California Department of Consumer Affairs, Boards, Bureaus, and Committees).

Restaurants
Advantages

- Represent a surprisingly large sector of the Los Angeles economy, attracting epicureans of all cuisines and pocketbooks.
- Often provide flexible work hours.
- Often provide lucrative tips depending upon the restaurant and scale.

Disadvantages

- Come and go quickly in any trendy city and may not always be a stable source of income.
- High-end restaurants, though lucrative, often involve internal politics of kickbacks and percentages expected to other employees.

Bars
Advantages

- No state laws regulate server training. The Department of Alcoholic Beverage Control offers a voluntary training program for licensees, called LEAD (Licensee Education on Alcohol and Drugs). The program focuses training efforts toward new license applicants, licensees employed in high-crime areas, and licensees who have violated ABC laws, as well as major special events and county fairs.

Disadvantages

- California liquor laws hold bartenders personally liable, with substantial fines, for serving an intoxicated person as well as for other violations.
- The after hours bar scene can easily harm a career for reasons too numerous to mention.

Hair Salons
Advantages

- The California Contractor's Licensing Board provides detailed information and study guides.
- The Board supports reciprocal out-of-state licensing.
- Once licensed, the Board offers online licensing renewals, unless one has run afoul of regulations.

Disadvantages

- The California Barbering and Cosmetology Act closely regulates and licenses stylists, barbers, beauticians, cosmetologists, manicurists, and electrologists.
- As with a variety of skilled vocations, substantial time and cost must be invested either to complete a course of instruction from a Board-approved school or to complete an apprenticeship program from a Board-approved sponsor.

Temporary Agencies
Advantages

- Agencies readily employ artists who have clerical business skills in all manner of office practices, such as reception, data entry, and secretarial services. Generally one must have proficiency in common software applications such as those in the Microsoft Office Suite. Those proficient in more advanced programs and/or in Web design and maintenance command higher rates.

Disadvantages

- Agencies generally pay only minimum wage, though some specialty skills can be negotiable.
- Some agencies prefer workers to make one- or two-week commitments to an assignment, often to replace someone on a vacation.

Gyms
Advantages

- No licensing or certification for personal training required by the state (although certification of some kind can help one's credibility).
- Provides a great place to network in the entertainment industry.
- Provides an opportunity to keep oneself in great shape.

Disadvantages

- Gyms hire trainers initially to train patrons, pay them minimum wage, and then double them as sales associates on straight commission.

Where do I look for employment notices?

Classified ads. Los Angeles may be a metropolis of millions, but the monolithic *Los Angeles Times* still attempts to micro serve the needs of this massive market with multiple daily, regional, and online editions all posting classified employment notices. As comprehensive as this approach may be, don't ignore Los Angeles's many other community, cultural, and trade papers and magazines:

- *La Opinion* (Spanish)
  http://www.laopinion.com
- *Santa Monica Daily Press*
  http://www.smdp.com
- *Hollywood Reporter*
  http://www.hollywoodreporter.com/hr/index.jsp
- *Variety*
  http://www.variety.com
- *Beverly Hills Weekly*
  http://www.bhweekly.com

- *LA Weekly*
  Los Angeles weekly alternative newspaper
  http://www.laweekly.com
- *Santa Monica Mirror*
  http://www.smmirror.com
- *Recycler*
  Los Angeles classifieds
  http://www.recycler.com/
- *Frontiers Newsmagazine*
  Gay community bimonthly magazine
  http://www.frontierspublishers.com/mags

Online. Online employment services remain subservient to the print media with several notable exceptions. Why? Cost-effectiveness. Perceived as more effective, the print media generally offers lower rates than online advertising, which favors corporate employers who bulk advertise. A few online services, such as Craigslist, offer a more comprehensive service, but buyer beware. While advertisers encounter liability for fraudulent employment notices in the print media, online services offer no such protections to the naive.

Employment agencies. Most employment agencies expect a long-term commitment from their clients and charge the employer that hires them a substantial fee. Be honest up-front. Though not necessarily a "temp" agency, an employment agency may on occasion accommodate an actor's need for flexibility with employers in need of temporary or on-call work situations. If the agency charges a fee for registration, they are not legitimate, so don't waste your time unless these are state licensing fees, or fees for fingerprinting or other governmentally mandated requirements.

Vocational schools. While most vocational schools offer employment services, it is usually only to their graduates. Whatever the value of the training, a grueling exam must be passed before being licensed. Schools may promise exam success, but be wary of any school that guarantees employment. Not only is this a violation of the Federal Trade Commission Act, but it's an all-too-common scam.

Targeted canvassing. Why not sell yourself? Do some research. Target local businesses. Ask for the owner or manager, and with resume in hand, announce your desire to be employed there. This method works occasionally, but not always. Still, a little determination, confidence, and chutzpah go a long way toward overcoming one's naiveté.

What jobs should I avoid?

First axiom to follow: If you are required to pay any fee or membership in order to work, it's not a job. Also, jobs that pay straight commission rarely equate to even minimum wage, which is the least one should receive for an honest day's work. But don't expect any benefits either. Union jobs usually pay well and offer substantial medical benefits but lack flexibility required by the serious working actor. If health insurance is an issue, you may need to rely upon community or municipal health services such as clinics and trauma care.

Managerial positions. The concepts of management and flexible hours are incompatible. Higher pay generally means more responsibility and less flexibility. As a result, career goals can soon become secondary, and while many a career has been sacrificed at the altar of financial need, don't fool yourself over the reason why.

Telemarketing jobs. Unless you need to improve your ability to handle rejection, avoid these jobs. They usually pay only a straight commission, so one's income can become a monthly gamble. While seductively offering flexible hours, employers may claim their product sells itself, when in truth the only thing moving out the door are former employees.

Drivers. Whether one drives a taxi, limousine, or a private vehicle, California now closely regulates commercial drivers. Licensing requires not only a medical test, involving standard drug testing at the applicant's expense, but also a written and physical driving test. Taxi drivers face long distances and high gasoline costs, making this a daily gamble as well. Higher paying limousine drivers and private drivers live on call and have little flexibility.

Entertainment industry related jobs. What seemed like a match made in heaven has often sounded the death knell of a career and been the excuse for a struggling actor to give up the quest. If you want to be a production assistant, then be a production assistant, but don't delude yourself into believing you're doing it to get more acting work.

What's better, employment or entrepreneurship?

Eventually, an opportunity to switch from employment to entrepreneurship may present itself. Owning one's own business, though perhaps not the best idea initially, offers the most obvious advantage of flexibility of hours once established. The disadvantages involve the financial investment that may be required and the establishment of a business that may compete with one's career. A simple guideline is needed: A business of one is manageable. A business with employees is not. Some vocations, though, lend themselves to this arrangement.

Stylists, barbers, beauticians, cosmetologists. Salon owners often prefer to rent the extra chairs in their salon rather than hire employees to work them. But for this to be lucrative, you must bring with you an established clientele.

Personal/sports trainers. Though in great demand, personal and sports trainers must constantly market their services. Clients may come and go, but the gym owner will still charge a monthly fee for its use. California requires no certification for physical trainers, but the sometimes fierce competition among trainers may require the pursuit of some credible certification programs.

Massage therapists. California also requires no certification or licensing for massage practitioners despite the obvious opportunity for misuse as a prostitution rather than as health service. Still, massage therapy thrives, with an estimated 14,000 to 24,000 legitimate practitioners in California, most of whom work as independent contractors (McRee, "Center for the Health Professions"). Here again, obtaining certification doesn't hurt one's credibility when building a loyal clientele.

Painters/landscapers. California regulates all practices of the construction industry. To work independently as a painter or landscaper requires a contractor's license as an independent practitioner. Undoubtedly, many nonlicensed painters and landscapers find work in Los Angeles, but they risk significant liability for doing so. Passing the contractor's exam will require some serious studying, but it will also provide a strong buffer from the financial liability one may encounter as an independent contractor. But once again, resist the temptation, as if your life depended upon it, to turn a vocation into a business.

HOUSING

Struggling actors find all manner of affordable, convenient, and supportive living spaces imaginable in converted garages, wealthy estate pool houses, hillside cottages, rooms in attics and basements, and in traditional apartments and homes. New residents will encounter corporate real estate company managers, mom and pop apartment owners, sometimes naive homeowners who are subsidizing a mortgage, and a renter or group of renters seeking a new roommate. Understand the ramifications of the financial relationship being discussed and its advantages and disadvantages. Once agreed upon and/or signed, the arrangement will be binding.

What do I do first?

First and foremost, you need to establish local residency and credit. Landlords rarely accept out-of-state checks. A cashier's check may have to suffice until you can establish a local bank account with your first paycheck.

Should I rent, lease, sublet, or live with someone?

This answer depends upon your unique needs and your financial realities. Are you alone or with family? Do you have special needs? Financial assets? First, carefully assess your anticipated monthly revenue. Housing should constitute no more than 33 percent of your monthly income. Then determine what you really need to sustain yourself in Los Angeles financially, physically, emotionally, and creatively. Do you need a five-room apartment, or just a guest room in someone's converted garage? One can survive quite handily with a blow up bed in someone's spare bedroom. I did. What assets are at your disposal in case of financial setback? A relative? A friend? A vocation? A trust fund? Whatever the answer, now is the time to be honest and to set a monthly budget. Rent in Los Angeles for a one-bedroom unit starts at a modest $1,000 per month, with two-bedroom units twice that. Even a single room will cost at least $500 a month. How does one afford this? Struggling artists make sacrifices. Many live with roommates, often four to a two-bedroom apartment. Some share a house in artist communes. Still others find live-in jobs that provide housing. You should pursue whatever financial relationship seems comfortable and affordable.

Rental. Generally based on a month-to-month written agreement, which permits the landlord to increase rent at any time with a thirty-day notice. The tenant also may choose to end the agreement with a thirty-day notice. This may be prudent for the short term, but it provides no financial stability.

Lease. A written agreement for fixed rent and fees over a fixed time period, most often a year. This provides long-term financial stability, but, should moving become necessary, it leaves the lessee financially liable for any remaining months, perhaps necessitating a sublease.

Sublease. Infinitely more complicated, this written agreement generally exists between a tenant with a lease who, for whatever reason, must live elsewhere, and someone in need of housing. The landlord also generally needs to approve and formalize the arrangement. The sublessee simply arranges to complete the terms of someone else's lease.

Roommates. Few single people live alone in Los Angeles, because of the high cost of housing. Roommates cohabitate in all possible arrangements, from the arcane to the sublime. While generally only a match made out of financial necessity, roommates do need to at least enjoy each other's company. Because of this requirement, the process needed to vet the living arrangements is crucial before making any agreements. Who pays whom, when, what amount, for what right, and with what conditions? This may involve a formal or informal agreement, usually requiring a deposit, a set monthly payment toward the rent, and some arrangement over utilities, food, household needs, and so forth. Such an arrangement may range from two persons in a small apartment to a dozen cohabitating in a large house. Often tenuous at best, roommate arrangements are predicated upon strangers living harmoniously. That's not always the outcome, and one participant who is short of the monthly rent can bring down the entire house of cards. (County of Los Angeles, "Rental Agreements and Leases").

Where do I look for housing?

Classified ads. The *Los Angeles Times* still dominates the classified market, but the cost of advertising here outweighs the need for all but large corporate real estate owners. Small apartment owners and homeowners can easily find cheaper advertising options, such as the smaller neighborhood papers.

Internet. The Web brims with rental services, but these are tailored more to business clients relocating on a moving allowance. Craigslist remains the best choice for individuals, but with the usual disclaimer.

Bulletin boards. Community bulletin boards in small grocery stores, community centers, and laundromats offer local listings.

Rental services. For a membership or weekly fee, one has access to "exclusive listings," published weekly. The problem is that the "teaser" listings disappear immediately or never actually existed in the first place.

Roommate services. A variety of services offer to match roommates of any age, gender, sexual orientation, or combination thereof. The client pays a membership fee to access a photo/info database of other members seeking roommates. The rest requires chemistry and accommodation.

On-site. Los Angeles landlords still prefer to advertise a vacancy with the old-fashioned posted sign, detailing the size of the unit, whether it is furnished or unfurnished, amenities, rental/lease rate, pet policy, and a contact number. Ultimately, one may find driving up and down residential side streets and jotting down phone numbers to be the most time effective and successful means to find an adequate apartment.

What should I look for when I inspect the unit?

Honesty! Landlords and managers seek honest, responsible clients as tenants, exactly what the tenant has the right to expect in return. Is the property and unit as advertised? The reality will tell volumes about one's future business relationship. A "view of the ocean" can mean one must open an upstairs closet, stand on a chair, and strain out a tiny portal to catch a glimpse of a shoreline. Let experience be your teacher. After a handful of inspections, reality will intervene and certain essential concerns should rise to the surface, reinforcing the fact that the consumer needs to beware and ask a lot of questions.

General physical condition. California law requires a unit to be "habitable," meaning leak-free windows, doors, and ceiling. In addition, plumbing, gas, heating, and electricity must be in good working order; the building must be clean and sanitary; the grounds must be free of debris, filth, rubbish, garbage, and rodents; stairs must be in good working order; and there must be working permanent smoke detectors (Pelisek, "Tenants' Rights"). Check for any signs of damage and ask lots of questions.

Paint. Has the unit been newly painted? Many jurisdictions require the painting of all units prior to new occupancy regardless of the length of the previous occupancy.

Carpet. Most jurisdictions require carpet replacement every seven to ten years, with generally no requirement to replace prior to a new rental. But if you ask about the carpet, a landlord must provide an answer. At the very least, carpets must be steam cleaned prior to a new rental.

Utilities. Check that the utilities work! If something doesn't, be clear about who pays, the tenant or the landlord. Ask how much utilities average per month and if any increases are expected.

Appliances. Are they gas or electric? Who pays? Are there additional charges? Do the existing appliances come with the unit? Landlords may charge extra for providing a refrigerator.

Bathroom fixtures. By law, toilets must work. Look for tell-tale signs of a leak, such as mineral deposits and discolorations. Nothing spells vacancy faster than a dysfunctional bathroom.

Parking. Is there any parking, on the street or elsewhere, or will you have to wake up at 5:45 a.m. each morning to move your car from a 6 a.m. restricted parking space. On-site, secure parking may cost extra, but depending upon the neighborhood it may be well worth the extra cost.

Laundry. Most large apartment complexes provide coin-operated laundry facilities, and their cleanliness and functionality are often a precursor to what one might expect about the facility in general. If these are not provided, locate a neighborhood laundromat. Waiters, bartenders, nurses, indeed service professionals of all ilk, may someday, as with life, live or die to a drying cycle or in search of one clean shirt.

Amenities. Landlords often promise pools, hot tubs, saunas, and fitness centers. Conduct a close physical inspection to see if they actually work.

Finally, before applying for a unit, walk around on your own and talk to the existing tenants. They may be more than happy to share their experiences with the management, both good and bad (CDCA, "California Tenants").

What application fees may I be charged to rent/lease a unit?

Depending upon the jurisdiction, landlords may charge the following application fees.

Credit check fee. A landlord may charge up to thirty dollars to conduct a credit check on each adult on the application. A copy of the report must be provided if requested, nominally to prove that the landlord didn't just pocket the fee. Consequently, a landlord cannot reject an application or charge a higher rental rate for bad credit, which is often a pretext to discrimination, unless this is evident on the credit report (County of Los Angeles, "Credit Checks").

Holding deposit. Nonrefundable and equal to one month's rent, this deposit removes the unit from the market pending results of a credit check. If required, be certain to establish how this deposit will be applied if approved (County of Los Angeles, "Holding Deposits").

Application fee. Charged mostly by larger corporate real estate companies, this fee covers the clerical costs of processing an application.

What additional fees can I be charged if I'm approved?

Most landlords use standard rental/lease forms, but read yours carefully. All charges, fees, and incremental increases must be delineated. California law and most municipal jurisdictions allow for a variety of additional charges and fees outside of the rental rate.

Security deposit. Depending on the result of that credit report, a security deposit can range from a nominal amount to twice the monthly rental fee (CDCA, "California Tenants," 25). Security deposits must be refundable by California law, but they may be increased only proportionately to an annual rent increase.

Late payment fee. Most jurisdictions allow a landlord to charge a late fee of less than 5 percent of the rental fee after three to five days of the due date (County of Los Angeles, "Rent Control").

Pet fee. Landlords generally tolerate cats over dogs. Often the "no pets" requirement really means "no dogs." But regardless, a landlord has the right to charge up to $100 per pet as a security against damage.

Registration fee. Many jurisdictions require landlords to pay a yearly registration fee for each unit. That fee may be recoverable from the tenant (City of Los Angeles, *Landlord-Tenant Handbook*, 5).

Systematic Code Enforcement Program (SCEP) fee. Another municipal fee, the $2.96 monthly surcharge for yearly code inspection may be charged to the tenant (*Landlord-Tenant*, 46).

Utility fee. If utility costs are included in the agreement, a 1 percent increase may be charged to cover the cost of their eventual increase (*Landlord-Tenant*, 20).

All in all, the initial cost of a rental or lease may equal as much as three times the monthly rental fee, which can require the tenant to lay down thousands of dollars just for the right to move into a space smaller than his or her mother's bathroom and nowhere near as good smelling. Some landlords count on tenants having little rental savvy. The solution? Get some. In whatever neighborhood you decide to settle, whether it is the county, city, or elsewhere, inquire as to what rights tenants have.

What are my renter's rights?

The rights of renters vary greatly between Los Angeles County, City, and other municipalities such as West Hollywood and Santa Monica, as does the degree of enforcement. Most landlords play by the rules, but discrimination exists sometimes with impunity. Whatever community you decide to settle in, research what rights renters have there. Basic California renter's rights are as follows:

- Landlords are restricted from inquiring about race, ethnicity, national origin, religion, sexual orientation, marital status, age, disability, or family status (having children living with you under age eighteen).
- Limits exist on the amount of the security deposit required.
- Limits exist on the landlord's right to enter the unit.
- Tenants are entitled to a refund of their security deposit, or a written explanation of what charges applied to it, within thirty days of vacating the unit.
- Tenants have the right to sue their landlord for violations of the law or the rental agreement.
- Tenants have the right to repair serious defects and to deduct the costs from the monthly rental fee.
- Under certain circumstances, tenants have the right to withhold rent.
- Tenants are granted protection against retaliatory eviction.
  (CDCA, "California Tenants," 19)

In addition, some jurisdictions have enacted additional renter's rights ordinances that provide for the following:

- Limits to the annual allowable rent increase are based on the Consumer Price Index (CPI) average for the Los Angeles-Long Beach-Anaheim areas for a twelve-month period ending September 30 of each year (*Landlord-Tenant*, 19).
- Security deposits are to accrue interest, 2.39 percent as of December 31, 2007, payable annually to the tenant (26).
- Tenants must be given a written explanation for eviction (19-22).

Knowing one's rights places one on equal footing with the landlord when negotiating an agreement. Many landlords make demands that violate local ordinances. Renters have recourse, but usually only after having suffered consequences. It is better to assert one's rights up-front.

TRANSPORTATION

Do I really need a car in Los Angeles?

The third tier of a business plan should involve transportation. Once you have established a revenue stream and a base of operations, sustainability requires that you learn the appropriate transportation means that connect your home, job, and the entertainment industry centers where auditions and industry related work will occur. Most actors find it difficult to exist without a car in this huge metropolitan area. Public transportation serves an amazing grid of city streets, but side streets and winding canyon roads fall outside of its system. Within the parallelogram of the entertainment industry, specific transportation corridors do exist, both freeway and side street, utilizing both public and private modes of transportation.

What are transportation corridors?

Los Angeles has many streets and boulevards that for whatever reason have evolved into major transportation corridors between certain points. Canyon roads such as Laurel Canyon and Coldwater Canyon connect the San Fernando Valley with the Basin. Fountain Boulevard connects Silver Lake with West Hollywood. Wilshire crosses mid-city, connecting the Westside to Downtown. Wherever one settles, these corridors provide a fast connection at various times of day in order to survive the sometimes unpredictable traffic flow in Los Angeles. While auditions and callbacks generally occur at studios and casting offices, location shooting can occur anywhere. Set your radio to KFWB News 980 on the AM dial, which provides traffic updates every ten minutes, and always check the DOT interactive Web site before setting out on a freeway jaunt.

An actor also needs to be just as familiar with the city streets as a taxi driver. A side-street route, though longer than the freeway, may make the difference between making or missing an important audition. Unless one has a GPS system, buy a Thomas Guide. Available in any 7-Eleven or bookstore, this book lays out the city in over a hundred sectored maps, allowing the user to focus on one detailed sector at a time.

What's with the freeway names?

Los Angeles's love affair with the automobile has resulted in an extensive system of freeways, connecting all the disparate parts of this great city (see appendix A, figure 1). These freeways have numbers and sometimes more than one name, which can be confusing. Angelinos generally refer to a freeway by its number, such as the "5" or the "101." In addition, depending upon the direction, the

10 Freeway may be the Santa Monica Freeway (west) or the San Bernardino Freeway (east). Likewise, the Golden State Freeway northbound becomes the Santa Ana Freeway southbound. It's easier just to call it the "5."

What are my public transportation choices?

Take your pick—light rail, train, subway, or bus? The Los Angeles County Metropolitan Transportation Authority, better known as LA Metro, has desperately attempted to keep up with unrestrained growth and provide public transportation options from sea to mountain and valley. One still needs an automobile to function in Los Angeles, but public transportation provides a real alternative to get most anywhere, if one has the time.

Metro Rail. Three light rail lines, one subway, and one shuttle service, each differentiated by a color, connect sixty-two stations that incorporate Downtown (Civic Center), Union Station (Amtrak), North Hollywood, Universal City, and the Los Angeles Airport (LAX).

Metro Link. Regional heavy rail systems that run through Los Angeles connect to this local rail system, providing commuter service to and from more distant suburbs.

Metro Bus. LA Metro provides four kinds of bus service and maintains 191 mostly CNG-powered bus lines along 18,500 stops on most all major boulevards of Los Angeles County. Orange buses designate local service; red buses are express. Additional bus services include Transit way and Bus way services on specific freeway routes. The system, though admittedly complex, certifies almost 34 million riders per month and intuitively aids the rider (LACMTA, "Facts at a Glance"). Bus stops display route numbers, LA Metro publishes weekly schedules that are accessible online, and bus drivers, to their credit, are known for their gracious manners. Don't be afraid to ask questions, such as, "What is the best way for me to get . . ."

Public transportation versus private vehicle

Owning an automobile in Los Angeles often gives one a false sense of security. Casting directors don't like to hear the words, "My car broke down"—talent agents and employers even less. A savvy newcomer will note bus routes and stops to and from various key places, such as work, home, classes, and casting, as well as train options, regardless of the current state of his or her vehicle. Distances magnified by traffic congestion may take hours longer by auto than by public transportation. The cost of gasoline is another factor in public transportation's favor. Public transportation does offer an important and affordable alternative.

- Basic fare—$1.25
- Transfer—$0.25
- Day pass—$3.00
- Monthly passes—$52.00

Public transportation can't serve every need, but LA Metro does offer cost cutting and time saving options. Still, though public transportation is affordable and comprehensive, the busy actor must primarily depend upon a personal vehicle or do a great deal of walking.

What about parking?

If one doesn't mind walking a few blocks, parking doesn't need to be a problem. Casting agents by necessity locate near available parking, both on-street and off-street. Parking garages, valets, and meters all cost money. But usually within a few blocks one can find free on-street parking. Watch the signs carefully, though, as most parking, metered or otherwise, comes with restrictions, permit requirements, and limitations. A missed sign can earn one a very expensive ticket.

Surviving in Los Angeles is really a matter of common sense and of using the resources at one's disposal. Learning the ins and outs of this city takes time, research, experimentation, networking with others, and trial and error—a lot of error! So ask questions and seek out advice.

Actors Forum

Like everyone else I thought I'm going to come here to conquer the city. They haven't seen me yet. Watch out Hollywood, here I come. You get grounded really fast because you soon discover there's a lot of people just like you in this town, wanting to do the exact same thing and they have more experience, maybe more talent, or are more trained than you are. They have tech savvy. Everyone does business by e-mail. Everyone's text messaging each other. You have to have a cell phone.

Tang Nguyen

The unions are having problems. If you put the television show on the cell phone, how are you going to pay the actors? They'll shoot in Canada so they don't have to pay residuals, and they really cut out your negotiating power. "Take it or leave it. We've got five hundred other actors who want the role." There are people up against me for one or two lines who have done a television series. It's just heartbreaking.

Jacque Lynn Colton

I was very lucky. The studio system collapsed in 1969. I came to do *Dynasty* on ABC, who had something that I don't think exists anymore called a Talent Development Program. ABC wanted me to play Adam Carrington before Aaron Spelling knew I existed, so I was spared all that corporate audition shit. It's just a lot of dead people behind a table who are basically lawyers or accountants with maybe one or two actual producers and, if you're lucky, a casting director's assistant. If you do become as lucky as I was for a while, anything you want you can have. You're going to want any sex, any drug, any car, any trip, any experience, anything to satisfy your appetite for living. And they're going to give it to you because you're hot, you're sexy, you're probably going to be famous, and you're going to make them even richer. And people know this. You don't know when you begin. I knew what I didn't want, so I didn't succumb. I didn't say, "Oh good, cocaine. I'll try it." I knew I didn't want that because I paid my dues.

Gordon Thomson

I've been in the business now for five years. You know what motivates me in this business, other than girls, is the money. The money that can be made in this business is so beyond sick. You don't even need to have talent. I'm not disrespecting an actor, but when you have an actor like Keanu Reeves who makes $258 million on *Matrix I, II*, and *III* and Stallone, "Yo Adrian!" who's made $300 million since 1976, they're not going to be getting any Oscars anytime soon. This business is about marketing. There's a reason why people will buy water from Norway, VOSS, for four dollars. You need to find your niche as an actor. Once you understand that as an actor you're a commodity, it's a process. It's not going to happen in a year, not going to happen in two. You better give yourself at least five years, and I'm talking balls to the wall!

Sajen Corona

4

The Business of Hollywood

It's somehow symbolic of Hollywood that Tara was just a facade, with no rooms inside.

David O. Selznick

The Hollywood Entertainment Industry Players

- 2,700 film and television production companies
- Over 600 casting directors
- Approximately 240 talent agents
- 600 management firms
- 117,000 members of SAG (Screen Actors Guild)
- Thousands of wannabee actors

Source: 2005 Hollywood Creative Directory

HOW DO I FIND A PAID ACTING JOB?

That's the $64,000 question, isn't it? Every actor in Hollywood would pay dearly to have the answer, and many casting services in Hollywood claim the inside track—for a fee, of course. But while Hollywood undeniably proffers the lure of great wealth and fame to wannabee actors, the incredibly competitive and complex nature of this industry flies in the face of these parasitic services that trade on an actor's dreams with simplistic promises. Actors, unfortunately, constitute a very subservient element of a billion dollar industry that markets dreams, visions, and a great deal of inferior pulp fiction. A few people make obscene amounts of money, or lose obscene amounts of money, all within a tedious infrastructure of legitimacy that harbors frauds, scams, and con artists. At best Hollywood is a gamble, and to be a player in this complex, multilayered marketplace, one must first understand its operating system and identify the real buyers and sellers in this high-stakes media poker game.

WHO ARE THE BUYERS?

Media companies that plan, commission, distribute, and produce principally film and television products represent the true buyers. On any given day in Los Angeles, on hundreds of studio sets and locations, large and small, union or otherwise, casts and crews spring into action, producing taped and film projects of all genres. But this billion dollar domestic industry, though still centered in Hollywood, has recently felt competition from north of the border. According to a report by the Center for Entertainment Industry Data and Research (CEIDR), domestic production expenditures declined by 17 percent in 2001, with Canadian film production expenditures increasing by 141 percent. The United States still represents 76.6 percent of all film production, but California and Washington have recently passed state initiatives to help lure production companies back to the United States (Katz, *Migration of Feature Film Production*, 1).

But the power to "green light" production still revolves around the half-dozen major studios that represent the last remnants of a once great empire of film magnates named Chaplin, Cohen, Warner, and Mayer. That golden age of the Hollywood studio system has long ago come and gone, and independent companies, such as Harvey and Bob Weinstein's Miramax and Ron Howard's Imagine Pictures, now produce most of the cutting edge, award-winning projects that dominate the public consciousness. But while independent film companies may produce more critically acclaimed projects, the major studios still control the business process. These studios own the facilities, the technical resources, and the distribution networks needed to produce more media products at a lower cost and at higher profit margins. Independent film companies, lacking these facilities and technical resources, must rent them from the studios, devouring a giant chunk of their production budget and gross profits in the process. Some independent companies form partnerships with the studios, often at their own peril. Witness Harvey and Bob Weinstein's recent split with Disney. A well-negotiated distribution deal with targeted product tie-ins can generate additional profit, but such deals rarely come without strings attached. To be sure, through direct production, rental, distribution, sales, and/or financial partnership agreements, the major studios in Hollywood have their fingers in the vast majority of domestic film and television projects and influence their content and marketing in many ways behind the scenes.

WHO ARE THESE "MAJOR STUDIOS"?

On the surface, the same acronymic television corporations from the past, such as ABC, NBC, and CBS, dominate the television industry, as the great corporations of film history, such as Warner Brothers, MGM, Universal, and Paramount still dominate the film industry. But today all these famous names are just subsidiaries of larger companies. Global megacorporations with broad interests in diversified markets engaged in a variety of commercial activities now own and control all the major studios. Japanese electronics giant Sony owns MGM; Viacom, itself controlled by National Amusements, an East Coast theatre management corporation, owns Paramount Studios and CBS; Disney owns ABC and Burbank Studios; and GE, with interests in both film and television, has acquired NBC and Universal Studios, itself bought and sold since the 1960s like an old war horse. Profit and profit alone drives these behemoths, not creativity or public service, despite their promotional rhetoric to the contrary. Script or casting decisions made today may be cancelled or fall victim tomorrow to a corporate merger, buyout, bankruptcy, or takeover, or to changing cultural trends, fads, politics, or celebrity foibles and whims.

The strange story of Warner Brothers serves as a metaphor for the entertainment industry: Be careful what you buy—it may eat you! In 1989 Warner Brothers merged with Time Inc. to form the media giant Time Warner. But in 2000, the high-flying head of AOL, Steve Chase, masterminded a takeover, opening the door for a massively powerful media giant to be controlled by a newcomer. Instead, AOL Time Warner floundered, and the stockholders banished Steve Chase and AOL to backstage status. The company's stock price continued to plummet.

The lesson to be learned for an actor? Each new twist and turn in the Hollywood corporate ecosystem puts dozens of projects, hundreds of actors, and thousands of technicians on notice or out of work. Nothing is for certain. Nothing is long term. The production process itself follows a treacherous path of focus groups, screenings, ratings, and budget meetings. Films lose funding and sitcoms are cancelled as collateral damage in the rise and fall of global entertainment politics. An actor may wait a lifetime for a break and finally get one, only to have it fall victim to a corporate scandal, the public whim, or a Michael Richards moment. C'est la vie! But knowledge is power, and the more an actor educates himself or herself on the internal workings of this industry, the better prepared he or she will be.

In the Box

One of the best auditions I ever gave was for a music video for an up and coming boy band. I had been called to audition for the role of a high school teacher. With fifteen years of high school teaching experience, I was more than prepared for that audition. With no script, I improvised each scenario I was given and nailed the audition. I was booked the next day. The music video was to be filmed at a local Los Angeles high school. My call time was the usual 7 a.m. for makeup and wardrobe. I arrived a few minutes early and sat and waited—and waited and waited. While this is not unusual, I couldn't help but notice that my scene kept being rescheduled. After the seventh hour of waiting, I finally asked the production assistant if this was a cruel joke and they would tell me I wasn't needed just in time to make rush hour traffic. As soon as I spoke the reason became clear. A limousine had just arrived, and its occupant emerged, a former television child star attempting a comeback via a cable reality program. The production company had set a deal with the reality show to publicize the video by including the former child star. As I soon learned, he was in and I was out.

HOW DOES THIS PRODUCTION PROCESS WORK?

Film and television companies must produce a product in order to stay in business. Whether it occurs within a major studio or an independent company, the production process follows a fairly straightforward approach. Investors form a production company that options or purchases a script. Typically a team of writers then develops the script and preps it for the camera (entertainment-speak for rewrites, revisions, and focus groups). Eventually, that preparation process involves casting. Rarely do the producers do their own casting. They hire one of the six hundred casting directors in Los Angeles to oversee the process. Some casting directors work exclusively for a specific studio (in-house), and some establish independent agencies. Producers occasionally opt to participate in the casting process, but most prefer to delegate the tedious process to the casting director and withhold judgment until the end. Either way, the casting director only makes a final recommendation to the producer, who rightly or wrongly and for better or for worse, will make the final decision either unilaterally, in collaboration, or as a surrogate for some nameless executive with a girlfriend who thinks she can act.

WHO ARE THE SELLERS?

Talent agents sell talent in this marketplace no differently than traders sell beef at the Chicago Commodities Exchange. The talent agent receives the casting breakdowns each day, reviews them, and then submits clients directly to the casting director either electronically or with hardcopy headshots. The casting director, or an associate, scans these submissions (usually numbering in the thousands per role) and narrows the selection to as few as ten or as many as a hundred for the first round of casting calls. A phone call to the talent agent, or the actor directly, sets the audition time. The casting director will often then make "sides" available to the actor to prepare for the audition. Out of this initial group, three to five finalists will be called back to read again, sometimes several times, before the casting director makes a final recommendation. After assembling an entire cast, a producer's audition may be held to confirm the choices before the casting director contacts the actor's talent agent to offer a booking. Once accepted, the actor signs the contract and is officially attached to the project.

While variations on this theme certainly occur, generally the acting business follows this standard process. Occasionally, open auditions or open calls (what are often called cattle calls) do occur, but these are usually done as a publicity stunt or for low paying extra work when producers need massive crowd scenes.

WHAT IS THE PRODUCT BEING BOUGHT AND SOLD?

Actors are what is bought and sold, of course. But it's a little more complicated than that. Hollywood is not looking for you, as of yet. Hollywood is looking primarily for types: cops, lawyers, younger leading metrosexuals, funny fat family men, female bombshells, and action heroes. More precisely, casting directors are looking for what they think young middle-American audiences think cops, lawyers, younger leading metrosexuals, funny fat family men, female bombshells, and action heroes look like.

The Screen Actors Guild's (SAG) *2004 Casting Data Report* reveals some sobering news for actors, especially minority actors. According to this report, television once again provided the lion's share of paying roles, with 86 percent of all roles cast. But while the film industry posted a respectable 4 percent increase over 2003, scripted shows on television actually lost a whopping 10 percent, the "reality" in reality programming. In truth, actors have seen a significant drop in their employment in Hollywood for four years in a row as a result of unscripted programming. SAG reports that the three major commercial networks, plus UPN and WB, "scheduled an average of 5.1 additional hours per week of non-scripted programs." This equals, according to SAG, the equivalent of "10 sitcoms or five drama series." Minority actors have taken the brunt of this decline.

HOW WELL DO ETHNIC ACTORS DO IN HOLLYWOOD?

Age, physical build, coloring, and facial features all serve to typecast actors and somewhat limit what roles will be open to them. One would like to believe that ethnicity shares no part in that limitation, but in truth, minority actors still predominately portray subservient and stereotypical roles. Caucasian actors still dominate the casting breakdowns, while minority actors account for only 25 percent of the total combined TV and theatrical casting (see chart 1).

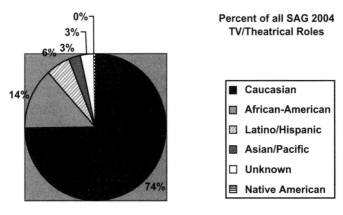

Chart 1. Source: *2004 SAG Casting Report*

Surprisingly, these figures at least roughly parallel the 2000 U.S. Census figures in which Caucasians represented 74 percent of the population, African-Americans 12.1 percent, Hispanics 14.5 percent, Asians 4.3 percent, and Native Americans 0.8 percent (U.S. Census Bureau, "2005 American Community Survey"). Chart 2 suggests that more lead roles have been awarded to minority actors since little difference exists between percentages of minority supporting roles and lead roles. But while these figures suggest that film and television casting does realistically represent the actual diversity of American society, a closer examination reveals the Hispanic market to be an exception.

It wasn't that long ago that minority organizations lauded Stephen Bochco's *Hill Street Blues* and Dick Wolf's *Law and Order* for challenging conventional sensibilities by casting ethnic actors to play district attorneys and judges. Creative casting has increased in practice, but the data show a decline in employment in most ethnic categories from 1999 to 2004.

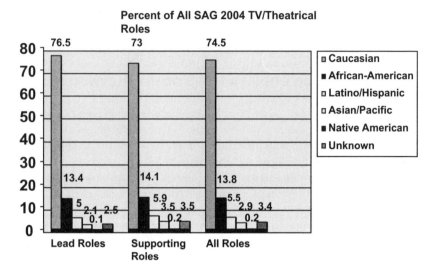

Chart 2. Source: *2004 SAG Casting Report*

As chart 3 indicates, most ethnicities, with the exception of Asian/Pacific, dropped in overall share of SAG casting from 2003 to 2004, while Caucasians increased by a whole percentage point. This is, of course, good news if you are a Caucasian actor, but if you are an ethnic Actor, it's plain to see that not all casting directors are as color-blind as they could be. Notably, the domestic Hispanic television market has significantly increased its share recently. As

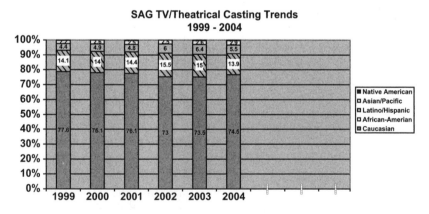

Chart 3. Source: *2004 SAG Casting Report*

14.5 percent of the population in year 2000 and growing each year, a 6 percent share of the casting represents a significant underrepresentation. No one will dispute the stereotyping of African-American and Asian roles in film and television casting, but both ethnicities benefit from well-established actors and directors who produce and market to their own communities. The Hispanic community has yet to establish actors and directors of that magnitude. But this is changing quickly.

Hispanic actors may take heart in one bright spot. The U.S Census Bureau estimates that the Hispanic population has grown by 58 percent in just the past fifteen years to now approximately 50 million. Analysts expect this figure to double by 2040 (McCabe, "San Diego Hispanic Television"). The Spanish language network Univision has grown to be the fifth-largest U.S. television network. Research conducted of Hispanic consumers indicates their preference for Spanish language programming, leading marketing and advertising firms to predict an explosion in Spanish language projects in the coming years to satisfy the demand for programming (Sonderup, "Hispanic Marketing"). Currently, daytime programming consists of the highly popular *telenovelas* produced in Brazil and Mexico, but increasingly one sees in the breakdowns calls for Spanish-speaking actors for Spanish language television programming. While actors of all types benefit from an increase in any market, Hispanic-American actors will primarily benefit from this rapidly growing market.

This is little solace, though, to the ethnic actor who must compete in a global market based in Hollywood when Asia, Mexico, and India all have vibrant film and television industries that import their best to Hollywood. Any ethnic actor coming to Hollywood must compete for limited roles with thousands of other actors coming from those countries.

Female actors, too, are at a disadvantage. As chart 4 demonstrates, despite a near 50/50 division in society, women fair far worse in the cultural mirror of television and film portrayals.

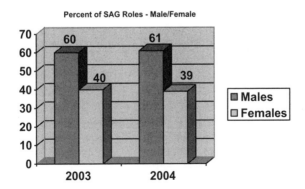

Chart 4. Source: *2004 SAG Casting Report*

Finally, Hollywood is still an industry dominated by under-forty-year-olds, for under-forty-year-olds. So, it's not surprising that most of the roles are written by twenty-year-olds for twenty-year-olds. Actors over forty appear nearly invisible in television casting and seem to be relegated to pharmaceutical commercials. And as chart 5 indicates, being over forty and female only makes matters worse.

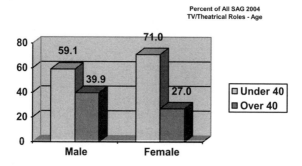

Chart 5. Source: *2004 SAG Casting Report*

The simple lesson to be learned from this data is that if one is a young, male, Caucasian actor in Hollywood, limitless opportunities await, but if one is an over-forty, female, ethnic actor, the challenge will be just getting in the door. But those who do and who have the talent to persevere will find a great deal of support among the rank and file working actors.

Actors Forum

It's really not that hard to find a good photographer. Generally the cheaper photographers are not the greatest. You really do get what you pay for. If you're strapped for cash, a lot of them are starting out and will do it for free for their portfolio. I do the digital because it's a whole lot easier. Any blemishes on your face can be taken out with Photoshop. I generally keep the clothes simple because they're not looking at your clothing; they should be looking at you. When I got roles after *American Dreams*, they asked for a demo reel. It's a new age and everyone's online now. A lot of times they want a hard copy of it so they can pop it in anytime they want, but it's just as easy to go on someone's Web site and click on their demo reel and push play.

Tang Nguyen

A woman who lived downstairs from me was a famous photographer. She told me if I took in her mail for six weeks she would take some headshots of me. They turned out awful because she didn't know me. She was just doing a favor. I met someone who was a *Newsweek* photographer and we arranged to go out to Central Park. Every shot this man took was beautiful. He would get me talking and take shot after shot. I was being me at my most real and funny. Every shot on the proof sheet could have been a headshot. The photographer has to love you in a way. I liked the proof sheet so much that I blew them up to 11 x 14 and put them in a book. Then I went to Actor's Equity. I showed them and they said, "You can't take proof sheets in for an audition." I went to an ad agency to meet a casting director. I showed her the proof sheets and she said, "These are adorable." Well, I started getting jobs at that ad agency. Don't believe what everybody tells you. When you see something that's good and you know it's good, then do it. Don't follow the crowd, because they don't always know.

Jacque Lynn Colton

I don't market myself well. I can't type. I don't do the Web site thing, and you should. Everything should be on DVD. If you can, get together what we used to call your demo reel. Pay for the best photographer you can. Finding a good photographer is very hard. Talk to your friends. In any camera shop, any film shop, there are always cards that photographers leave. They all have a Web site. Check them out. The most effective photographs I've ever had taken have been the ones where I was as relaxed as I could possibly be. No cutesy pooh, no character. None of that crap. Look as much like yourself as you can. It's essential probably that you don't dislike each other, at least.

Gordon Thomson

For an actor it's so important to get your own Web site. Ten years ago you'd have to mail out a VHS tape and be lucky if it actually went into a machine. Now, at a click of a stroke, they can watch your reel. I called Earthlink because I was having trouble with my Internet. I talked to this guy in India and told him I wanted to be a movie star. He Googled my name and within seconds he was able to go to my Web site and check out my reel. Pitch cards are very important for an actor to have, too. I went to Sundance. I didn't have the money for a pass, but I was on the street pitching. You've got to be prepared, though, to find your pitch card in a urinal face up at the premiere party! That's okay. It just made me stronger. It just gave me better stories to tell on Leno.

Sajen Corona

5

Marketing Tools

To market, to market, to buy a fat pig,
Home again, home again, dancing a jig;
To market, to market, to buy a fat hog;
Home again, home again, jiggety-jog;
To market, to market, to buy a plum bun,
Home again, home again, market is done.

Mother Goose

Actors' Online Forums, Chat Rooms, and Discussion Boards

Showfax Actors Resource Discussion Board
http://www.2nd-tier.com/showfax_bbs/

The Bone-Yard
http://pub59.ezboard.com/ftheactorsbonefrmThe Bone-Yard

Planet Shark Productions' Insider Industry Forum
http://pub64.ezboard.com/bplanetshark

Caryn.com Acting Resources
http://www.caryn.com/film/caryn-film-discussb.html

Actors Websource
http://www.actorswebsource.com/forums/index.php

The Actor's Forum
http://p206.ezboard.com/fthemoviefanforumfrm4

The Green Room
http://www.tvistudios.com/cgi-bin/ubbcgi/ultimatebb.cgi

American Association of Community Theatre Online Forum
http://www.aact.org/cgi-bin/yabb/YaBB.cgi

Hollywood a meat market? Hollywood remains its own worst enemy, and this image still rings true, although it is a bit simplistic. Without a doubt, actors both young and old represent a commodity, meat or otherwise, worshiped here on the altars of youth and sexual gratification. Any novice to this industry must confront that reality. Many fall victim to its expectations. The smart ones focus on developing that which makes them unique or different from the rest. Any marketing analysis begins by identifying that quality and then communicating it to potential customers.

WHAT MARKETING MATERIALS DO I NEED?

Twenty years ago an actor needed only a black and white headshot and a resume to launch a career. Today the digital and corporeal worlds have collided. Increasingly, the entertainment industry relies upon electronic casting for most projects. Yet hard copy headshots and resumes still remain the industry standard. Why? For the same reason that some people still prefer a typewriter. True, computers now provide instant digital access to an actor's marketing information: audio, video, and photos that are easily downloaded, categorized, and stored, eliminating crates of submissions and facilitating the screening required for the exacting casting process. But for some, nothing satisfies like the aesthetic of the mechanical process, and the casting director occasionally needs a photo to hold and physically handle, display, categorize, compare, or discard. Casting breakdowns often stipulate, "Submit electronically, then follow up with hard-copy submission." As a result, an actor needs to provide hard copies of photos and resumes as well as digital versions of each. From there, in order to compete in this marketplace, the actor must also eventually create a variety of specialized marketing materials such as business cards, photocards, an actor's reel, and a Web site.

Headshots

If casting is done electronically, do I still need headshots?

An actor's headshot functions as a business card. Casting directors spend on average only a second or two scrutinizing each of the thousands of photos that cross their desk for each project. Imagine looking at a thousand faces a day? Most will remain a blur, but certain faces may stand out. Why? A smile? A look in the eyes? A body? That helps, but an actor's headshot must convey more than a beautiful body. An actor needs to create a persona. True, it may be enhanced by wardrobe, makeup, or a spectacular setting, but the photo must catch the casting director's eye within that two-second window of time. An actor must therefore have good professional photos to compete in today's global marketplace, not amateur snapshots by well-meaning friends or loved ones.

An actor must have confidence in that headshot's ability to produce bookings. Finding the right photographer takes a systematic search. Even the best headshot eventually gets old, however. Casting directors expect actors to look like their headshots. Nothing will end an audition more quickly than an actor who arrives five years older, twenty pounds heavier, and twice as bald as advertised. Every actor needs new photos taken every few years. Each time can be like a born again experience. Hope springs eternal. If the last headshot didn't produce work, maybe this one will!

How do I find a good photographer?

Los Angeles teems with hundreds of professional photographers whose entire stock in trade is theatrical and modeling photos—no weddings, no proms, no bar mitzvahs, just headshots and portfolio shots. These photographers have an almost symbiotic relationship with actors. They need actors and actors need them. They advertise in every industry resource, from the trade papers to electronic casting services. But selecting the proper photographer involves dynamics not unlike choosing a good dentist. One really shouldn't just select a photographer randomly out of the Yellow Pages unless it's an emergency. Photographers have vastly different styles, equipment, and price schedules, as well as different personalities. Feeling comfortable with the photographer ranks as the primary consideration. A good photo shoot requires an actor to reveal his or her inner self and risk looking ridiculous in the process. Ask a few questions and do some simple research before hiring a photographer.

Ask Talent Agents and Managers. Word of mouth remains the best recommendation. When first representing an actor, a talent agent or manager may request new photos and may recommend a photographer. He or she may even arrange a discount. But beware! Talent agents and managers have been known to recommend a photographer in exchange for a commission or kickback. This setup is unethical but not illegal. On the other hand, some talent agents and managers do have contacts with well-known photographers. Check them out carefully. You might find a bargain, or just a photographer struggling to keep a studio open.

Check out other actors' headshots. Other actors provide the best source of referrals. When at auditions, workshops, readings, and so forth, make friends, ask questions, and purposely look at other actors' headshots, especially those of a similar age and category. Look for a style that catches your eye. Ask questions about the photographer and collect a name and telephone number. Actors usually give a more authentic recommendation than a Web site or advertisement.

Consult electronic Web sites. Most electronic casting Web sites have advertisements or resource lists of photographers, which may include links to their Web sites where samples of their work may be viewed. Once armed with a name, post a query on one of many online actors' forums, chat rooms, or discussion boards. Other actors will share their experiences, positive or negative, and warn about unprofessional, unethical, or unsavory photographers. Women especially should exercise caution. Unfortunately, the entertainment industry draws its share of predators masquerading as professional photographers.

Check out photo duplicating shops. Most photoduplicating services, in order to impress potential customers, plaster their entry walls with the headshots of their more successful clients. It may or may not impress, but it does provide a great comparative source of poses, styles, or looks employed by gainfully employed actors. Styles do change. Once again, scan for a photo that stands out, then look for the photographer's name, often printed somewhere in small print.

Interview selected photographers. Insiders recommend that an actor interview up to eight different photographers before making a decision. Those consultations offer each the opportunity to ask questions and to meet. Look for "chemistry," a symbiotic energy, something that suggests that this person can capture and eternalize one special moment in time. Interview the photographer, but also closely scrutinize his or her portfolio. Are the photos clear or muddy looking? Is the background obtrusive? Do the poses look stiff or posed? Does the photo draw your interest? What's happening in the eyes?

What questions should I ask the photographer? The photographer will make a series of recommendations regarding wardrobe, hair or makeup, photo location, and shooting style. Listen to the photographer's suggestions, but make certain the following questions are answered to your satisfaction.

How much will it cost? A headshot session of several hours can cost anywhere from $200 to $2,000, depending on the photographer. First, establish the fee and what it includes. Photographers generally charge an hourly rate for studio time, but this usually includes approximately seventy shots, proofs, and perhaps two or three 8x10 prints, rarely more, so beware of the "packaged deal" pitch. Conventional wisdom also might suggest that the more expensive the photographer the better the photo. But sometimes one needs to follow unconventional wisdom. If you are strapped for cash, seek out a beginning professional photographer who is looking to build a portfolio. Check out Craigslist to find photographers willing to shoot for free in exchange for the use of the photos.

Digital or 35mm photographs? Digital cameras have reached professional quality, but many actors, reluctant to switch, believe 35mm remains the superior format. Regardless of one's preference, both a digital file and a hard copy photo will ultimately be required. Either format has advantages and disadvantages.

35mm Cameras	Digital Cameras
Superior quality	Quality will soon surpass 35mm.
Requires costly film	Requires only a reusable memory stick or card
Prints are cheaper	Prints are more expensive
Hard copy photos must be scanned	Digital files download instantly into a computer
Defects must be airbrushed	Photoshop easily corrects blemishes and defects
8x10 prints are easily copied	Headshot reproduction services prefer submission of digital files.

With either format, the photographer generally shoots a set number of exposures for a set fee and provides contact prints. But contact prints don't always display sufficient detail. Enlargements will suddenly reveal imperfections and distractions. You will want to choose half a dozen or more exposures for enlargement in order to have a satisfactory selection. Photographers may provide final prints and/or a disk of the digital photo files, usually in a high-resolution format.

Studio lighting or natural light? Photographers live or die by their lighting technique. Some have elaborate studios with complex lighting equipment, and others provide only the basics. Still others prefer to work outdoors, dueling with Mother Nature over sunlight angles and shadows. Outdoor photos lack the smoothness and the subtlety of indoor photos, but they offer a variety of backgrounds that suggest role-playing.

How many clothing changes are allowed? Wardrobe requires a series of individual decisions based upon what persona the actor wishes to portray. Photographers may suggest three, four, or even more clothing changes. Just remember, the fee pays for the photographer's time. The more time you spend changing clothes, the less time you will spend in front of the camera. In addition, glamour shots require an extensive wardrobe and makeup. Fantasies need to be costumed elaborately and can cost serious money. On the other hand, photography inspires improvisation. Take a close look at your wardrobe, check out local thrift and value stores, find something that looks really good, and go with it.

Always remember that wardrobe selection, whether formal or informal, ethnic or generic, hip or professional, sexy or wholesome, should reflect positively upon the product—namely, you. The photographer will provide suggestions for style and color. Set the number of wardrobe changes and types of clothes, and organize wardrobe pieces in shooting order.

How do I prepare for the photo shoot?

Once you have chosen a photographer, agreed upon the fee, services, and a specific time and place, the work has just begun. Whether you are male or female, laundering, grooming, and gathering remain imperative.

Wardrobe. If possible, let the photographer preview the selections. If not, bring a variety of choices and trust the photographer's suggestions. In general, avoid black and white, green, yellow, and orange. Inspect the clothes and try them on. Just because something fit two months ago doesn't mean it fits today. Clean, press, and organize each item in filming order. Make them transportable in garment bags, easily loaded and unloaded.

Grooming. Whoever you are, male or female, young or old, make definitive decisions about hair color, style, and length. An actor must commit to those decisions. Having a beard for a headshot means appearing at an audition with the same beard. The same is true for hair color, general length, and style. Gather grooming and makeup paraphernalia for the shoot. Some photographers offer makeup and hair technicians to assist. Either way, bring rescue tools: hair dryer, curler, gel, spray, and hairpins.

Makeup. Men should bring face powder. Photographers prefer actors to move, often to music, to set a mood. Powder periodically applied removes the sheen from a sweaty face. On the other hand, a spray bottle may be used to create a hot and sweaty appearance. Any veteran stage actor knows how to use an eyebrow pencil to correct any imperfect eyebrow features, and a mascara brush instantly masks gray in a beard or mustache.

If they can afford it, women should have makeup professionally applied just prior to the photo shoot. If they cannot, they should seek out an aspiring makeup artist who needs practice. Make a deal! Or, bring a friend to keep the chaos organized.

What should I expect during the photo shoot?

You have the right to expect professionalism. The photographer has the right to expect the same. If at any time the situation turns uncomfortable, speak up. A good photographer should create a comfortable atmosphere, whether that involves burning incense, setting lights, playing music, or jabbering about the morning news. Many actors bring their own CD to set a mood. Photographers generally offer a selection as well. The rest depends on the camera and the subject, with the assistance of some verbal and nonverbal communication. The photographer should follow the actor's lead, if he or she has one; otherwise, the photographer may suggest poses and looks. At this point, the personalities of the photographer and the actor engage, and the result hopefully emerges artistically and aesthetically satisfying.

How do I choose a headshot?

The photographer should provide contact sheets of proofs, small exposure-sized prints that show little detail but when viewed with a magnifying glass provide enough clarity to enable you to choose the shots you would like to have enlarged to 8x10s. The final choice will ultimately be subjective and may not even be yours to make. Talent agents or managers generally preempt the actor's choice based upon their expertise. But if given the choice, consider the following questions.

To smile or not to smile? Thirty years ago a nonsmiling photo suggested an actor with bad teeth. Today it reads as a dramatic actor but still not necessarily as a commercial actor. Theatrically, Actors still need to appear more neutral, mysterious, or downright seductive. Versatile actors may need two different headshots—a commercial one and a theatrical one. This gets pricey, but it solves the conundrum.

Body shot or close-up? A headshot should, at the very least, flatter the actor. Most photographers will shoot both body shots and close-ups unless the actor directs otherwise. The final choice may depend ultimately on what the actor wishes to sell. A body, a face, or both?

Where do I have headshots printed?

Photo reproduction services flourish in Los Angeles for obvious reasons. One needs only a digital file or an 8x10 photo to have bulk headshot reproductions processed. Most offer approximately the same services and charge similar fees.

Sizes. Bulk reproductions of 8x10 headshots, photo postcards, and zed cards, which display three or four different high-fashion poses.

Quantity. Ordered in groups of one hundred. Package deals usually offered.

Formats. Portrait, landscape, bordered or borderless, color or black and white. Color printing, now cheaper than in the past, has become the industry standard, though black and while photos still offer a stylish alternative. A recent in-house survey by casting director Bonnie Gillespie reveals that 92 percent of actors submitted color headshots as opposed to black and white (Lawrence, "Los Angeles Acting Blog").

Finishes. Gloss finishes are prone to fingerprints. Pearl finishes provide a kind of luster but tend to look manufactured. A matte finish weathers better but is cheaper—and may look as such.

Text. One's professional name, talent agent or logo, and union affiliations all may be imprinted.

Resume

What should I put on my resume?

A resume always accompanies a headshot, sized to 8x10 inches, either printed directly on the back of the headshot or on an attached sheet. As with any professional, the resume represents one's professional accomplishments, training, and special skills, and it may drop a name or two along the way. But what if all you have is training and skills?

Everyone begins a career at the beginning. Other than college and community credits, a newly graduated actor may only have training and skills to report. If this is your situation, list those college and community theatre productions, but, when possible, mask their amateur status by eliminating the words "community" and "college" from the listing. Needless to say, replace these credits at the earliest opportunity. Always a work in progress, an actor should update a resume each time more experience or training has been earned, always eliminating lesser credits in favor of those with more weight. Consider the degree of difficulty, versatility required, and prestige attached to each new role in weighing its placement on a resume.

How should I organize my resume?

Just as in other professions, the entertainment industry has a resume standard. Hollywood insiders recognize a newcomer's resume in one of two ways: it may lack organization or it may not be stapled to the back of the headshot's upper left hand corner. The latter reflects laziness to the casting director. For the professional standard, try the following template.

Nameplate The top three inches of the resume forms the nameplate and should contain some essential information.

Name (or a stage name). The actors unions collectively require a unique name for membership. Check with SAG first. Even if you are not a union member now, if you aspire to be one in the future, it is best not to build a career around a name that will eventually have to be changed.

Union affiliation(s). List membership in any of the four sister unions, but don't lie. Many Actors join AFTRA, an open union, just to list something here. But be prepared to pay a $1,300 initiation fee, in addition to current dues. College honor societies don't count.

Height and weight. Be honest here as well. Casting directors expect an actor to appear for an audition as advertised, not ten pounds heavier or two inches shorter.

Body type. List this attribute only if you are comfortable with the category. Casting directors hire actors with heavy set and chunky bodies as well as slim and athletic bodies, but for admittedly different types of roles. Actors may want to specialize in a particular body type.

Vocal range (if any). List this attribute only if you wish to advertise this talent.

Credits Credits are divided into genres: television, film, music video, and stage, generally in that order, although television and film are interchangeable. Understandably in a film town such as Hollywood, stage ranks lowest even though it might include the bulk of one's credits.

Television. Arrange in three columns: (1) project title, (2) contract rate of the role (principal, day player, guest star, etc.), and (3) network or production company. Place in parentheses the name of any celebrity connected to the project as a director, producer, writer, or actor. Rank each credit chronologically, or cite your best roles first.

Film. Also arrange in three columns: (1) project title and writer's name, (2) contract rate, and (3) production company. Once again, list the director, producer, or actors if noteworthy. Student, educational, and industrial films count as well.

Commercials. State only "Commercials provided upon request." Why no commercial credits on a resume? Even the entertainment industry harbors a hierarchy, and commercials rank near its bottom. Unless you plan to specialize in only commercials, most talent agents recommend stating in small letters, "Commercials provided upon request."

Music Videos. Once again, arrange in three columns: (1) performer and song title, (2) role played, and (3) production company and director. Film directors, both new and experienced, often direct music videos to showcase their talent.

Stage. Arrange in two columns: (1) title, venue, and theater company, and (2) role performed.

Related Skills and Training List sports, stage skills, dialects, language proficiencies, or any other extraordinary skills. Using a separate line entitled "Training," list academic degrees, programs, awards, acting schools, coaches, and trainers and their specialty.

What should I NOT put on my resume?

Never provide personal and private information on a resume, such as home address, Social Security number, marital status, date of birth, or even exact age. Cultivate a sense of mystery. Some resumes simply provide an "age range." When possible, use a talent agent's or manager's phone number, not a personal number. The same goes for e-mail addresses. Academic curriculum vitae are definitely unnecessary, as are corporate styled subheadings such as "Career Objectives" and "Salary Requirements."

Do actors lie or exaggerate on their resumes?

Actors routinely pad their resumes, dropping a name, listing a cancelled production, elevating a role, or even switching productions and venues. Any working actor who denies padding his or her resume at some point is lying. But true working actors don't need to lie. They have the credits. Only novice actors without serious credits need to fill that void, but they take a risk when they invent roles for themselves. Consider this example supplied by Academy Award winning actor Michael Caine:

> I wrote down as part of my experience that I had played George in *George and Margaret*. I was summoned to an audition, and when I walked into the theater the first thing the producer said to me was, "It says here that you played George in *George and Margaret*?" "So I did," I replied. "You are a bloody liar all right," roared the producer, "or you would know that the plot of that play centers on the fact that the entire cast spends the whole duration of the play waiting for George and Margaret to turn up, and they never do!" (Caine, *What's It All About*, 88)

Inside Hollywood beats a small-town heart. Padding a resume can eventually lead to an embarrassment. Casting directors recognize past projects, especially if they cast them. Better to list high school, college, or community theatre credits, dress them up a bit, and then systematically replace them with each new student film, Equity-Waiver theatre, or nonunion project. Eventually, you will accumulate enough union credits to replace them all.

How should I format and reproduce my resume?

Since a resume attaches to the back of an 8x10 headshot, format the resume to fit that size, even though it will be printed on standard 8½x11 paper. Simply size the paper to the resume and then trim to match. Not doing so will appear unprofessional. Photocopies will suffice, but always treat a resume as a work in progress. Maintain it as a computer file and print copies as needed. You can even print directly on the back of the headshot, saving paper, staples, and time. Experiment and see what works.

Photo Cards

Occasionally actors may wish to send announcements regarding an upcoming television role, stage appearance, or film release. Most casting directors, but not all, appreciate receiving updates on an actor's work, if known to them, as do some producers, directors, and other actors. So actors mail out photo postcards, which are printed by photo reproduction services at a bulk rate with a headshot on one side and the announcement on the other. Add the cost of postage and labels and the expense can be considerable, but as in all advertising, over time the residual effect may lead to more auditions and more work.

Do I need photo business cards?

Business cards carrying an actor's headshot are certainly not a necessity. Most actors function without them unless they are promoting a second business. But networking requires some type of promotional tool. Business cards tucked into a wallet provide a cost effective alternative to bulky and unwieldy headshots. A simple business card with one's headshot in miniature and contact information does provide a relatively inexpensive option.

Actor's Reel

The term *Actor's reel* initially referred to the actual metal reel on which actors kept clips of their best scenes to show to producers and casting directors. The digital age has transformed that metal reel into a DVD that displays those clips on a computer or television screen. Today's actor's reels are easily reproduced and transported, and casting directors often request them in their daily breakdowns. The actor's dilemma lies in collecting those clips.

How do I get clips of my work?

Nonunion or deferred pay film projects often lure actors with the promise of "copy, credit, and meals." But securing that "copy" can be problematic. Production companies come and go, move, warehouse projects, and ultimately have no real requirement to provide actors with copies of any finished product. All too often actors must beg, steal, borrow, or buy their copies in order to secure documentation of their work. Always record any television project when it airs. Film projects will eventually appear as DVDs or downloads, but not for some time. Music videos generally can be downloaded. Student films or industrial/educational projects may be more difficult. Commercials, though, offer a particular challenge. Unless you plan to record long blocks of television airtime, you must contact the production company personally to obtain a commercial project. Most companies will provide a copy, but for a fee.

How do I go about making an actor's reel?
A DVD consisting of a five- to ten-minute montage of video clips from an actor's past television, film, commercial, and even stage projects, represents the digital equivalent of an actor's reel. Creating this montage need not involve expense or complication. Several software programs easily transfer videotape to a digital file and allow the user to edit and produce the actual DVDs. Many businesses provide this same service at an hourly rate.

Personal Website

Should I have my own Web site?
In the twenty-first century, cyberspace is creating virtual explorers of everyone, each of us pioneering new domains and establishing new digital communities, homesteading with personal Web sites or "spaces." Performers need a virtual "booth" that is accessible to all with a computer, in which they can display their promotional materials easily and cheaply to prospective clients. Digital resumes may be sent electronically with an active link to one's personal Web site. Some production companies provide links on their Web site for each cast member's personal Web site. Clips and photos can easily be changed and one's resume updated, providing one with a 24-hour, 365-days-a-year product showroom.

How do I establish a personal Web site?
Actors, verily anyone in the performing arts, have a variety of options:

1. Younger actors, those who have grown up with YouTube and MySpace, have created cost-free virtual spaces in which to post film clips, resumes, photos, and blogs. But the formats display less than professionally, and questions still remain regarding infringement of copyright laws despite the truce between YouTube and the television networks (Montopoli, "CBS to YouTube").
2. Most electronic casting services offer a personalized Web page as an incentive for membership. Options are usually limited unless one pays additional fees.
3. Several online services allow clients to "build their own" Web site, giving them a variety of options and tools from which to choose but often requiring fees to maintain their sites.
4. For the most individualistic, maintaining a personal Web site can provide a flexible and cost-effective marketing tool. The primary cost involves

hiring a Web site designer. Once established, the Web site costs only a monthly fee to maintain, though additional fees may apply for updating.
5. Web creation software such as Dreamweaver provides powerful tools to build, maintain, and update one's own Web site but generally requires some tutoring to learn the complicated coding involved in HTML creation.

Whichever way you choose, if you build it, they will come.

What is the *Academy Players Directory*?

The Academy of Motion Picture Arts and Sciences represents over 6,500 film-makers whose achievements have placed them at the top of their craft. Perhaps most notable for its Academy Awards, this professional honorary organization has historically published the *Academy Players Directory*, a casting bible of every working professional actor in the entertainment industry. For decades, producers and casting directors have relied upon this coffee table tome for quick reference and casting ideas. Unfortunately, its usefulness of late has declined with the proliferation of online services. Most casting directors prefer the flexibility and convenience of online services, and the *Directory* may have become somewhat of a relic of the past. In 2006 the *Academy Players Directory* published its final edition and was sold to Now Casting Inc., which has merged it somewhat with its online electronic casting service (Academy of Motion Picture Arts and Sciences, "History and Structure"). To be included, an actor must have membership in an actor's union, either domestic or foreign. The printed version still only lists the actor's name, one photo, credits, and representation. The online version provides an option for additional photos and inclusion of an actor's digital reel.

Actors in Hollywood will find no end to the marketing tools at their disposal. Over the years, they have tried every nontraditional approach imaginable, such as billboards, skywriting, singing telegrams, and elaborate staged presentations. It all costs lots of money, and its effectiveness is consistently difficult to analyze. All too often one must spend a dollar to make a dime in the hope that someday that dime will multiply a hundred times over.

Actors Forum

The key thing is to have an agent that will push for you, that will fight for you, and that has some kind of pull. They may not be able to get you in. They may not have the pull, but at least they're on top of it and know what's going on. It is a hassle. You have to check in almost every day, because new things are coming in all the time. Don't rely upon your agent to get you auditions. They're there to negotiate the money when you do book a role. It's really up to you to be in charge of your own career. Your agent has enough to do without babying you. You've really got to do it yourself.

Tang Nguyen

I have a relationship with an agent again, finally. When your agent dies and you're over thirty or over forty, it's very, very hard to get anybody excited about you. And if you don't have an agent that's excited about you, forget about it.

Jacque Lynn Colton

It's a very important relationship. Avoid one-man offices. I would also suggest avoiding big offices. I remember I was with William Morris, and on a list of actors over fifty was Bill Cosby. I thought, this is not an agency I want to be with, but I had already signed with them. They treated the biggest star in television at the time as simply a name in a category. It was grotesque. That's the attitude of that kind of agency, and there are several of them around. When you find an agency, they'll check you out very carefully. You check them out too. I had a manager that was charming as hell. She was bright, imaginative, attractive, and she had all this pizzazz. And she was the laziest woman I've ever come across. I hired her on my agent's recommendation, who was on coke most of the time and extorting money from this agency as well as from me, and I knew nothing.

Gordon Thomson

The last four years I've been through about five agents. I got my agent doing the drop. I went to Samuel French. They have labels for about 260 talent agents and you do the drop, mail a headshot to all of them. You only need one. My agency dropped me while I was at Sundance. I had their name all over my promotional materials. When I got back to tell them that I had booked a movie, *Gettin' It*, they said, "You didn't get our letter?" How hard would it have been for an agent to pick up a phone and say, "Look, you don't fit our criteria"? They won't even tell you when they drop you. They'll just send a letter. You have to find the agent that believes in you, and I'm still in that process.

Sajen Corona

6
Talent Agents and Personal Managers

I'm not selling Cadillacs. I'm selling human beings. I'm selling artist's souls. I'm looking for brilliant actors that I think can break, who either have hopes of breaking or who come very close to breaking. An actor must respect my efforts, and if he doesn't think I take care of him on that level, then he needs to leave me.

Scott Manners, Stone Manners Talent Agency

Talent Agent and Manager Resource List

Association of Talent Agents (ATA)
9255 Sunset Blvd., Suite 930
Los Angeles, CA 90069
(310) 274-0628, Fax (310) 274-5063
http://www.agentassociation.com/

California Division of Labor Standard Enforcement
(cases involving talent agencies)
http://www.dir.ca.gov/dlse/DLSE-TACs.htm

Screen Actors Guild—Hollywood Agents List
5757 Wilshire Blvd.
Los Angeles, CA 90036-3600
(323) 549-6733
http://www.sag.org/sagWebApp/application?origin=page1

Wikipedia's list of Hollywood agencies and management companies
http://en.wikipedia.org/wiki/
List_of_Hollywood_agencies_and_management_companies

Talent Manager's Association
http://www.talentmanagers.org/

WHAT IS A TALENT AGENT?

Hollywood films and television have cemented in the minds of Americans the image of the Hollywood talent agent as a wheeling-dealing, ego-driven, type-A control freak who hobnobs with Hollywood moguls and makes or breaks actors' careers. While some agents may fit that stereotype to one degree or another, the reality is much more mundane. Except for a few mega-agencies, most talent agencies operate from small offices, tied to the world of electronic casting via the Web, telephones, e-mails, fax machines, booking slips, and an ever changing contract environment, affording agents little time for the so-called Hollywood social scene.

The role of a talent agent includes marketing and promoting his or her stable of clients by submitting their headshots and resumes to casting directors, networking with personal managers, processing contracts, and advising clients on the legal complexities of union regulations and production company requests. In their spare time, talent agents may attend workshops and theatre productions or showcases, always on the lookout for fresh faces to represent. For their efforts, talent agents receive a union-capped 10 percent commission on each client's income (SAG, "Codified Basic Agreement").

WHAT DOES A TALENT AGENT DO FOR THE ACTOR?

Part den mother or father, part business partner, and part mentor, a talent agent provides a buffer, a filter, or liaison for an actor, acts as an advocate who markets, promotes, and even packages the actor's talents, and then serves as a mediator during contract negotiations. Some negotiations proceed smoothly; others, not so much. An actor may choose to stay in the background, providing distance and deniability, or not. If successful, the agent processes the contract and shepherds the actor through its documentation. Many bookings don't issue contracts until after the shoot. A good talent agent will secure a deal memo of some type, providing a guarantee as to the final terms of compensation. The agent bills the producer for the actor's services and, when payment is received, deducts and transacts payroll deductions, disburses the actor's net earnings after commission, and records the transaction.

The unions provide complicated and legalistic contract guidelines to safeguard actors' rights. Talent agents must understand the complexities of union requirements, and when requests exceed contract terms, they intervene when warranted. If issues arise on the set, the talent agent acts as an advocate. The talent agent protects and defends the actor for one important reason: the more the actor makes, the more the talent agent makes. But a talent agent is not an attorney, although many successful talent agents have degrees in entertainment law. On matters of contract law, a talent agent should refer an actor to an entertainment law attorney for counseling.

In the Box

As I sat talking to my talent agent, her ubiquitous phone rang and she answered. I overheard a brief conversation in which one of her other clients, who was working on a film, was calling to claim that he had been required to perform an action sequence that clearly fell within the realm of stunt work, despite the fact that he had not been hired for such. The agent calmly instructed the actor to sit quietly and do nothing until she called back. She then dialed the number of the production company in question, identified herself as the actor's talent representative and asked to speak to the production manager. The conversation proceeded civilly but pointedly. The actor had been hired as a day player and had now been required to perform stunt work, which entitled him to an additional day's pay. The production manager appeared to disagree, at which time the agent pulled out the SAG Basic Codified Agreement and read him the specific requirement to which the production company was a signatory. Having reached agreement on the additional compensation, the agent called back the actor on the set and instructed him to go back to work now. The entire conversation took less than three minutes. The agent apologized and calmly continued our conversation. I felt less than inconvenienced, though, since I had witnessed firsthand exactly why an actor needs a knowledgeable talent agent to represent his or her interests in this competitive business.

ARE THERE DIFFERENT KINDS OF TALENT AGENTS?

Some talent agents may specialize as either commercial agents or theatrical agents (film and television), but many represent both. (Some actors prefer to engage a talent agent to represent them in both, while others prefer to have two agents hustling their talent. Some talent agents may require dual representation as a condition to signing an actor.) Some may handle only voice-over clients or stunt actors. Still others represent only children, teenagers, or models. An agency may also have a literary department that handles writers or agents who specialize in representing directors. The largest agencies, such as William Morris, Creative Artists (CAA), United Talent (UTA), and International Creative Management (ICM), employ a small army of agents, exclusively representing only star players and covering every base of the creative process. This range of clients provides them with the ability to package a project in-house from soup to nuts: the writers, the directors, and the actors. At the other end of the spectrum are the mom and pop agencies that, in order to make ends meet, must represent all categories.

HOW DOES ONE BECOME A TALENT AGENT?

A talent agent in the state of California must be both licensed and bonded. A prospective agent must make written application to the California Labor Commission, providing:

- name and address;
- the business address of the proposed site where the business will be conducted;
- previous employment history;
- names and addresses of all business partners and the percentage of their investment;
- letters of recommendation from two members of the entertainment industry attesting to the applicant's moral character;
- two sets of fingerprints;
- a $225 license fee and a $25 filing fee; and
- a surety bond of $10,000, placed in a trust account. This protects the actor against potential fraud, since an actor's salary is generally processed through the agent, who deducts taxes and commissions before disbursing the remainder.

(Association of Talent Agents, "Laws Relating to Talent Agencies: Excerpts from the California Labor Code")

Upon receipt, the commission conducts an investigation into the character of the applicant and the proposed business premises. If approved, the commission grants a ninety-day temporary license. As a condition of licensing, the applicant must agree to:

- file a schedule of fees to be charged and collected in the conduct of the business;

- file all contracts with the Labor Commission;
- abide by state Dispute Resolution Rules; and
- never split fees with an actor's employer.

Additional conditions apply when seeking employment for minors.

MUST AN ACTOR HAVE A TALENT AGENT?

An actor may self-submit for any project, but union signatory producers use talent agents as a screening process, assuming that any legitimate actor would have representation. They submit their breakdowns exclusively to licensed talent agents, who immediately submit their clients. Unrepresented actors must learn of pending projects from the trades, often long after completion of primary casting. For the most part, Internet casting services only post nonunion projects that pay little to nothing. Union projects occasionally appear, but only because the casting director needs to troll a broader ocean. Most television and commercial casting occurs quickly. But whether for the sake of credibility or to facilitate the process, actors generally need a licensed talent agent to submit them in time to a SAG signatory project.

HOW DO I FIND A LICENSED TALENT AGENT?

An actor doesn't find a talent agent, the talent agent finds the actor. Most agents represent a stable of clients, perhaps a dozen in each age, gender, and ethnic category. If an opening occurs, talent agents may solicit actors for representation. They may respond to an actor's direct solicitation for representation or attend showcases and workshops looking for interesting faces. After a face-to-face meeting, several potential clients will receive verbal acceptance of representation for a probationary period. In other words, the actor that works gets the contract; the actor that doesn't, will walk. Yes, talent agents constantly search for fresh talent to bring more cash into their agency, but talent agents also build their agency upon the working actor who generates consistent commissionable income. They will sign that actor to either a SAG Agency Contract if they are SAG franchised, or to a General Services Contract if they are not.

HOW DOES A TALENT AGENT FIND NEW ACTORS TO REPRESENT?

In the 1980s, talent agents explored Hollywood's considerable talent showcases, such as "comedy houses" or "music rooms." Today's talent agents can preview an actor's reel in the privacy of a den. The trick is getting their attention long enough to view the goods. Veteran actors recommend the following three strategies.

The Drop. Potentially the most effective approach, but also the most expensive, an actor mails a headshot, resume, and possibly an actor's reel to every talent agent in Los Angeles. Care should be taken to separate out agents who represent only children or other categories out of one's expertise. Legitimate online casting services, such as NowCasting, LACasting, and Actors Access, provide label-formatted downloads of current names and addresses of all legitimately licensed California talent agents. Bookstores and magazine kiosks sell complete packets of preprinted labels. Next, several hundred photos and resumes must be assembled into 9x12 envelopes with a well-written cover letter requesting a meeting, and then "dropped" into the mail. The odds favor a 10 percent response rate. Telephone follow-up calls are an acceptable practice.

Showcase. Find a good theatre company, showroom, or comedy venue to audition for, and when performing, send invitations to those talent agents with whom you've become acquainted. The role should be substantial, not the second spear holder in *Julius Caesar*. If interested, a talent agent will make contact and offer to observe a performance. Proper etiquette is to offer complimentary tickets, usually for two. Expect the agent to come backstage after the performance. (If the agent doesn't, that isn't a good sign.) You will know quickly whether or not the talent agent has any interest. He or she may proffer a business card and request a phone call to set up an appointment. The rest will be up to you.

Referral. Actors have little to offer other actors except for experiential advice, but the act of referral represents one exception. An actor may ethically recommend another actor to the same talent agent. But, always mindful of one's integrity, they do so with great discretion.

WHAT SHOULD I EXPECT WHEN I MEET WITH A TALENT AGENT?

Expect to be evaluated, appraised, assessed, and generally assayed on various scales pertaining to potential productivity. An agent must believe you will make him or her money. The enthusiasm with which the agent represents an actor directly relates to the degree to which the agent perceives the actor to be a "hot property." Most mentors will advise the actor to just be himself, admittedly a simplistic answer. Actors must be everything and anything. True, authenticity counts, but so do professionalism, poise, and confidence. This polish is what convinces a talent agent that an actor can hold his or her own in a casting director's office. The agent may ask questions about training, experience, resume credits, and personal interests, looking for versatility. The agent will also ask to see a memorized monologue, perhaps two contrasting pieces, so come prepared to perform in a busy office full of interruptions.

IS IT IMPORTANT TO HAVE A SAG FRANCHISED AGENT?

Yes and no. SAG's Global Rule 16 (g) requires all members to accept representation from only SAG franchised talent agents (SAG, "Codified Agency Regulations"). Ostensibly, this rule protects actors from the many disreputable scam artists claiming to be talent agents. But in a recent attempt at union busting, legitimate talent agencies, such as the William Morris Agency, have dropped their SAG franchise, leaving union actors in a quandary.

On the surface this conflict appears to stem from what SAG recognizes as commissionable income. Different standards have been negotiated in different regions. In Los Angeles the union upholds the right of an actor to receive a minimum salary, known as scale. All SAG television and theatrical contracts recognize only income above and beyond this minimum as commissionable. Casting directors generally offer scale plus 10 percent in their breakdowns in the Los Angeles market. Additionally, reimbursement income, such as per diem, mileage, and wardrobe allowances, doesn't fall under SAG's definition of commissionable income. But, others disagree.

The dissident talent agents have other complaints as well. All these issues are currently undergoing a dispute resolution process between the unions and the Association of Talent Agents (ATA), a nonprofit trade association representing the interests of over one hundred member agencies and the National Association of Talent Representatives (NATR) in New York. As an act of good faith, SAG most recently suspended its Global Rule 16 (g) of its Codified Agency Regulations (*Screen Actors Magazine*, "General Service Agreements"). SAG members may now accept representation from any non-SAG franchised talent agent who belongs to ATA or NATR. But buyer beware. The General Services Agency Contract (GSA) offered by these talent agents differs significantly from a SAG Franchised Agency Contract (see Appendix C, document 1).

WHAT IS THE DIFFERENCE BETWEEN A SAG AGENCY CONTRACT AND A GSA?

Commission rates. SAG caps a talent agent's commission at 10 percent across the board on all applicable income. GSA Contracts may stipulate up to 15 percent and even 20 percent.

Commissionable income. SAG sets a minimum wage (scale) for actors in all television projects. Commissions may only be paid on amounts over and above this minimum wage, and SAG restricts many other residual payment conditions. GSA contracts consider all an actor's earned income commissionable, including all travel and living expenses and reimbursements for travel and mileage, even though this may have been paid up front from previously commissionable earned income.

Term of contract. SAG contracts restrict initial contracts with talent agents to a one-year term, renewable for up to three years. GSA contracts require longer terms.

Limit to representation. SAG limits an agency's representation to a fifty-mile radius, except in Los Angeles, which extends its jurisdiction throughout the state of California. This limit allows an actor to have different agents in different cities. GSA contracts revoke this limitation and stipulate worldwide exclusive representation.

Conflict resolution. In the event of a conflict, SAG provides binding arbitration for the dispute. GSA submits its members' conflicts to the California Labor Commission for declaration. SAG has no legal standing in such instances (*Screen Actor's Guild Magazine,* "Important Message").

WHAT IS THE DIFFERENCE BETWEEN A TALENT AGENT AND A PERSONAL MANAGER?

A personal manager provides an actor with a variety of services once provided by a talent agent, including advice, promotion, travel arrangements, networking, and mentoring. The talent agent of yore no longer exists in this more technologically bound and competitive market. Personal managers offer a more objective and personal approach to career building. Their personal contacts and experience inside the industry may provide them an insider's advantage with insight and access, but there are limitations, and actors can pay handsomely for their services.

- California state law licenses talent agents but not personal managers. As such, while personal managers may build relationships in the entertainment industry, they may not solicit employment or enter into contractual negotiations on behalf of actors (Association of Talent Agents, "Laws Relating to Talent Agencies: Excerpts from the California Labor Code").
- SAG caps talent agent commission rates at 10 percent. No such restriction exists for personal managers, who charge as much as 25 percent (Association of Talent Agents, "Talent Agency Act").

Still, the distinction between the two professions can become blurred in some areas, such as in recording contracts, creating an ambiguity noted by state entertainment commissions but never resolved (California Department of Industrial Relations, "California Entertainment Commission Report").

Many actors succeed without the services of a personal manager, but when personal managers help actors achieve success, actors usually find them indispensable. Actors must decide for themselves whether or not the benefit to their careers offsets the added cost of a personal manager.

HOW DO TALENT AGENTS AND PERSONAL MANAGERS WORK TOGETHER?

Talent agents and personal managers work together in this industry every day. Personal managers carefully scrutinize the daily breakdowns and request submissions to the talent agent on behalf of the actor. A personal manager coordinates promotional materials based on the talent agent's needs, and a personal manager pursues personal contacts and shares this information with the talent agent. Daily communication between these two team members optimizes an actor's visibility. This all occurs to the benefit of the actor, but conflicts can arise.

Double submissions. Without careful coordination, an actor can be submitted twice for the same role, which is a pet peeve of casting directors, not to mention an additional cost to the actor.

Inequity in commission. Talent agents are often reluctant to cooperate with personal managers who earn a higher commission rate and may threaten to drop the actor. They cite their business license as the primary authority of employment, and truly, an actor can ill afford to lose a talent agent.

Stepping on toes. While personal managers can provide essential services to an actor's team by making follow-up calls after auditions, forming initial contacts, or acting as a liaison on behalf of the actor, the talent agent must set the ground rules to avoid miscommunications and territorial blunders. Giving mixed signals can quickly end a casting discussion.

HOW DO I KNOW A MANAGER OR MANAGEMENT COMPANY IS LEGITIMATE?

Actors should scrutinize a potential personal manager or management company as they would a lawyer, therapist, or physician. The Los Angeles Better Business Bureau, the Association of Talent Agents, and the California Division of Labor Standard Enforcement all offer actors assistance by providing information on incidents of complaint or of current violations and prosecutions. Often just a message on an actors' forum or listserv yields sufficient positive or negative feedback to make an informed decision.

WHAT SCAMS SHOULD I WATCH OUT FOR?

1. **Talent scouts who will make you a "star"** or who have "selected you," implying credibility where none exists (Federal Trade Commission, "If You've Got the Look").
2. **Personal managers who promise employment.** Only licensed talent agents in the state of California may solicit theatrical employment for an actor. Personal managers may advise and network for the actor but may not enter into contractual negotiations.
3. **Talent agents who charge advance fees for services or required classes.** Whether called "registration," "consultation," or "administrative" fees, a scam by any other name would smell the same. Legitimate talent agents earn their income strictly through commissions, not from fees for photographs and career counseling. Those who charge "advance fees" are not talent agency but services, and are neither licensed or SAG franchised. State law allows an actor ten days after signing such a contract to cancel. Extra casting services prove the exception, as they may charge an administrative fee for processing into their database because they actually do the extra casting for the production company.
4. **Acting schools that promise employment.** Legitimate modeling and acting schools earn income by charging fees for instruction just as talent agents charge a commission—but neither should be doing both. Therein lies the conflict of interest (Los Angeles Better Business Bureau ("Modeling and Acting Scams").
5. **Anyone who prefers to work without a contract.** Though legal, verbal agreements often end in conflict, are heavily litigated, and are expensive to the loser.
6. **Any acting or modeling contract requiring the performer to "pay to play."** An actor may need better photos or a class in acting technique, but other than providing a referral, an agent may not require an actor to purchase those services from a specific source without violating California state law.

Be aware that these scam agencies use names similar to well-known legitimate talent agencies, drop the names of celebrity clients, and dangle the glittery promise of fame and success with flattery and ego massages. Their offices look legitimate, with a lobby filled with photos of famous actors and a waiting room filled with gullible wannabees. But in the end comes the high-pressure sales pitch for "screen tests" or a "photo book" and the demand for money. If you find yourself in one of these situations, stop, take a deep breath, and remember that you came to Hollywood to be paid to act, not the other way around.

All in all, talent agents and personal managers provide a very important service to an actor. Celebrity bios are rife with stories of corrupt and fraudulent agents and managers. Finding ones that are honest, straightforward, and effective will be your greatest challenge. Once you are represented, though, doors will begin to open and your legitimacy factor will increase. Success may still not be ensured, but you will finally be a true player in the industry.

Actors Forum

My first two SAG vouchers were from doing extra work, and then they had the big commercial strike several years ago and whoever picketed for some eighty hours automatically was eligible, so instead of doing more extra work I signed up for that. The route most people go is to do extra work. Some people get very lucky and somebody wants to hire them and Taft-Hartley them immediately. Some people get it right away and some take years. Try to get in good with a production assistant and do as many SAG shows as possible.

Tang Nguyen

In New York I got a job at a magazine as a proofreader. I could do the Saturday and Monday shift so I could go audition for Broadway jobs. Then I did some play at the Publick Theater. I went in and sang for Joe Papp. They asked me if I'd be willing to go on the road with the touring company of *Two Gentleman from Verona*. So I packed everything I could and went on the road. When I arrived in LA, I was doing the fifth lead in a Broadway hit. My name was on the marquee and I had a couple of solos. I knew somebody who was a casting director. I called him and he gave me a list of other casting directors to call. I got in the door. I did twenty-two commercials in my first year and a half in LA and made enough for a down payment on a house.

Jacque Lynn Colton

The only thing I was smart enough to ask for, because I was getting basic minimum wage in terms of SAG, was for them to get and pay for my green card and with a very blue-chip firm in downtown. It took them three and half years to get my green card, but Aaron Spelling paid for it. Not the kind of story you probably get much of talking to people here because it's particularly arcane. But I think it's probably just as bad now as it was then.

Gordon Thomson

I got my SAG card way back. I hustled. I did it the old school way. I got the three vouchers. I'm AFTRA and SAG. So many actors don't want to join AFTRA. When I first got into this business, I joined AFTRA because I was going to radio school and you have to be a member. AFTRA's a walk-in union. There's nothing worse than seeing on a resume "AFTRA eligible." I think they're just too cheap to put the money out. For an actor coming to this town, it's so much better for them just to join AFTRA. Why wouldn't you join a walk-in union that has a hundred-plus shows you could be on? But if you're coming to Hollywood and thinking you're going to get your three vouchers in a year, it ain't going to happen unless you're sleeping with somebody.

Sajen Corona

7
The Unions

You can only protect your liberties in this world by protecting the other man's
freedom. You can only be free if I am free.

Clarence Darrow

The Four Performing Arts "Sister" Unions

Actors' Equity Association (AEA)
http://www.actorsequity.org/home.asp

The Western Region
Museum Square
5757 Wilshire Boulevard, Suite One
Los Angeles, CA 90036
(323) 634-1750

National Headquarters
165 West 46th Street
New York, NY 10036
(212) 869-8530

Screen Actors Guild (SAG)
http://www.sag.org/

National Headquarters
5757 Wilshire Boulevard
Los Angeles, CA 90036-3600

(323) 954-1600 (main switchboard)
(323) 549-6648 (deaf performers only: TTY/TTD)
(800) SAG-0767 (outside Los Angeles)

American Federation of Radio & Television Artists (AFTRA)
http://www.aftra.org/

260 Madison Avenue
New York NY 10016-2401
(212) 532-0800

5757 Wilshire Boulevard, 9th Floor
Los Angeles CA 90036-0800
(323) 634-8100

American Guild of Variety Artists (AGVA)

National Office
184 Fifth Avenue, 6th Floor
New York, NY 10010
(212) 675-1003

Nothing provides validation like union membership. But in most working trades, professional status means only joining one union. If pursuing a career as an electrician, one joins the International Brotherhood of Electrical Workers; a miner, the United Mine Workers of America, and so on. But to work as an actor, one may need to join as many as four separate unions: Actors' Equity Association (AEA) for stage, the Screen Actors Guild (SAG) for film, the American Federation of Television and Radio Artists (AFTRA) for television and radio, and the American Guild of Variety Artists for ice shows, circuses, and hotel/casino variety shows.

Collectively these "sister" unions often create for an actor a tangle of jurisdiction, contracts, dues, and residuals. This is why God made talent agents, to sort out these employment entanglements, but an actor should still understand each union's jurisdiction, benefits, and costs before doling out what might represent one's life savings or mother's pin money just to join one.

A BRIEF HISTORY

As the financial optimism of the 1880s gave way to the working class angst and violence of the 1890s, the turn of the century saw the birth of the union movement. Amid frequent "rebellions," several attempts to form an actors' union failed, until May 26, 1913, when 112 performers gathered at the Pabst Grand Circle Hotel to adopt the Actors' Equity's Constitution and elect its first president, comedian Francis Wilson (Actors' Equity Association, "About Equity"). Their strike ended the iron-fisted dominance of the Theatrical Syndicate, a consortium of producers whose monopoly over contracts and bookings controlled wages below free market levels and set subhuman and unsafe work conditions. The preamble to Equity's Constitution begins:

> We hereby constitute ourselves as a voluntary association to advance, promote, foster and benefit all those connected with the art of theatre and particularly the profession of acting and the conditions of persons engaged therein; to protect and secure the rights of actors; to inform them

as to their legal rights and remedies; to advise and assist them in obtaining employment and proper compensation; to procure appropriate legislation upon matters affecting their profession. (Actors' Equity Association, "Constitution")

Equity served the acting profession well through the Golden Age of Broadway in the 1920s as well in its continued growth during the '30s and '40s. But as the film industry evolved, Equity's attempts to organize film actors met stiff opposition from Hollywood megamogul Louis B. Mayer, head of MGM films.

Rather than bow to the demands of disgruntled artists in his employ, Mayer formed the International Academy of Motion Picture Arts and Sciences, not as a vehicle for honoring excellence in filmmaking as it exists today, but as "a thinly disguised studio pressure group designed to keep further unionization at bay" (Holden, *Behind the Oscar*, 89). Mayer pitched the Academy as an organization that would be mutually beneficial to the various working groups that constituted the film industry, a kind of "League of Nations for the motion picture industry," as Mary Pickford called it (89). Its charter empowered the Academy to set fair wage and working condition guidelines. But Mayer controlled the Academy from the beginning, using his own studio attorneys to draft the organization's bylaws and then pressuring MGM actors and technicians to join. His plan worked for a while, dividing dissident actors, some convinced that the Academy had their best interests at heart—until 1933.

At the outset of the Great Depression, the Academy responded to Roosevelt's call for industrial self-regulation by mandating a 50 percent pay cut for all film industry employees—everyone, that is, except studio executives. Even MGM actors bolted from the Academy in response. That year saw the birth of both the Writers Guild of America (WGA) and the Screen Actors Guild (SAG). Over the years, actors benefited with increased wages, benefits, and safer working conditions, while film companies struggled to maintain control over their actors. But Congress and the courts dealt the fatal blows to the old studio system with antitrust legislation, finally liberating contract players to become independent contractors, now represented by SAG franchised talent agents.

Television created an entirely new business within the entertainment industry. Immediately, actors formed two temporary guilds in 1950 to set fair work standards for this new medium. In 1952, the Television Authority and the American Federation of Radio Artists merged to form the American Federation of Television and Radio Artists (AFTRA) to represent actors in both electronic mediums. This merger led to some discord with rival union SAG. Eventually the two organizations agreed to split jurisdiction based on the format utilized to record the actor. If the television program was "filmed," SAG had jurisdiction; if the television program was "taped," AFTRA had jurisdiction.

WHAT DOES A UNION DO FOR AN ACTOR?

It is difficult to imagine what exploitation would ensue in an unregulated marketplace. But while union membership provides no guarantee of work, the doors it opens guarantee mandatory work standards and standardized wages. Over the past ninety years, actors unions have won important victories, establishing:

- minimum pay scales and residual compensation rates;
- health benefits under two Earned Eligibility Plans depending upon the level of an actor's earnings;
- pension credits that may be earned toward participation in a benefit plan to which SAG signatory producers must contribute;
- nonexploitive work hours and safety conscious work conditions; and
- specific steps regarding hazardous conditions, overtime, nudity, privacy, and method of payment.

As a result, actors now participate in the financial success of their work, receive fairer compensation for dangerous or extreme work conditions, negotiate their own projects through their talent agents, and need not endure sexual harassment in order to obtain work. All professional actors can relate at least one horror story in which the union provided a buffer between themselves and an inappropriately demanding studio, director, or producer. In the supply and demand of the Hollywood celebrity market, often enflamed by the ambrosia of fame and fortune, one can only imagine to what extremes an actor might resort to secure a role and to what extremes others might exercise to exploit him or her.

In the Box

I had been cast as a one-line day player on a television series. The production assistant had been very clear in his e-mail. My call time at the location site was 6:00 a.m. I would meet a shuttle bus in a parking lot that would transport me to the film site. I arrived that morning promptly at 6 a.m. along with a dozen other sleepy actors and waited patiently for a bus that never arrived. An hour later, one actor contacted a studio assistant via cell phone who informed us of the startling fact that the shoot was really scheduled for 6 p.m. This created a problem for me, as I was already committed to a stage performance that night. I regretfully called my agent to turn down the role.

Later the production assistant called to apologize for his error. He explained with great apology that despite his having made the mistake and my showing up at the assigned time and place after having turned down other work for the day, the studio wouldn't be paying me for the missed job. He assured me instead that he'd "keep me in mind for future roles." I politely thanked him, hung up, and called the SAG hotline. I gave them the details, forwarded the PA's e-mail, and received a check two weeks later. That production assistant no longer works for the studio, but guess what? They have since called me for an audition.

WHICH UNION(S) SHOULD I JOIN?

As the product of a college theatre program, I take particular pride in carrying my Actors' Equity card. It validates me as a professional actor. But SAG remains the only union that an actor must join to succeed in Hollywood. Not surprisingly, it's also the most difficult to join. AFTRA, on the other hand, has open membership: "Any person who has performed or intends to perform professional work in any one of AFTRA's jurisdictions is eligible for membership" (AFTRA, "How to Join").

WHY DOESN'T EVERYONE JUST JOIN AFTRA AND NOT SAG?

Many beginning professional actors do just that. But that is too easy. Remember that SAG has jurisdiction over film, AFTRA over tape. Most television producers, though, film their content. Tape is used mostly for reality-based programs in which participants are expected to be amateurs or contestants, as well as for talk shows, news programs, and an occasional sitcom. Additionally, advertising companies rarely tape commercials. So not only does SAG have jurisdiction over film and most television production, but the entire commercial industry as well. That's why a SAG card can open casting doors while an AFTRA card will get you invited to workshops. Membership in AFTRA will not buy you into SAG either—not, that is, until you have worked first as a principal under AFTRA's jurisdiction.

HOW DO I JOIN SAG?

Until 1946, unions were mostly closed shops, and union membership was required in order to be hired. In that year, Congress passed the Taft-Hartley Act, prohibiting, among other things, the closed union shop. It required an opening in which an employer might hire an individual despite his or her nonunion status. The individual would be expected to join the union thereafter and may be required to pass a proficiency test or pay an initiation fee. The producer would also have to pay a penalty, but no longer could labor unions control their own membership. Beginning actors must look for this portal.

SAG has one great restriction. One must first be offered a contract before SAG membership can be obtained. Since most casting directors only consider union members, how does one overcome this Catch 22? Several ways exist, thanks to Taft and Hartley.

The Right Place at the Right Time

Sometimes the actor who gets the role is still the one who fits the costume, or has a unique skill or an odd size, or resembles someone famous, or just has a quirky persona. Rarely does one achieve one's first SAG contract on talent alone. Physical appearance plays an important role. Television programs and commercials thrive on fresh new faces. Breakdowns often specify size, coloring, ethnicity, skills, and odd physical characteristics. Sometimes casting directors need to match faces and body types, such as in the television series *Cold Case*. And, of course, young beautiful bodies, male and female, still get noticed, as do very unusual character faces of all ages. Casting directors receive thousands of pictures from nonunion actors, and while they generally only consider union actors, commercial casting directors often cast nonunion actors with unusual looks and skills. Either way, if you have the look casting directors are after or the skills they seek, you will be offered a contract, and the production company will be required to fill out a Taft-Hartley report to the union (see Appendix C, document 2).

The Casting Couch

Though it is not the most professional approach, more than one actor has slept his or her way to Hollywood with a producer, a director, a casting agent, or any one of a veritable sludge pool of other industry decision makers. But this approach often backfires. Hollywood crawls with opportunists who make promises they can't keep. Anyone can print business cards as a producer or casting associate and claim to have a project in development or know someone who knows someone. The casting couch very much exists, a fact that most actors must confront at some point in their career. How you respond will be a personal decision, but remember to know your talent and what it is worth.

Be an Extra Body

Atmosphere or background casting still represents an actor's best chance for professional status. Actors, union or nonunion, simply register with a handful of agencies specializing in atmosphere casting, such as Central Casting.

Production companies contract these extra agencies to provide the needed background actors for each day of shooting. Under a SAG contract, the first ten extras hired for a project must be union; thereafter, they may be nonunion. A nonunion actor can work most every day, but the work is boring, tedious, pays half as much as union work, and offers few perks other than the catering wagon, unless one finds fulfillment in degrading anonymity and mindless inactivity. Still, proximity to the industry and the opportunity to work on a film can justify the trade-off for such thankless work. Scripts often contain one-line roles not crucial to the plot but for which the cost of casting is prohibitive. Some producers or directors prefer to cast these roles on the set from the pool of extras. Still other directors prefer the creative flexibility of improvisation and may invent new speaking characters on the fly. Either way, if chosen to speak a line, any small meaningless phrase, one may request to be "Taft-Hartley-ed" into the union.

The Waiver Game

SAG provides another portal for background actors through a waiver system. SAG requires producers to hire a certain number of union members before they are permitted to hire nonunion actors. Once booked, if a union actor fails to show, a nonunion actor's status may be "bumped up." That actor receives a waiver for each workday this occurs. After obtaining three waivers, the nonunion actor may now join at full SAG rates and conditions. Unfortunately, accumulating those three waivers requires lightening to strike the same location three times. Meanwhile, unscrupulous casting directors and producers exploit nonunion actors' eagerness with fake waivers, switch and bait tactics, and a financial con game (SAG, "Tip and Tools"). Several scandals and criminal investigations have tainted the process, leading SAG to undertake the task of revising this portal by developing a point system in which union and nonunion jobs, along with educational seminars and sanctioned events, count toward eligibility.

In the Box

One of my former students moved to Hollywood, registered with a nonunion extra casting agency, and soon found himself working as a permanent extra on a weekly network sitcom. The daily pay was meager, but the production assistant in charge of extra casting had made him a promise: hang in for three years and be rewarded with three waiver forms, the number needed for SAG membership. Three years was a long commitment, but the promise of union membership seemed fair and worthwhile. The next year, sagging ratings forced a reassignment of the production crew. The production assistant moved on, and the new production assistant knew nothing about this arrangement. The student was screwed. The lesson: always, always, always get it in writing. If they can't put it in writing, then you'll know exactly what that promise is worth.

Use the Stage Door

Membership in one of the four "sister" unions opens the door to the others. Performers may join a sister union once they are paid-up members of an affiliated performers' union (ACTRA—Alliance of Canadian Cinema, Television, and Radio Artists—AEA, AFTRA, AGMA—American Guild of Musical Artists—or AGVA) for a period of one year and after they have worked at least once as a principal under that union's jurisdiction. One cannot just join AFTRA and then join SAG the following year. Equity membership, though, especially for those with established stage careers, provides the best side-door entrance to SAG membership. Equity requires producers to set aside time for nonunion actors, and though one must still be offered a union contract before obtaining an Actors' Equity card, after one year of membership in Equity an actor may join SAG, and vice versa. Live stage work in Los Angeles has increased tremendously in the past twenty years as more and more Equity theatres have flourished, though civic theatres, dinner theatres, and theme park productions still predominate.

Regardless of how one cracks the SAG seal, success incurs a startling initiation fee, currently $1,600 and soon to increase as per a membership vote. Mindful that this presents a huge financial obstacle for many actors, most unions provide payment plans and options. But whether you have or have not obtained work, the unions will bill twice a year for dues. Nonpayment results in suspension of membership rights until paid in full. The first question a talent agent will ask when notifying an actor of a booking is, "Are your SAG dues paid up in full?" If they are not fully paid by the end of the day, that booking can be revoked.

Nothing says validation like union membership. But while membership has its privileges, it has responsibilities as well. With membership come professional standards of conduct. Union membership means professionalism: arriving on time to calls, preparation, commitment to the project, and loyalty to the union for its auspices. In addition, turning professional tends to realign employment opportunities into two distinct categories: union and nonunion, one acceptable and one now forbidden. By accepting union membership, one has agreed to certain restrictions. Working for less than fair wages is one of them. One cannot automatically assume that union employment will follow union membership, and if it does not but nonunion employment still does, an ethical crisis may result.

Actors Forum

Everybody in LA gets the breakdowns illegally somehow. I know people who have actually created a fake management company to submit themselves. There are so many agencies and management companies out there; they're not going to care who you are. If they like your picture, if they want you, they'll call you into an audition. I have a friend who set up his own management company. He's got his own separate phone line. He forwards the message, saying this is so and so management company. People leave messages for him. He calls them back and acts like he's the manager, gets all the details and then goes on the audition. The bottom line is, if they want to see you, they don't care who represents you.

Tang Nguyen

Self-promotion is the hardest part of the business end of this profession. When I'm rehearsing a play, I'm usually too deeply ensconced to think about all the people I need to invite. By the time we're opening, I'm not sure it's as good as I want it to be, and by the time it's as good as I want it to be, it's almost over and it's too late to invite anybody. I would like to be more organized or computer savvy and push a button and have everybody read my reviews. If you belong to a group, you can put stuff about yourself in the newsletter. You want to send them postcards with your reviews on them. Keep your name out there so casting directors will look at your name and say, "I've heard of you."

Jacque Lynn Colton

I got a job on *Ryan's Hope*, a soap opera in New York. I was playing an Egyptologist because of the fact that I was not American and didn't sound American. And I said, "Why are you bothering with all of this nonsense of going to Canada and England?" And they said, "Well, people who look like you or as old as you with your kind of resume are on the West Coast making ten times the amount of money." And I thought, "Gee, I wish I was one of them." And it turned out that literally two or three years later I was doing just that with a television series called *Dynasty* for seven of its nine years.

Gordon Thomson

I'm of mixed race. My mom's Mexican and my dad's Iranian. People call me an Irexican. But technically I'm Latin. I don't consider myself Latino because I'm not that ethnic. I don't speak Spanish, but I see a huge market that's been untouched, and I don't see a lot of Latino talent out there that has universal appeal. I have universal appeal and I have comedic ability. I would go on these auditions, and they would always say, "We're looking for someone more Latino." I'd say, "I could bring my leaf blower. It's in the car." When they're thinking Iranian, they're thinking Afghanistan or Pakistan. I can only portray who I am. My acting coach told me it's going to be very difficult to get in because I'm more a character. When you think of a Mexican, you don't think of me, you think of someone at Home Depot. If I had been white I might have gotten more work. If I had been black I might have gotten more, and if I was a woman, I'd work it. Girls don't know how easy they've got it.

Sajen Corona

8

The Casting Game

Anyone who has ever been in the position of casting a project will testify that casting is at best a guessing game. Casting directors never make choices with 100 percent certainty and often base them on intangible as well as tangible qualities. Simultaneously, actors play a game of "Guess what the casting director is looking for." Age? Hair color? Ethnicity? An attitude? A look? The actor is the commodity being bought and sold in this marketplace. And while talent agents do earn their commissions promoting actors, no one should be better at selling you than you. But an actor can't play the casting game if the actor doesn't know how.

HOW DOES AN ACTOR GET AN AUDITION?

College theatres, as well as most professional theatres, usually hold open auditions scheduled well in advance for actors to prepare by reading the play. But the film and television industry works much differently. Casting directors could never possibly accommodate every actor who wanted an audition. Casting directors hold private auditions scheduled by appointment only. Scripts are closely protected and rarely provided in advance, except for specific sides that will be used for auditioning purposes. For the professional actor, then, the challenge is just to get in the door.

Casting directors see hundreds of actors every week either in auditions or general interviews. But don't be naïve enough to think an actor can just pick up the phone to make an appointment. The casting director contacts the actor or the actor's talent agent via telephone or email to schedule an audition. But first an actor must get the casting director's attention. The actor must first send a headshot, like a calling card. This can be accomplished either as a mass mailing or as a submission for a specific role.

Some actors do yearly mass mailings of their headshot and resume to the casting directors in Hollywood—all six hundred of them. Many electronic services and bookstores sell packets of names and addresses. But general submissions generally go into a pile that the casting director or an associate will scan later when they have down time, such as during summer hiatus or Christmas break. If an actor wants to be considered for a specific project, he or she must submit for that specific project.

HOW DOES AN ACTOR LEARN WHAT PROJECTS ARE BEING CAST?

The trade papers publish production notices that often list the casting director, but those notices don't include role breakdowns. At best they provide short plot summaries that rarely provide much insight into what the producers want beyond gender and age. For an actor, then, it's all about access to those casting breakdowns, knowing what's being cast and what matches their characteristics. Gender? Age range? Ethnicity? Physical attributes? That's why, of course, actors need talent agents who receive the daily breakdowns.

WHAT ARE BREAKDOWNS AND HOW DOES ONE GET THEM?

When producers prepare to cast a project, each licensed talent agent receives a "breakdown" of each role and its description. Talent agents may then submit any of their actors that match the breakdown. Once upon a time, before computers, talent agents subscribed to a business service called Breakdown Services and received hardcopy daily breakdowns submitted by the major studio casting directors. Talent agents scanned them for compatibility with their stable of clients, assembled packets of pictures and sent them out with the afternoon mail, or paid expensive couriers to deliver those packets directly to the casting directors. Unless one worked in a talent agent's office, one had little if any access to those breakdowns. Occasionally the trade papers published casting notices, but mostly actors waited by their phones. Electronic casting has changed all that!

WHAT IS ELECTRONIC CASTING AND HOW HAS THE CHANGED CASTING?

Talent agents still receive their morning breakdowns from Breakdown Services, only now electronically, and they can now submit headshots electronically. The clear advantage for the talent agent lies in the lack of expense and labor; there are no hard copy photos, pages of resumes, 8×10 mailing envelopes, or postage needed. Breakdown Services is still a subscription service, but today talent agents go to an access-controlled Web site to view the breakdowns casting directors submit daily. They then make submissions simply by clicking on particular roles and then choosing from their clients' photos displayed on a pop-up menu. While infinitely easier, a talent agent or associate needs to monitor those breakdowns hourly, as important projects get posted at all hours, often with a short audition notice.

The casting director's advantage lies in time management. A casting director bids on a project and generally receives a lump sum payment for his or her casting, regardless of the time required. Sifting through and sorting mountains of photos is time-consuming work and requires additional staff. With electronic casting, a television casting director, for instance, can publish breakdowns on Monday morning, receive submissions the same day, book auditions directly with the actors for Tuesday and Wednesday, hold callbacks on Thursday, and schedule a producer's audition or a booking by Friday to set next Monday's filming roster.

DOES EVERYBODY USE ELECTRONIC CASTING NOW?

Stage, film, and television projects all now use electronic breakdown services, but television and commercial casting rely upon them almost entirely. Film casting directors still prefer to receive hard copy photos to mix and match, as they generally have the luxury of time to methodically complete the casting process. But a television season is demanding, and time literally represents money. From page to stage, the casting process generally takes a week per episode. An actor would never have time to submit for a project except through electronic casting services.

CAN ACTORS SUBSCRIBE TO THIS SERVICE?

Only licensed talent agents may subscribe to Breakdown Services, but casting directors occasionally prefer to post selected breakdowns to a wider talent pool. They may be looking for a very specific look, an unusual skill, or to physically and facially match another actor.

The Jerry Bruckheimer detective drama Cold Case serves as an excellent example. Each week the detectives solve a "cold case" involving a murder that happened in the past. They interview suspects in the present as we, the viewers, see the suspects' actions in the past. Each pair of actors must be convincing as older and younger versions of the same character. The producers routinely post breakdowns on these actors' access electronic casting sites to give the roles more exposure and to help ensure that the casting director will draw from a large pool of talent with a greater chance of a perfect match. Thus, Breakdown Services now offers access to actors with its aptly titled Actors Access, a free service, up to a point, that provides access to some casting breakdowns. Nonmembers can review casting breakdowns and upload and manage photos and resume information, but they will incur a nominal charge per submission. Those nominal charges can add up and thus provide the motivation for actors who use the service to subscribe and receive unlimited submission privileges. Membership also provides other services, such as the ability to upload one's slate or video, giving advance notification of suitable roles, and providing free sides. But don't be fooled into believing you have access to the complete breakdowns. Breakdown Services still only provides complete access to licensed talent agents who are subscribers.

> ### In the Box
>
> It was during a casting director workshop that the truth hit me. The evening's guest asked an actor, "Do you get the daily breakdowns?" "Yes," she answered. Astonished, I leaned over and said something to my new friend, a dead-on lookalike for Doris Roberts. She nudged me in the side and said, "Oh honey, you've got a lot to learn. She just buys them online. Just go talk to her at break. She'll tell you how."
> Break came and I sought out the woman in question. Awkwardly, I asked her. She chuckled and pulled out a pen. "Here," she said. "Call this person. It comes a day late, but it's exactly what the talent agents see." I thanked her and walked away amazed at how the information pipeline cuts through any attempt to restrict it.

WHICH ELECTRONIC CASTING SERVICES SHOULD I SUBSCRIBE TO?

Electronic casting provides a tremendous service to actors, but dozens of Internet services have now sprung out of the lure of fame and fortune. Those services promise access to legitimate Hollywood breakdowns, but in truth provide nothing of value. The majority of the postings are nonunion projects or duplications of projects from other legitimate services, posted too late for submission. Some post breakdowns of suspicious origin about unconfirmed projects or from disreputable sources. Others have gone so far as to post fake projects just to entice hopeful young talent in Kansas to buy a year's subscription with the promise of a film or television role. The legitimate Web sites allow visitors to register and view the casting notices for free. They charge only for the use of their submission services, either through a fee for service or a membership fee. Prospective subscribers can examine the casting notices in advance to determine if the service is worth their while. If you have to pay first, refuse to play the game. Talent agents and working actors acknowledge only four legitimate and reputable electronic casting services that actually provide the services to the actor they claim.

Actors Access

This subservice of Breakdown Services provides a package of services through its Showfax Web site to union and nonunion actors for a yearly membership fee. Besides providing access to legitimate casting notices, Actors Access allows actors unlimited submissions to casting directors, and they can download sides and upload and manage their photos, demo reels, and resume information all for one yearly membership fee.

Now Casting

This relatively new business in Burbank offers many of the same services as Actors Access, with some notable exceptions. It provides more information about the many actors' services in Los Angeles and a great deal of helpful information through newsletters and online articles from casting directors and working actors. Some network casting breakdowns appear that aren't posted on Actors Access, suggesting that this company works directly with some casting directors. That's good news for actors and makes it worth the extra monthly expense to subscribe to two similar electronic casting services that otherwise duplicate each other.

LA Casting

Commercial talent agents require their clients to register with LA Casting, since most union commercial casting proceeds through this service. LA Casting provides free registration for represented talent and charges no yearly fee. You can register online, but you must bring photos to one of four offices to be uploaded. They will scan the first photo for free but will charge for each additional photo added or changed—$25 for the first added photo and $10 thereafter. Bring all your photos at the same time to save on that $25 first photo charge.

If unrepresented, actors can still register for this service, but other than commercials, it offers little more than other electronic services, duplicating most film and television casting notices. LA Casting's Web site does offer other helpful services, such as downloads of label sets or reports of current casting directors, talent agents, and management firms. LA Casting also provides a database of businesses that provide a host of services to the actor, such as photographers, private coaches, and demo reel services.

Craigslist

Craigslist is a national classified advertising Web site that is also an online community and is for the most part free. In 1995, Craig Newmark started electronically posting a list of cool events in the San Francisco Bay area. The service gained popularity, and Craig wrote new software to provide accessibility for others to post e-mails in various categories.

Today Craigslist has morphed into a nonprofit organization called Craigslist.org, and is accessible from almost anywhere in the world. Major U.S. and international cities post their own Craigslist Web site. One of the many categories of ads is "TV/Film/Video." One will find job postings for talent and crew listed daily. Craigslist is open and unrestricted and provides fertile ground for scammers and schemers, so ask lots of questions when responding to an ad. Just notice the number of ads for "XXX Adult Actresses" posted on any given day to understand what's happening there. But other ads can simply be misleading and confusing. Still, I booked several legitimate projects through Craigslist. Music artists have been known to post their video breakdowns, as have famous directors who want to cast something themselves, quietly. It serves as a kind of back door for casting from the grassroots of the LA entertainment community.

Craiglist isn't as hi-tech as the other services either. It provides no active links for electronic submissions. As with all the Craigslist categories, the ad provides an anonymous e-mail address for response. One responds as with any other e-mail submission, providing a headshot and resume as an attachment. Craigslist has an upload limit, so keep the photos small or risk having your message bounced back to you by the system administrator.

WHAT DIFFERENT TYPES OF CASTING NOTICES ARE POSTED ON ELECTRONIC SERVICES?

All casting notices are not created equal. They divide into media groups—*television, film, Internet, print*, and *live entertainment*—and then into genres, such as *episodic, drama, reality, commercial, music video, feature film, industrial, infomercial, student film, stage, Internet*, or *voice-over*, or whether they *taped* or *filmed*. Next they divide into *union* and *nonunion* projects. Union notices break down into the type of union contract, such as *low budget, ultra-low budget*, or *experimental* for film. Nonunion notices just break down into whether or not there will be pay, or just the promise of a meal and a copy of the project. Unfortunately, the nonunion, nonpaying projects well outnumber the paying ones. Some are based on no more than a hope and a prayer. Many will never get to production but will waste your time with auditions, callbacks, promises, and maybe even a few rehearsals.

In the Box

I remember wasting three weekends auditioning for a film company at a film acting school with a high-rise Hollywood address and fancy offices. No one seemed to be in charge. Audition times had been long forgotten. I spent an hour rehearsing one role only to have the associate casting director (really the author of the screenplay) ask me to read a different role. I never did get to read for either role but instead read for a different one altogether. Callbacks the next week were even stranger. I was paired off and given an hour to rehearse a scene. Two hours later I was finally called in to read not for that role, but for the role I had originally submitted with a partner I had never seen. Imagine my surprise when I booked the project. I was told to clear the next weekend for rehearsals and wait for a call as to where and when. That call never came. Nor were any of the messages I left returned. In fact, I never heard from them again. But a year later I noticed a film project in the breakdowns that just didn't seem right. I checked the production information and, sure enough, it was the same team. I passed this time.

HOW DO YOU KNOW IF A PROJECT IS LEGITIMATE?

No electronic casting service guarantees the legitimacy of the breakdowns posted. As with everything else in Hollywood, the buyer must beware of both union and nonunion projects. Nonunion projects that fall outside of union jurisdiction, such as music videos and local advertising, are inherently suspect, but even union projects can fall apart at any point in the preproduction process. All actors can do is to follow their professional instincts and gather as much information about the project as possible.

Electronic casting notices provide the actor with a lot of information that will help him or her determine whether or not to submit for the project, especially if it's a nonunion project. First, the casting notice will provide the names of the writer, director, producers, production company, and the casting director. Look for those known as legitimate players in Hollywood, and avoid those known from experience or reputation to be flakes. Also, the notice will list the audition, callback, and production dates. If these dates are TBAs, this is a good warning sign that the project may be still more a hope and a dream than a reality. Finally, the notice will list the type of contract, the contract status, the rate of pay, and the film format. Once again, the less information given, the more suspicious one should be of its solid ground.

IF EVERYBODY USES ELECTRONIC CASTING, WHY DO I NEED HEADSHOTS?

1. **Casting directors generally delete electronic submissions once they have cast their project.** A hard copy photo will therefore have a longer life in a casting director's office.

2. **One never knows whom one will meet and where.** Always carry a headshot to an audition, always have them on hand when showcasing, and always have a few in the car just in case. A casual conversation can end with a request for a headshot just as a similar conversation in a different industry might end with a request for a business card.

In the Box

I was at the closing night of a play in Los Angeles on New Year's Eve. The theatre held a special party after the performance. Champagne flowed while the mostly industry crowd mingled and schmoozed. Suddenly a woman recognized me from a play I had performed twenty years earlier. She introduced herself, talked about a play she was directing, and asked for a picture and resume. I remembered I had one in my car and quickly retrieved it. Several weeks later I found myself rehearsing a play written by the legendary Broadway producer Stewart F. Lane, directed by that same woman, for a special benefit performance honoring him. My performance was seen by hundreds of industry professionals and eventually led to other projects.

---

3. **Subscribe to bootleg Breakdown Services casting notices.** With a little networking, an actor will find someone who will provide the Breakdown Services list via email each day for a monthly fee. It's common practice in Hollywood. The breakdowns comes a day late and have no active links for electronic submission, but they do provide the actor information for hardcopy submission. Some talent agents will provide trusted actors and managers with their access code to make their own submissions.

4. **Film casting directors prefer hardcopy submissions.** While television relies almost entirely upon electronic casting, film does not. Casting directors for film prefer to scrutinize hard copy photos. They can shuffle the photos on a table as they mix and match character relationships, coloring, and looks. This approach provides perhaps more homogeneous casting, but as they have more time to complete the casting, they usually charge the producer a bigger fee.

5. **All casting directors keep files.** Even though television and commercial casting directors rely almost exclusively on electronic casting, they still keep hard copy files. These submissions may be placed in a separate stack that won't get scanned until a hiatus but will eventually be scrutinized and either kept for future consideration or for general interviews, or tossed. Some

electronic casting notices will specifically request a hard copy in addition to an electronic submission.

6. **Consult the Trades.** Some casting notices requiring hardcopy submissions can still be found in the trades. Stage, student films, music vides, theme parks, music videos, and tech jobs regularly advertise in the trades, more specifically, Backstage West, the Los Angeles version of New York's Backstage East. Subscription, though pricey, offers a wealth of information and casting news both union and non-union. The Hollywood Reporter and Variety can be informative but provide more in terms of business information and little in the way of casting notices.

HOW DO I CREATE PROFESSIONAL-LOOKING HARDCOPY SUBMISSIONS?

Actors have much more control over their careers now than at any time in the past. Most working actors spend the early morning hours scanning their electronic casting services for possible submissions, or they call their talent agent to do this for them. But actors need not rely entirely upon a talent agent. An actor may decide to mail as many as ten to twenty headshots a day, a tedious and labor-intensive process unless well organized. As with any other small business, a daily process of research, data gathering, manual preparation, and delivery requires organization and mass production.

Besides storage space and a work area, an actor will need a stock of headshots, printed resumes, 8½×11 mailing envelopes, Post-It Notes, and postage stamps. The mass production of daily submissions requires the careful organization of these materials. Running out of envelopes or stamps can mean interrupting the day with a supply run, so purchase your supplies in bulk.

Headshots. Many photo duplicating services exist in Los Angeles. Three hundred photos will cost about $100, but they will last about a year. Actors often want several different headshots: for comedic, dramatic, and commercial projects.

Resumes. Resumes can easily be photocopied and then stapled to headshots with one annoying complication. Headshots are 8×10, and standard paper is 8½×11. Resumes must be cut to match the headshots and then stapled to the headshots. One simpler solution exists. Most computer printers can print a resume directly onto the back of a headshot, saving both paper and time.

Mailing envelopes. Mailing envelopes can be bought in bulk at any office supply store. The color doesn't matter, but make certain they have clasps. Casting directors hate to open sealed envelopes because of time and paper cuts.

Stamps. At present the cost of mailing a headshot is $0.97. The U.S. Postal Service offers no discount for bulk purchases, but buying stamps in bulk will cut down on the time one stands in line at the post office.

Post-It Notes. Casting associates open most hard copy submissions to screen and organize them. While many talent agents enclose cover letters, many just use Post-it Notes to communicate with casting directors, specifically to include the project name and the role(s) for which an actor is being submitted. Placed at the top of the headshot in an unobtrusive spot, the Post-it Note helps the casting associate to organize the submissions into piles—that is, those that pass the associate's preliminary criteria.

Return address labels. Microsoft Word or any other word processing program can produce a full page of the same label. It takes no time to print multiple sheets, thereby providing an ample supply.

How should I address the envelope?

First, print the name and address of the casting director or the production exactly as given in the casting notice. At the bottom of the address, print in even bigger and bolder letters "Attn: [name of project]." Occasionally, the casting notice will ask you to specify the role on the envelope as well. After placing your headshot and resume in the envelope, *do not seal it!* It takes twice as long to open sealed envelopes.

If organized, an actor can complete this daily process by noon. Casting offices then will receive the submission the next morning. A later posting may delay the submission and miss the deadline, especially in television casting.

Between electronic casting, hard copy submissions, and a talent agent's efforts, a conscientious actor has a variety of options to ensure that he or she is a player in the casting game. Casting directors discourage duplicate submissions, but unless one has a close working relationship with a talent agent, most actors never really know for what roles they have been submitted. Often they just sit, waiting for a phone call. Those actors don't work as much.

Actors Forum

There are a million reasons why they don't hire you. You could look like their brother, and they don't like their brother. I'd come into an audition process really prepared with my work, doing my best and just leaving it like that. And if they hire you, great, and if they don't, don't take it personally. But if you consistently put out good work, somebody will eventually recognize it. A lot of the times they don't really know what they're looking for until they see it. You make up your mind how you want your scene to go and you do it, and if they ask you to do it a different way, then you tweak it a little bit.

Tang Nguyen

When my agent would send me out on commercial auditions I would go in and there was all this social chitchat. And I thought, they don't even see me. I'm an invisible person here. I'm not part of this little clique here. So I would slate my name for the camera and say something like, "Hi, I'm Jacque Lynn Colton, star of stage and screen." The director would look at me. You have to be a very good actor to do commercials. I mean, you really must have mastered that you believe in the situation without being precious or cute.

Jacque Lynn Colton

I hate auditions. They're never easy, even if you are absolutely spot on the mark in terms of casting type and everything else. Relax as much as you possibly can. This is essential. Be as familiar with the text as you possibly can to the point of being able to be off book, but always carry your pages. If you don't carry your pages, they think that's what you're going to do. They think that's your performance. That's all you can do. Carry your sides. You have to be ready as if you don't need them, but carry them. Be as relaxed as you can possibly be, and that's the most difficult thing in the world to do. Be as prepared and as familiar. Don't try tricks, technical tricks. Make natural choices, not just strong choices. Sometimes they may see making a strong choice as an extreme choice, like giving a character Tourette's syndrome. Make strong choices that come to you as you become familiar with the material. That's why being familiar with the material is essential. Pretend that everything you're doing is written by Chekov. Really, take it that seriously.

Gordon Thomson

Come prepared! Make a strong choice on the character. When you get the sides overnight, or if you get them the day before, or let's say you get them right before the audition, leave, take the sides, and go away for a half hour. Make a strong choice that brings the words to life. I would come dressed for the role. I auditioned for some print work for a hospital as a male nurse. I showed up in scrubs and a stethoscope. I got the job and made $600 for the day. The guy taking the picture told me I was the first actor to show up in scrubs. But it's better to be well prepared.

Sajen Corona

9

Auditioning

*The agent and the casting person are not employers, they are frankly
impediments standing between the actor and the audience. Does that mean
they should be ignored? Well, many times they cannot be. There they are. But
they, and their job, should be kept in perspective.*

David Mamet, *True and False*

Audition Resources

Out of the Closet Thrift Stores
http://www.outofthecloset.org/locations.htm

Junk for Joy
13314 West Magnolia Boulevard
Burbank, CA 91505
(818) 569-4903

Norcostco (costume and makeup supplies)
3606 West Magnolia Boulevard
Burbank, CA 91505
(818) 567-0753
http://www.norcostco.com

Quartermaster (police equipment, security and military uniforms
2543 West 6th Street
(213) 351-9632
http://www.qmuniforms.com/FAQs.asp

@ LA (uniforms, apparel, dancewear)
http://www.at-la.com/biz/@la-uniform.htm

Easy Background Check (entertainment industry)
http://www.easybackgroundcheck.com

eHow—How to Do Just about Anything!
http://www.ehow.com

SAG Actor Bulletin Board
http://www.sagactor.com/bb/

Unlike college and community theatre projects, open auditions rarely occur in
Hollywood film and television projects. Auditions happen by appointment only,
beginning with a phone call or an e-mail from a talent agent or directly from the
casting director. An invitation has been delivered, a date, a time, a location, an
opportunity, a *business* opportunity. For whatever reason, your submission, electronic or hard copy, has reached a set of eyes that discerns something worthy of
closer inspection. Actors prepare auditions for casting directors no differently
than a salesperson prepares a presentation for a prospective business client. The
form may change, but the intent remains the same—to sell a product. An audition must be viewed no differently. The first thing an actor must do is get to
know those gatekeepers, the casting directors.

WHO ARE CASTING DIRECTORS?

Casting directors oversee the casting process for the producer of a film, television,
commercial, or sometimes a theatrical project, generally from start to finish.
They may be independent contractors or employees of a studio or production
company. They are not "agents" and receive no commission. They may be former
actors, former production assistants, or just someone drawn to talent procure-
ment. They pore through thousands of headshots and electronic submissions;
audition hundreds of actors; attend casting workshops, showcases, and local
theatre events; and generally keep both eyes open for talent and striking looks.
Finding both in the same package can make a career. To do this job, casting
directors hold:

General interviews. When time allows, casting directors with no project in mind interview actors who have caught their interest, simply to become familiar with these actors.

Initial auditions. Thirty to a hundred actors are chosen to read or be interviewed for each role after casting associates have screened thousands of submissions.

Callbacks. The list of actors dwindles to five to ten, and additional readings or meetings are scheduled.

Final audition. A complete cast is presented to the producers.

While neither California nor Los Angeles has any formal requirements for the licensing of casting directors, the casting couch mythology has necessitated the formation of two organizations dedicated to setting professional standards: the Casting Society of America (CSA), established in 1982, and the Commercial Casting Directors Association (CCDA) (CSA, "Who We Aren't"). Recent conflicts between producers and casting directors over health benefits have led to a growing unionization movement within these societies. Many casting directors, former actors themselves, have come to their position by virtue of theatrical or production backgrounds. They view their relationship with actors as collegial and their role as empowering and rewarding talent, not as being adversarial or judgmental arbiters of talent.

WHAT IS THE CASTING PROCESS?

A producer works closely with a casting director to establish exactly the kind of talent desired for a project. Well-known actors may already be attached to the project or are being courted. The casting director prepares breakdowns for open roles and posts them through Breakdown Services and occasionally the trades. Talent agents and individual actors respond with submissions, both hard copy and electronic. Casting assistants sift through and organize these thousands of faces. The casting director scans the fruits of their labor to choose approximately thirty to a hundred actors to audition for each role. Casting assistants then make phone calls to talent agents or unrepresented actors to set audition times for reading and taping during the next few days. The casting director reviews the tape, sometimes with the producer, and selects a small group of actors for callbacks. Casting associates again make appointments for the callback readings, often held with producers, directors, or writers in attendance. Often a casting director makes the final casting decision, but this is always contingent upon a producer's approval. At this time the casting director holds a producer's audition to present the completed casting. Generally, the producer relies upon the casting director's expertise, but producers have been known to override the casting director, sending the whole process back to square one.

In the Box

I had gone through three days of grueling auditions for a major role in a new Los Angeles–based soap opera. The casting had been overseen by an in-house television network casting director, and all that remained was for the producers to approve the completed casting. I thought I'd finally made it and had already gotten out the party hats. Several days before this scheduled meeting, my talent agent called to inform me that the meeting had been cancelled. I asked when it would be rescheduled, and he replied that it wouldn't be. It seems the casting director had been caught in a compromised position with one of the actresses he had cast. "They fired him and the entire cast," said my agent. "What did this have to do with me?" I asked in disbelief. "Nothing," he replied. "It poisoned the well. They've blacklisted everyone he cast. You can't even submit again." Needless to say, I put the party hats away.

IS THE CASTING PROCESS THE SAME FOR ALL PROJECTS?

Different kinds of projects require different approaches.

Commercial casting. Casting associates shepherd hundreds of hopeful actors through the casting offices each day, searching for some special look or talent, a spokesperson, a character actor, someone to wear a costume, provide a voice-over, or portray some humiliating, stereotypical public Joe. A laugh, a quirky smile, a dry wit or the ability to fall down convincingly may seal the deal. Commercials often involve little or no dialogue but require strange talents for comic situations. Polaroid photos may be taken, as might be measurements for costuming or prosthetics. Actors may be given time to familiarize themselves with a prop of some kind. Commercial casting directors often employ improvisation and role-playing games to screen potential actors. Actors may have to demonstrate an action or skill such as pratfalls. Sometimes casting directors only need a look-see, and are satisfied to simply conduct and tape a conversation with the actor. Commercial casting can be slow, with continual consultations between the triumvirate of client, advertising agency, and casting agency, with actors caught in the middle.

Television casting. Generally with tighter budgets, television projects complete casting quickly. An hour episodic breakdown can be posted and cast within a five-day workweek. Casting directors usually stick to a strict schedule of five-minute audition slots and specific prepared sides from the script. Sides are specially prepared excerpts from the shooting script provided to the actor for auditioning. Casting directors have little time for interviews and no time for role-playing. Before the end of the week they must provide the producer with a tape of their preferences for each role.

Pilot casting. Casting directors carefully screen actors for television pilots. A successful television series does not happen by accident. Ensemble casting requires creating the right chemistry with the right actors the first time around. Hundreds of actors may be read for each role. Scripts and characters may still be somewhat amorphous. Casting directors may even assemble dual casts, anticipating two competing stylistic directions of the project.

Reality show casting. Reality programs fall into several categories:

Contest: Actors are hired not as actors but as contestants in some kind of increasingly bizarre game show where they will win prizes, not paychecks. To be certain, reality shows audition contestants much the same way as actors in other shows are auditioned and will rely heavily upon improvisation and role-playing. Be prepared for the ten-page application form and an on-camera interview. Potential contestants generally go through intense background checks before being offered a contestant contract and a scary confidentiality agreement to sign, neither of which is covered by union jurisdiction.

Feel-good shows: These reality shows perform a "good deed" for somebody and thus make viewers "feel good." Producers hire actors to host, cohost, or participate in the restoration, transformation, or reformation of something or somebody. The carpenters, dressers, fixers, and hair stylists of these programs generally have acting aspirations. Accepting employment on such programs requires considerable deliberation as a career decision, since reality show stars rarely move on to any other substantial projects.

Reenactment: These programs dramatize past events such as medical emergencies, court proceedings, or police activities. Sometimes casting directors, armed with only a photograph, must accurately match the actor to a real-life counterpart without placing acting technique secondary. Some auditions require more intense preparation and technique as a historical reenactment or a documentary. Casting directors may request a certain type of clothing, such as from a specific historical period.

Film casting. Larger budgets often mean extra time for casting. Film casting directors plan a lengthy process of sifting and matching, generally preferring hard copy submissions and time to match and balance a film cast. Actors may be asked to read three or four times in front of casting associates; an assembled group of creative personnel such as directors, writers, and producers; or just the camera.

Stage casting. Theatrical auditions still rely mainly upon either cold readings or an actor's prepared monologues as an initial screening process, but they may easily turn to improvisation and informal rehearsals for callbacks.

ARE THERE AUDITION SCAMS I SHOULD AVOID?

Use a simple rule. If money must exchange hands in order to be considered for casting, it is considered a paid audition, a violation of California labor laws. The same may be said of any expectation of sexual favors in exchange for casting.

Casting agencies. Newcomers to Los Angeles will soon notice rip-off extra casting notices stapled to telephone poles. "Begin your career today. Just call this number." Of course, these "casting agencies" require the actor to purchase a photo package before being submitted to their clients, most likely nonexistent. Hollywood has seen many variations on this theme, involving management companies and talent agencies as well. To be fair, legitimate extra casting agencies do charge a one-time registration fee to process an actor into their database, but these agencies actually do the casting rather than merely submitting to phantom clients.

Management companies. Again, promising employment and even fame, these fast talkers pledge access to auditions for a fee, not directly, but through photos, postage, envelopes, portfolio, and so forth. Promotional packages range from basic to "the works," costing naive actors their life savings. Legitimate management companies never ask for an up-front fee. They make their investment back on commissions from actors' earnings, just as talent agents do.

Casting workshops. These workshops have grown in popularity. Sponsored by acting companies or entrepreneurial actors, they feature well-established casting directors and associates who observe scenes performed by actors who have paid a fee to participate. The casting directors generally make opening remarks about casting and then pair off the actors, who are given sides to rehearse. Each is observed and critiqued. Actors learn not just from their own efforts but also from the performances of others, not unlike in acting classes or workshops. An added inducement obviously derives from the hope of impressing a casting director. SAG has deemed this exercise a violation of its Rule 11, prohibiting any financial inducement for the right to audition. (Troster, "Agent Information"). While the value of the casting director's critique to the actor may justify one's participation, one cannot deny that the implied allure to actors remains the hope that their performance may open a door that might otherwise have been closed.

Other casting directors have chosen a different strategy, choosing to teach workshops, often in collaboration with an organized weekend seminar or similar event. This brings legitimacy to their purpose and satisfies the SAG Rule 11, since actors presumably don't audition for the casting director so much as listen and learn.

Reality casting calls. The growth of reality programming has spawned its own scam artists. Watch for open calls for reality programs or talent search programs that require a "refundable" registration fee. Good luck getting the refund.

Pay to play. Never pay a producer for a role. That might seem elemental, but one might not recognize a scam when the producer offers a role in exchange for helping to finance the film. Essentially, the actor pays to play and, while the risk may seem equal between all parties involved, be assured that the producers will emerge from this project richer, and you, poorer.

WHAT INFORMATION SHOULD I REQUEST WHEN I RECEIVE AN AUDITION CALL?

Talent agents generally receive audition requests in the late afternoon for the next day's appointments, giving an actor little time to prepare. However, much will be expected, so much must be done. A great deal of information should be provided. Take note of the following.

Role and rate. Day player? Guest artist? Background? Make certain to understand the pay structure and any restrictions. Whether union or not, no one likes surprises when it comes to one's paycheck. Make certain the terms are spelled out to your satisfaction. Confirming the audition infers agreement to play the role if cast. Be certain it's a role you will be comfortable playing. "Princess of the Underworld" could well end up representing one's legacy.

Audition date and time. Note how much time you will have to prepare.

Location. Special directions may be e-mailed, such as maps and parking instructions.

Sides. Most auditions, but not all, involve sides, or excerpts of dialogue chosen to audition each roles. They may be e-mailed directly to the actor or accessed online through electronic casting services for a fee.

Dress. Actors may be directed to dress in a certain manner or to wear a particular item of clothing.

Special requests. An actor may be requested to bring something or to prepare in some way, usually in reference to some special skill that he or she must demonstrate, such as martial arts or a foreign language.

HOW SHOULD I PREPARE FOR AN AUDITION?

Preparing for an audition is the subject of innumerable books, seminars, workshops, and classes, and the different perspectives on successful auditioning tend to contradict themselves:

> Make strong choices / Play it safe
> Be yourself / Be in character as soon as you enter the room
> Memorize the sides / Don't memorize the sides
> Create a specific character / Be yourself

Most casting directors agree that the more successful actors arrive well prepared for the audition. A well-prepared actor will observe the following rules.

1. **Arrive on time.** Carefully consider the audition location and travel time needed. Take into consideration traffic, parking, and wrong turns. Casting directors schedule auditions every five to ten minutes. When your time arrives, you need to be there. Be sure to allow time to prep before the reading. While arriving early may earn you an earlier slot, arriving late will say to the casting director that you are unprepared and unprofessional.

2. **Don't memorize—"know" the sides.** Sides may or may not be provided. Some projects, such as music videos and some commercials, will be dubbed or will use a voice-over. If sides are provided in advance, the casting director will expect that you are at least familiar with the lines so that you don't have to rely entirely upon the script. Casting directors don't expect a word-perfect audition. Some may even exhort an actor to throw the script aside and to improvise. But casting directors do expect actors to know what they are saying and why.

3. **Research the project.** Find out everything possible about the project and its producers, director, writers, or other actors. Current television episodic and sitcom programs have Web sites with links to video. Go online, watch some video excerpts, and strategize how to fit in. Trade references may also pop up, as well as past episode summaries. Look up the producers or directors on the Internet in order to familiarize yourself with their work. Walk into the audition having done your homework and knowing exactly for whom you are auditioning and for what reason.

4. **Create a character.** Having learned as much about the project as possible, you may begin to develop certain aspects of the character. This process evolves no differently from a theatre audition. Look for clues in the sides about social status, educational level, profession, health, or anything that is not obvious from the dialogue. Consider vocal inflections, accent, and rhythms. Look for emotional range and the character's objectives. Making

strong choices is a gamble, but most casting directors prefer actors who make an impression over others who play it safe.

5. **Rehearse, rehearse, and rehearse.** Know the scenes inside and out. Work on presenting the dialogue in a variety of ways. Casting directors often rely upon improvisation techniques. Consider how the character might react to a variety of stimuli or circumstances. Be ready for whatever may be thrown at you.

6. **Don't overdress for the role.** Casting directors seem wary of actors who have overaccessorized or made obvious costuming choices about the character. They are auditioning an actor, not a costume, and the actor runs the risk of being upstaged by his or her own costume. If you are truly playing an outrageous character, then dress outrageously, but otherwise don't go overboard unless specifically requested by the casting director.

On occasion casting directors request actors to wear particular types of clothes, perhaps specifying casual, conservative, or outdoor wear or even period or uniform dress. Los Angeles's many thrift stores and vintage clothing shops provide actors with a variety of resources in these cases. As a general rule, avoid white, shiny material and loud patterns, as they don't film or videotape well.

WHAT SHOULD I KEEP FOCUSED ON DURING THE AUDITION?

There are plenty of reasons why you might be anxious before an audition. You may fear arriving late. Sides may have been changed. Parking instructions may be complicated. Studio security guards require a driver's license or other picture ID for entry. Directional signs may be posted but confusing. A maze of studio buildings and hallways must be traveled in search of some phantom room or wing. The more seasoned actors arrive early and relax into the role. But if traffic or circumstances intervene, a simple phone call to your talent agent or the casting office can often lead to a later audition time.

Your objective will ultimately be a small office suite where a casting associate with an ominous clipboard will greet each actor by taking the actor's headshot and resume and providing additional instructions. Listen carefully. Ask questions if you are confused. Use this time wisely to ask questions concerning any pronunciation or relationship ambiguities in the sides, but don't waste the associate's time playing twenty questions; the associate may be consulted later concerning actors' attitudes.

Sign in. Somewhere will be posted a sign-in card or form. Nonunion projects may use sign-in sheets of some kind but may not stick to them. SAG signatory projects must submit an audition report that documents each actor's name, talent agent, call time, time in, and time out. Many may require a Social Security number, a potential identity theft opportunity, so use your SAG membership number instead.

The waiting room. Vocal, physical, and emotional warm-ups should be completed prior to arrival, but if you were not able to do this, find an innocuous hallway and prepare. Otherwise, sit quietly and wait. Actors often share stories and information. This collegial time occurs by accident, yet it often leads to new friendships, contacts, and sometimes work. Also, take a second to scan the competition. Certain personal similarities should appear obvious, offering a small glimpse into the casting director's vision of the character. On the other hand, don't psych yourself out by worrying about having a different look. Your uniqueness may be the edge you need.

In the Box

I was sitting in the casting offices for Fox's *The Shield*. It was for a recurring role, a big deal for me. I had done due diligence in preparation and found myself sitting there fairly relaxed and enjoying the opportunity to participate at this level. I surveyed the other actors in the room, all characteristically dark, good looking, and middle aged. Some were nonchalantly reading the morning paper or doing a crossword puzzle. Others sat in stony silence. Still others recognized each other from a film shoot not quite a year ago. Some desperately studied the sides, while the rest of us who had gotten them yesterday sat holding them patiently. Suddenly a short, bald man emerged from the men's room. He daubed at his face and neck with a handkerchief as he surveyed the handsome faces of his competition. He then began to pace up and down the hallway with increasing panic until be bolted for the men's room door. Five minutes later he emerged, only to do it again. By the time he was called to read, he had reduced himself to an exhausted, physically stressed, and psyched out wreck. Perhaps a brilliant actor, he fell victim to his own insecurities rather than overcoming them, the first real test of one's aptitude for professional life.

On deck. When called, an actor will follow the associate into a room that may have one to a dozen individuals waiting to observe the audition, which begins the minute the actor walks into the room. Actors must "own" the room and fill the space without appearing cocky or overbearing. Some acting coaches instruct actors to arrive in character from the moment they enter the casting office, while others preach authenticity. The casting director should introduce each of the other participants, such as casting associates, directors, writers, or producers. The handshake has gone out of fashion in these circumstances, mostly due to health concerns. Take a hand if offered, but otherwise don't touch anyone unless directed to.

Reading the room. Learn to read the room, to understand the dynamics involved and to adjust accordingly. Casting sessions vary; they can be hot one minute and cool the next. This producer's not happy, this director wants to chat, this casting director's all business, this one jokes and encourages. Actors must follow the casting director's lead, think on their feet, react accordingly, and keep focused on the matter at hand.

The reading. At some point the casting director, if filming, will direct you to a mark on the floor. Take note of the camera—its direction, distance, and type of lens. Some instructions may be given: where to look, who to read with, and so forth. Feel free to ask any intelligent questions regarding characterization, pronunciation, or the instructions, but rhetorical or fawning questions only waste time and often gain nothing but the casting director's annoyance. Slate for the camera, stating your name and the audition role. Take a good strong beat and then begin, observing these guidelines.

1. No matter how secure you may feel with the script, always carry it. No worse sin exists than dropping a script with some bravado, and then going up on your lines.
2. Treat the camera as the audience and adjust your volume and performance according to its distance from your mark.
3. Listen carefully to any suggestions or adjustments given before doing a retake. The casting director may be testing your ability to listen and follow directions. Take a moment to consider them, and then attempt the reading once again.
4. If you are not happy with your performance, you may appropriately ask to repeat the reading, although this is always at the prerogative of the casting director. Just be prepared for your request to be denied, an occurrence that is often fatal to less experienced actors. Never let them see you sweat, and never let them see you cry!

In the Box

I received an audition request via e-mail in response to an electronic submission I had made to a casting breakdown for *The Office*. But as it hadn't aired yet in the United States, I assumed it was for the British show. So I dutifully practiced the rather short sides with my best working class London dialect, all along a bit confused as to why the BBC was casting in Hollywood.

The next day for the audition I was line and dialect perfect. I took my mark at the audition and dropped my script. The lines were simple and I wanted to show off this time. Then, as I waited for the casting director to set the camera, I asked, "This is for the BBC, right?" to which she replied, "No, dear, it's a pilot for NBC." I swallowed hard and then asked, "So I suppose the British working class accent I worked on all night is unnecessary?" She smiled blithely and said, "Yes, dear, it is. Now are you ready?" I wasn't, but I said yes as I struggled to change my character's nationality and native tongue. Gone was my focus. Gone was my concentration. I went up on lines so badly that I finally had to reach down and humbly pick up my sides from the ground and find my place. I couldn't leave quickly enough. I didn't get the part.

The exit. A polite "Thank you" indicates the casting director has seen enough. Thank him or her in return and then promptly and professionally leave. Do not complain, make excuses, criticize the script, or offer suggestions. Any additional soliciting will be viewed as begging and only serve to magnify your pathos—not the most professional impression to leave behind. On the other hand, a confident and unobtrusive demonstration of talent and a humble exit accentuates one's professional competency. Finally:

- Have passion.
- Have fun with the role, even if it's the second spear holder.
- Be patient and ask questions to clarify pronunciation, characterization, or instructions.
- Bring extra headshots and resumes in case others in the casting office ask for them.
- Be friendly but not overly chatty. Make every word count for something.
- Be nice to everyone, from assistant casting associates to fellow actors in the waiting room. One never knows what star will rise tomorrow—or fall.

WHAT SHOULDN'T I DO DURING THE AUDITION?

- Avoid excessive perfume or cologne. Casting personnel often see hundreds of actors a day, each with their own personal "scent."
- Props are unnecessary unless requested. Warriors need not arrive wearing samurai swords, and military personnel may leave their assault rifles at home.

- Never touch or physically involve anyone else in the casting office in the scene reading, including your reading partner. Their purpose is merely facilitation, not manipulation.
- Avoid chewing gum unless it's a character choice and even then only if it's essential.
- Never bring friends, relatives, or pets to audition calls, even just to wait in the lobby—that is, unless you have concerns about the legitimacy of the audition. Then by all means bring a friend to sit in the lobby!
- Never ask to read for a different role than the one for which you have read.
- Never make excuses. Self-deprecation is not a strategy. If you think you can do it better a second time, then ask to do the reading again. Otherwise, leave your personal life at the door.

WHAT SHOULDN'T HAPPEN DURING AUDITIONS?

- Auditions should happen in offices, never in private residences. If you are ever directed to report to a private residence for an audition, bring a friend, preferably a fatherly type.
- Nudity of any kind, male or female, even if mandated in the script, may not be demonstrated during initial auditions as per SAG directive. Not until final callbacks and only under clear rules may a casting director or producer require an actor to audition in any state of nudity. SAG policy is very clear on this, and even if the project is nonunion, it is a standard respected by all but the sleaziest of filmmakers.
- Actors never pay to play. If anyone at any time during the casting process discusses payment as a prerequisite to obtaining employment, it is time to say goodbye.

WHAT COULD HAPPEN AFTER AN AUDITION?

Always sign out and leave. A talent agent or personal manager may place a follow-up call to solicit feedback. Many actors maintain a journal or computer spreadsheet to document each audition, date, time, project, mileage, and outcome, a practice that is valuable not only as professional documentation but also for tax purposes. Then the waiting happens. The casting process can transpire in either days or months. One never hears unless one is hired, and when too much time has transpired, hope can turn to resignation. Letting go becomes the hardest aspect of an audition process. All actors second-guess their performances, whether good or bad. And in Hollywood, where the stakes are so much higher than in community or college theatre, so too is the obsession. But unlike in community or college theatre, the entertainment industry doesn't nurture actors. Business drives all decision making, especially casting. The better actor will be passed over for one with a bigger bust. One never knows exactly why the phone doesn't ring. One just knows that it doesn't. Learn to let go—unless the phone rings with a callback!

A callback represents success in a way, a giant step toward achieving a booking. The casting director now knows your work and has pitched it to the client, who now wants more input. You will be asked to repeat the audition in much the same way as before, this time before a different or larger group of people. You may be given new directions. Casting directors occasionally utilize a more game-oriented or role-playing technique. Sometimes an actor is asked to cold read a new script or to improvise some kind of role-playing. This represents the raising of the bar, and the actor must be prepared to meet the expectation.

More often than not, nothing happens. Someone else got the job. You didn't. Or maybe you did. If the phone rings and a casting director offers a booking, no matter how small the role, the universe suddenly becomes possible once again. But if not, then the practice of auditioning must be its own reward. Move on to the next audition or project.

Actors Forum

For the first five years I didn't do much of anything except work. I did extra work here and there. I also had a skill as a martial artist. I trained and started networking at the gyms where I spent a lot of my time. Get people's cards. Be in contact with them and just surround yourself in that environment. In the back of my mind, I was thinking perhaps I might find work from these people or perhaps even meet someone who could possibly hire me. The auditioning process is not the only way to get cast. There are a lot of people making their own films and a lot of people who will hire their friends. Most people who come out here don't have their SAG card. Most people do a lot of extra work, get their vouchers and pay to become SAG, but once you become a SAG member, you don't work as often. Nonunion work is out there all the time. But what they do is not use their screen name but use their real name. But not everyone can do that.

Tang Nguyen

I had my Equity card first, then AFTRA and SAG. I was a real pain in the ass, but it's because I was trained as an actor. I was doing a TV show with William Devane. I was like a receptionist that got fired. I had one little speech, and then I would exit. Well, I brought a raincoat with me and a shopping bag, a box of Kleenex, and a plastic vase with a flower in it. I would gather everything up and start to leave. Then I saw the little vase, turned around, went back, picked it up, put it in the shopping bag and exited. And all these old famous actors told me they loved to see me do that scene. But it was my theatre training that led me to fill in the details. People would recognize me and say, "You're the one who went back to retrieve the vase." It's the little tiny details that make a little tiny part seem big.

Jacque Lynn Colton

I loved doing soap operas. It's hard work. It's harder work than most people know, because audiences are very savvy and the older you get, the savvier they get. They recognize bullshit when they see it. If you're doing an hour show you're probably churning out ninety pages of mostly crap a day if you're lucky and the writers like you. When I was doing *Santa Barbara*, arguably the best-written soap opera ever, the money was absolutely wonderful, but I was doing 165 pages of new dialogue a week, so there was no time to take a deep breath and think, "Look what we did today." It was go home and learn thirty-nine more pages. It was exhausting.

Gordon Thomson

I did a couple of reality shows that I thought were going to launch my career, which was probably the biggest mistake of my life. An example would be *Blind Date*. I'm embarrassed by it, but I did it. They sent me to Acapulco for three days. I bit the anchovy. I thought, how bad can it be? It was the worst experience of my life. The girl was hot! But we were complete opposites. They set us up for destruction. I'm a guy with a lot of drive. I want my wife driving a supercharged Range Rover. She said, "Isn't that materialistic?" I said, "Excuse me, I could raise a family in an apartment for the rest of my life and be happy." Of course, they edit this part out. They made me look like a deer about to be circumcised. I thought it was something that was going to launch my career, and it never did. My attorney called me up and told me, "Dude, you're on the Hall of Shame." So stay away from reality shows. They're unscripted, which means you have no talent and everyone is just blah, blah, blah, blah. Talking heads, that's all it is. Unless you're a name star like Flav, no one takes them seriously.

Sajen Corona

10
Working in Hollywood

All this nostalgia about the "golden age" of Hollywood is almost laughable.
Hollywood hasn't changed in the ways that count. No matter how we
romanticize them, the golden years were hard work, as they are today. The
fight is still between the artists and the money men.

Bette Davis, *This 'n' That*

Background Casting

Sandee Alessi Casting
13731 Ventura Boulevard
Sherman Oaks, CA 91423
(818) 623-7040
http://www.sandealessicasting.com

Creative Extras Casting
2461 Santa Monica Boulevard #501
Santa Monica, CA 90404
(310) 391-9041
http://www.la411.com/Creative_Extras_Casting.cfm

Headquarters Casting
(310) 556-2626
http://www.headquarterscasting.com

Central Casting
220 South Flower Street
Burbank, CA 91502
(818) 562-2700
http://www.centralcasting.org

Bill Dance Casting
4605 Lankershim Boulevard #401
North Hollywood, CA 91602
(818) 754-6634
http://www.billdancecasting.com

On Location Casting
1223 Wilshire Boulevard #409
Santa Monica, CA 90403
(310) 770-7492
http://www.onlocationcasting.net

Prime Casting   Idell James Casting
6430 Sunset Boulevard #425   (310) 230-9344
Los Angeles, CA 90028
(310) 230-9344
http://www.primecasting.com

For an actor, working begins with a phone call, referred to as a *booking*. A talent agent, casting director, or producer will call to offer the contract and to provide call information such as dates, times, and places. This booking may first take the form of a verbal offer (which may be canceled up until noon of the day preceding the start date), a booking slip, or an offer letter. These documents may precede the phone call if your talent agent and casting director have already engaged in some negotiation over salary, duration, travel, expenses, and many additional terms or conditions applicable to the project. Daily or weekly contracts may follow, or in more advanced scenarios where the actor participates in some other aspect of the production, a deal memo may be issued, specifying the salient details agreed upon by the talent agent and the producer.

WHAT KIND OF CONTRACT AND BOOKING INFORMATION WILL I RECEIVE?

The casting director will provide and request confirmation of the following information:

Dates of hire. A booking may require a variety of work dates and report times for:

- Costume fittings
- Rehearsals
- Makeup or prosthetic fabrication
- Filming or taping
- Retakes
- Dubbing or redubbing

The actor must agree to report on a given day and time for work assignments. Some flexibility may be granted, but the inability to do so may jeopardize the booking. An actor may have to choose between a booking and a daytime job that generally pays the bills. An actor may also be given an "on or about" start date that may create uncertainty, but a start date cannot be moved backward once it has been agreed upon, only forward.

Work rate. The casting authority will offer a rate of pay, negotiable in some cases, depending on the size of the role and the experience of the actor. Union contracts define a hierarchy of acting roles and specializations for which a minimum scale or rate for a workday applies, as well as for postproduction tasks. These various ranks are:

Principal performer
Supporting player
Series regular
Guest star
Day player
Dancer/singer
Extra
    Background
    Body double
    Hand model
    Stand-in
    Omnies
Voice-over
Stunt performer

In addition, the contract should specify the services and compensation rates, if any, required for preproduction and postproduction. Nonunion projects generally use the same terminology but not the same compensation rates, which generally range from approximately one-half of union rates to merely "copy, credit, and meals."

Usage. Though not always definitive, the contract should delineate the following:

Platform: Is this for theatrical release, television airing, DVD, Internet, Webcast, podcast?
Range: On what basis will it be released? Nationally, regionally, in syndication, internationally, locally?
Period of time: This may be left open-ended for principal players or regular or recurring characters, or a deadline may be stipulated such as with a television or commercial contract.

Usage rate. Actors receive compensation for each rebroadcast of a project. The usage rate refers to the residual compensation the actor will receive per airing on television. Film actors have in the past received a residual rate per unit sale of VHS cassettes, but with the advent of DVD and Internet downloading, the producers now pay the actor nothing and refuse to negotiate any form of residual compensation. This contractual issue could lead to a protracted union strike in the future.

Screen credit. Whether or not an actor receives screen credit and, if so, where it is placed in the opening credits and advertising requires negotiation and knowledge of the industry standards. An actor has truly reached celebrity status when his or her name lists above the project title.

Each of these items requires expertise in negotiation. An actor may attempt to negotiate any or all of an offer, although it is unwise to do so without the services of a talent agent or manager. If an actor is unrepresented, a simple phone call to any talent agent will cure the problem. No agent will turn down an easy commission.

WHAT SHOULD I EXPECT OF A UNION CONTRACT?

Global Rule 1 of the SAG Constitution and Bylaws states, "No member shall work as a performer or make an agreement to work as a performer for any producer who has not executed a basic minimum agreement with the Guild which is in full force and effect." Every SAG performer agrees to abide by this, and all the other SAG rules, as a condition of membership in the Guild. This means that no SAG members may perform in nonunion projects that are within SAG's jurisdiction once they become members of the Guild (SAG, "Constitution").

Production companies that have signed contracts with one of the unions must issue a union compliant contract, either a standard union form or a negotiated contract. Extra casting and day player contracts generally entail a standard form whether union or nonunion. A booking of a role for more than five lines usually requires a talent agent's services to negotiate the best terms possible for the actor and to explain each clause and its stipulations. But a talent agent does not have to live with the consequences of a contract, and, as in most legal contracts, the language favors the employer. An actor should understand exactly to what he or she has agreed. A few contractual clauses beg clarification.

"Name and likeness." Most contracts give the producer the right to use the actor's name and likeness for the purposes of promoting the project in perpetuity. But what about merchandising and commercial tie-ins? Does the actor participate in the profit sharing of those? Look for the words "in perpetuity." This provides consent for the use of the actor's name, image, and voice commercially throughout the life of a product. For a film, that's forever; for a television program, life after cancellation spells syndication. Either way, a "bomb" is forever!

On the other hand, commercial contracts contain an automatic renewal after twenty-one months unless the advertising company receives a letter from the actor, sent no later than sixty days before the twenty-one-month expiration, revoking consent for use. Why would an actor cancel a commercial? Conflict. Commercials fall into categories, and if an actor appears in one pharmaceutical ad, it disqualifies him or her from appearing in any other for the life of that commercial. Appearing in a Ford commercial, for example, places the actor in conflict with all other automobile advertisers as long as the Ford commercial runs. Beyond that time, advertisers often renew a commercial on contingency without actually running it, thus providing no income to the actor, who in the meantime must refuse commercial work from conflicting advertisers (SAG, "Commercials Contract Digest").

"Insurance." Producers may purchase insurance covering the actor's life and health as a condition of employment in order to protect their investment. If the actor fails the medical exam or is denied coverage for any reason, the actor may be terminated. In addition, the insurance company will have the right to restrict or prohibit the actor's activities as a condition of coverage. As such, a studio can legally bar an actor from sports activities, such as skiing or mountain biking, or from traveling, and one does not even want to discuss the issue of pregnancy (SAG, "Codified Basic Agreement")!

"Promotion and publicity services." A producer may require the actor to consider any "reasonable request" to participate in promotional activities, such as photo sessions, interviews, premieres, or television or radio appearances. Actors generally receive some compensation for these obligations. But what constitutes a "reasonable request," and how much notification an actor receives in advance of such activities lies in the negotiated details.

"No obligation to proceed." In short, the producer has no obligation to use even one frame of footage of an actor's performance in the project. Many an actor's performance has ended on the cutting room floor for any number of reasons, such as a poor performance, the demands of a jealous star, or an actor's unreasonable demands or behavior. An actor may easily be discharged for a variety of reasons, a new actor engaged, and the original footage discarded.

"Assignment." This clause gives the producer the right to sell or assign an actor's services. Many actors have woken up one morning to a new employer and discovered themselves a commodity, an asset of a corporation that had been sold without their participation. Now such actors are obligated to perform for a new master not of their choosing.

"Favored nations." Not always found in a contract, this clause provides that no principal actor will receive more advantageous terms over the others. Though intended to prevent long and tedious negotiations, this clause occasionally backfires on the producer when an actor takes a gamble and holds out for a better deal, perhaps unintentionally providing all the other principal actors a simultaneous upgrade (SAG, "Codified Basic Agreement for Independent Producers").

"Breach of contract." This clause relates to an actor's work conduct—for example, tardiness, incompetence, drug or alcohol use, medications, and any behavior or practice that might hinder an actor's ability to perform. The producer must give warnings and a twenty-four to forty-eight hour notice of termination or suspension, but producers rarely take such action because they want to avoid bad press. A "newbie" may safeguard against such an occurrence by understanding that landing a guest actor role does not entitle the actor to suddenly demand star treatment and make outrageous demands such as only red M&Ms in their trailer (SAG, "Codified Basic Agreement for Independent Producers").

"Employee conduct." The agreement may contain morals clauses that prohibit the actor from violating public conventions of "decency, morality or social propriety," or "tending to result in scandal, ridicule or contempt to the Corporation" (Litwak, *Contracts for the Film and Television Industry*, 110). In the past these clauses kept homosexual actors in the closet or restricted an actor's political involvement with the implied threat of termination. Today producers have less leverage, but one must assume that actors whose sudden public apologies or publicized excursions to rehab clinics have not always been voluntary.

"Termination or suspension." If a producer wants to fire an actor, the producer will find a reason. Loosely written, this clause allows the producer to fire or suspend an actor if his or her behavior "provokes any retaliatory action or boycott against himself or the Company" (Litwak, *Contracts*, 117). An actor's bad manners or behavior in the press can lead to the ridicule of a production company with which the actor is associated. This clause allows that production company to sever ties with the actor and cut its losses.

"Exclusivity." An actor under contract may not work under a competing contract until the term of the preceding contract expires. For instance, an actor in a television series may not work with a competing network, series, or film unless the producer signs a "loan-out agreement" giving permission in exchange for some form of compensation.

Contracts may also include language about the following:

Studio zones. In the past, production companies took their film companies outside of Los Angeles city limits to escape stringent city and union rules. SAG eventually created studio zones, which grant less restrictive use of background actors outside of a certain radius of the studio's operational base. In other cases, studio zones may require rest periods and overnight accommodations for actors filming far outside a certain radius (SAG, "Codified Basic Agreement").

Per diem. Production companies generally provide craft services, but when this is not possible, actors may receive a set amount of money to purchase their own food.

Wardrobe allowance. An actor who has been asked to bring wardrobe or even prop items for use in the project receives compensation. Extras receive a set compensation amount for each wardrobe outfit requested, whether used or not, while principals receive compensation only for the outfit actually worn.

WHAT ARE THE CONTRACTUAL DIFFERENCES BETWEEN THE VARIOUS KINDS OF PROJECTS?

Each designated union and a consortium of studios and producers have negotiated separate agreements for each genre.

Film

Studio and independent film producers have up to now each followed a different set of expectations, regulations, and requirements negotiated with SAG. But most recently, a Basic Codified Agreement has been negotiated to create one unified set of expectations covering:

- Performer rates
- Residuals
- Number of mandatory union background actors employed before nonunion actors may be engaged.

In addition, this agreement sets forth specific requirements for, among others:

- **Hours per workday**—A normal workday consists of eight hours and ends at 5 p.m. If these limits are exceeded, overtime kicks in or the actor receives an additional day of pay.
- **Drop and pick up**—After the completion of filming (six months for film and four months for television), the producer may recall an actor to film additional scenes without payment for the intervening time.
- **Overtime pay**—Most actors receive an additional increment of pay for every hour beyond the normal eight-hour workday.
- **Rest periods**—Most union contracts require a twelve-hour consecutive rest period between call times on consecutive filming days.
- **Meal periods**—The union requires a thirty-minute meal period within six hours of the call time under penalty, regardless of the filming circumstances. Nevertheless, a producer faced with expensive equipment rentals and a complicated setup may force actors to work beyond this limit and will pay the penalties set forth by the union.
- **Safety requirements**—These specific, and nonnegotiable, accommodations are required by the union in hazardous situations such as working in smoke or extreme weather.

- **Transportation**—Relates to a myriad of situations regarding location shooting. Producers must provide first-class air transportation unless six or more performers travel together.
- **Travel time**—An actor may be compensated for the time required to travel to and from locations.
- **Overnight accommodations**—Contractual requirements involving studio zones and the "sixteen-hour rule" require producers to provide housing and/or pay for an additional day's work. Housing must consist of single room accommodations.
- **Use of extras**—Contractual requirements regulate the number of union extras required and their use.

In recognition of the inequality of film budgets, SAG has agreed to modify contracts based upon budgetary levels and project format. The following modified contract agreements have been adopted with larger budgeted projects held to higher standards. This modification allows smaller budgeted films to work with union actors without having to conform to the stricter requirements for compensation required of larger budgeted projects.

	Low Budget	Modified Low Budget	Ultra-Low Budget	Experimental	Student Waiver
Budget not to exceed	$2.5 million	$625,000	$200,000	$75,000	$35,000
If agrees to diversity in casting*	$3.75 million	$937,500			
Theatrical release	Required	Required	Entitled	Film festivals only	Classroom only
Must shoot film in U.S.	X	X	X	X	X
Performer rates	2/3 of basic	Significantly lower	$100 per day	Deferred	None
Reduced overtime	X	X	Prorated	Prorated	None
Background	Fewer union required	Negotiated	Negotiated	None required	None required
Residuals	Lower %	Lower %	Lower %	None	None

Source: SAG, *Film Contracts Digest*, 2005
* **Diversity in casting**—Producers meet this requirement when members of these four protected groups comprise 50 percent of the total speaking roles for 50 percent of the total days of employment: (1) women, (2) senior performers (sixty years or older), (3) performers with disabilities, and (4) people of color (Asian/Pacific Islander, Black, Latino/Hispanic, and Native American Indian).

Television

Television contracts are complex and cover a range of subjects beyond the terms covered in film contracts, such as:

Length of final project (in half-hour increments)
Time period

- **Extras**—Background actors generally book for one day at a time, though they may be asked to commit to two days. The second day does not always equate to a booking but is only a condition of employment in case the production company needs the same players the next day to complete filming.
- **Day player**—Similarly to film, the actor, often as a supporting player, commits to a one-day rate with the possibility of extension depending on the filming schedule.
- **Three day**—Only a television option and often offered for guest star roles, these contracts guarantee three days of filming.
- **Less than thirteen weeks**—A new series may receive a thirteen-week conditional commitment from a network, contingent upon a week-by-week renewal notice for principal and recurring players.
- **Thirteen weeks guaranteed**—A new series has received a guaranteed thirteen-week commitment from the network.
- **Recall**—A series has been picked up or renewed.
- **Term contracts**—A series has been renewed for an entire season or for a longer term.

Platform

- Free television (domestic)
- Basic cable
- Pay per view

Format

- Movie of the week
- Episodic
- Sitcom
- Foreign telecast

Occurrence

- **Rerun**—Each rebroadcast on its original platform triggers additional compensation.
- **Syndication**—A series generally needs to run for 3½ seasons to qualify for syndication or sale to a new platform.

(SAG and Alliance of Motion Picture and Television Producers, "Television Agreement")

Commercials

A commercial actor must not only navigate the same contractual minefield and categories as in film and television but must also contend with:

- convoluted designations such as "on-camera nonspeaking featured role" that commonly accompany the off-camera voice-over narration;
- the length of the commercial; and
- usage specifications, whether running nationally or in regional markets classified as Category A (paid for by local dealers), Category B (paid for by the national manufacturer), or "wild spots," which are scheduled at the behest of the local advertiser.

National commercials fall within subcategories such as "seasonal," "foreign broadcast," "theatrical" (for commercials that run in movie theaters) or "industrial" (inhouse). The platform may specify free television or basic cable. The length of time a commercial runs is its "cycle," the number of weeks it may run under a specific rate structure. Public service commercials command their own special rate structure (SAG, "Commercials Contract Digest," 2003).

Extras filmed in commercials also require special consideration, not unlike in film. Individual extras may be contracted, but under commercial contracts. Producers may lump background actors into extra groups and request waivers for special compensation. For instance, crowd scenes, often a staple of commercials, may employ a number of nonprofessional, unpaid extras. Undirected scenes, or individuals filmed as part of crowd scenes, public events, or accidentally as part of a street scene, may be asked to sign a release form that waives payment to them if they are not members of a professional actors union.

Finally, advertisers often run edited versions of the same commercial. A principal or featured actor may receive a "downgrade" during a new cycle, meaning the commercial has been edited and the actor's face no longer appears or is unrecognizable. The actor may still receive payment, but at a reduced rate. Consequently, an actor may also receive an "upgrade," in which, after editing, the actor's face becomes featured, thus requiring additional compensation under union rules.

New Media

We live in a brave new world of Internet, cell phones, BlackBerries, iPods, and who knows what. No one knows where technology will go tomorrow, and so the union has negotiated an open-ended contract that requires signatory producers to negotiate their terms with union actors. The New Media Contract and the Special Internet/Online Agreement impose no minimum compensation rate or conditions other than standard workplace requirements consistent with the Basic Codified Agreements. Actors and producers may freely bargain for fees—session, use, extended or unlimited editing rights, and exclusivity as separate areas of negotiation—which is another reason why serious actors need a talent agent to represent their best interests for compensation in such matters. Pension and health benefits are set at a nonnegotiable rate of 14.8 percent of gross compensation. Producers must inform actors at the time they are hired of their intentions with regard to the number of commercials and their intended use. Actual use requires substantial compensation rates as long as the actor has checked the box on the front of the contract that requests bargaining rights. This contract undergoes constant transformation, as does the technology, so stay tuned.

Theatrical

Actors Equity Association has similarly modified its basic agreement—which now is specific to individual cities, regions, and stage venues—to bring as many professional and semiprofessional productions under its umbrella and to provide as many stage actors with compensation, safety, and a professional environment. In Los Angeles, actors often encounter so-called Equity-Waiver theatres, which permit producers to pay actors a very small per performance stipend but that also guarantee certain working conditions. Actors may also encounter LORT agreements (League of Resident Theaters), from a consortium of larger nonprofit regional venues that produce quality productions and pay actors somewhat below commercial rates.

Industrial/Educational

Corporations often produce in-house training or promotional videos. Educational institutions may create documentary films to chronicle research or scholarly investigation. SAG's Industrial/Educational Films and Videotape Agreement provides compensation and work accommodations, such as prompting devices for scripts containing medical or technical terminology, but also additional compensation should these videos ever find their way into theatrical or television distribution (see Appendix C, document 4).

Interactive Media

This segment of the industry, which includes computer games and software, is growing quickly. Producers may use actors for computerized images or for voice-over. SAG's Interactive Media Agreement dictates compensation rates but, sadly, no residual compensation.

BACKGROUND ACTORS

SAG's Standard Background Agreement (see Appendix C, document 3) requires producers of film, television, or commercial projects to treat extras as human beings, not chattel. In general, they receive:

- a set pay rate for an eight-hour day;
- individual chairs;
- gender-specific dressing rooms; and, for extraordinary circumstances,
- additional compensation for

    - handling hazardous materials;
    - working in extreme weather conditions; and
    - suffering through physically demanding costumes or makeup application.

Wardrobe allowance. Producers often request that background actors bring at least three different wardrobe selections to the set. Production assistants may take advantage of naive actors by counting only the wardrobe pieces actually worn for compensation, but the contract stipulates that each outfit schlepped to the set by the actor counts for separate compensation.

Prop allowance. Handbags, luggage, sports equipment, books, cameras, electronic equipment, and so forth qualify as props. Background actors, if asked to use their own, receive compensation at set rates listed on the standard contract.

Mileage. When required to report outside of a thirty-mile studio zone, the actor is due a mileage reimbursement at the current rate of $0.30 per mile. (The IRS allows an alternative of $0.485 per mile if claimed on a federal tax return.)

Auto. Actors often register their automobiles with an extra casting service for use in a parking lot, a congested highway, or some other filmed scenario. The union stipulates that the producer must pay mileage to and from the set as well as a specific daily rate for the use of an actor's personal vehicle.

Vouchers. Union signatory producers must hire a minimum of union extras. Beyond this number, nonunion actors may be hired. If a booked union actor fails to show, a nonunion actor may be "bumped" to union status, entitling him or her to a voucher toward eventual union membership and an increase in pay rate for the day (SAG, "Background Actors Contract Summary").

WHAT OTHER LEGAL DOCUMENTS MUST AN ACTOR KNOW ABOUT?

Nondisclosure agreement. Studios and producers zealously guard scripts and the results of unscripted projects such as reality programs. Actors who receive advance copies of film and television scripts or who participate in reality programs must sign nondisclosure agreements that contain severe financial penalties for violation. Make no mistake, they mean it! Premature disclosure of a script ending or the result of a reality program contest can result in incalculable financial losses to a studio or producer, who will take out their anger with help from their considerable legal resources.

Nudity rider. This amendment to a contract obligates the actor to appear nude, seminude, and/or to perform simulated sex acts on camera. The emphasis here is on "simulated." Both SAG and AFTRA require strict adherence to their guidelines. SAG requires signatories to follow these guidelines:

- An actor must receive notification prior to auditions if the role requires nudity.
- An actor may wear pasties and a G-string during the initial audition or interview.
- The actor must receive at least a $500 bump in pay.
- The actor must receive in advance a general description of the extent of the nudity and physical contact.
- The actor must provide written consent.
- The actor may remain clothed during rehearsals.
- The film set must be closed, with all nonessential personnel removed.
- No still photos may be taken without the written consent of the actor.
- The actor may request a body double if he or she is uncomfortable with the situation.
- The actor may not revoke consent after filming has been completed. (SAG, "Codified Basic Agreement")

Extra release form. Originally used to inoculate producers against the use of amateur actors or a passerby unintentionally filmed, this form is rarely encountered anywhere but in nonunion projects where actors receive little or no pay and sign away any or all future claims of compensation for the use of their image.

WHAT SHOULD I DO TO PREPARE FOR FILMING?

Production personnel leave nothing to chance. Either a production assistant or your talent agent will provide all necessary call information, generally by e-mailing a call sheet that specifies the following detailed information.

Call time. Expect a call time of 6 a.m. or earlier, depending on the degree of makeup and costuming required. Film companies often need to exploit every second of daylight and expect all actors to be ready at first light unless they are shooting a night scene. Either way, late actors don't work again and can be blacklisted.

Actors may receive a "weather permitting" call, issued only prior to the report time, that allows the producer to cancel photography or hold the actors in costume for up to four hours until a determination to continue or suspend filming is made and a half paycheck is issued to those released from work.

Location. The shoot may take place at a studio or on location. If at a studio, you will be given an address and directions. If on location, you may be directed to an Internet service that provides location maps. Either way, smart actors use a Web site such as Mapquest to plan a specific transportation route. Even at 5 a.m. traffic can be tricky in Los Angeles, and often the most direct route is not the quickest.

Contact person. A name and a telephone number will be provided. Whether hired as a principal, a guest star, or an extra, you will report to someone upon arrival.

Wardrobe/props. If asked to provide wardrobe or prop items, iron clothing first. Costume assistants appreciate the effort even if they must redo the work.

Script. A script has most likely been provided either digitally or by courier. Directors expect actors to arrive line perfect. Production time costs money, and an actor who flubs lines or clearly has not done the work looks less than professional. And no, they don't use cue cards.

WHAT SHOULD I BRING WITH ME TO THE SET?

The production crew generally reports to the set a good hour or two before the actors and so has little patience for actors with tardy excuses. Rule number 1 is to be on time and prepared. A production assistant will phone or e-mail information detailing where and when to report with perhaps an online map as well. Always bring the following:

1. **Production company contact number**—Traffic happens, as do accidents and confused directions. A preemptive call eliminates the need for a panicked call and all its ensuing embarrassment and explanations.
2. **Driver's license (or an additional form of identification)**—Studio security requires an acceptable form of photo ID regardless of role.
3. **Union membership card**—Although not a requirement, this is a good idea.
4. **Thomas Guide**—A missed freeway exit can propel an actor miles in the wrong direction. Narrow canyon roads twist and turn and change names without warning. Badly engineered intersections often compound the complication with missing or confusing signage. This essential map book of Los Angeles provides a safety net. Don't leave home without it.
5. **Cell phone**—For many reasons, an actor may need to contact his or her talent agent, manager, babysitter, significant other, or day job. However, cell phones are usually banned from the set to prevent an otherwise perfect take being ruined by a rogue call. Turn it off upon arrival and, if possible, leave it in a secure location with other personal items.
6. **Change**—Parking may require feeding a meter. A parking garage may require payment in advance, with a refund at day's end.
7. **Laptop, books, and iPod**—All great distractions when shooting turns into a hurry up and wait syndrome. Production companies generally provide principals, guest stars, and supporting actors private and secure dressing rooms or trailers. Day players occasionally receive the same, but extras are entitled only to a rest area, never secure dressing rooms, so inquire in advance as to whether the production company provides a secure location. It's a good idea to bring things to occupy your time whether in public or in private.
8. **Pencil and paper**—These are useful for documenting work times, names, and dates, or writing down names and numbers of new friends and contacts (SAG, "What Actors Should Remember," 42).

WHAT SHOULDN'T I BRING TO THE SET?

1. **Food**—Unless you are on a special diet, leave your lunchbox at home. Production companies provide craft services, which are often elaborate and generous.
2. **Friends or relatives**—This is never appropriate unless you have been given permission in advance.

3. **An attitude**—Leave this at home regardless of any insult to your professionalism. Report any ill treatment or inappropriate request immediately to your talent agent or on-set representative.

WHAT SHOULD I DO WHEN I ARRIVE?

1. Report to the assigned contact person and sign in. All extra casting services will have an on-set representative. Principal actors will report to a production assistant.
2. Fill out any paperwork.
3. Wait. Costuming and makeup follow a schedule as does filming. Whether these are held in a trailer, dressing room, or holding room, an assigned production assistant keeps actors informed and on task.

In addition, here are a few behavioral guidelines:

1. Don't touch anything unless asked to.
2. Be silent during filming. "Quiet on the set!" means what it says.
3. Stay calm. Boisterous behavior doesn't go over well with producers.
4. Learn the names of the crew members. They can make an actor's day a dream or a nightmare.
5. Thank everyone, twice!
6. Fill out all necessary paperwork before leaving. SAG or AFTRA can't help an actor without completed vouchers or production time sheets.
7. Don't throw anything away. Keep and file all call sheets and production information.
8. Sign out before leaving the set. The producer must submit a Production Time Report to the union as an official record for payment. Your signature confirms the hours worked. Bring any mistake to the attention of a production assistant, or call the union if you believe the report is in error.

WHAT CAN I EXPECT FROM NONUNION PROJECTS?

Unfortunately, when calculated against the total volume of all film, television, and commercial projects in Los Angeles, nonunion projects represent the greatest number. They fall into five categories:

1. We have a good script and some money.
2. We have a bad script and some money.
3. We have a good script and no money.

4. We have a bad script and no money.
5. We haven't a prayer of ever getting this project produced.

An actor must learn to differentiate between each category and know when to say, "No thank you." All nonunion projects pose as legitimate projects, but if this were true they would have signed agreements with a union. Some projects, such as categories 1 and 2, have good intentions but simply lack resources. How does an actor tell the difference and avoid exploitation? An actor learns to notice certain warning signs. Do auditions proceed chaotically? Is information posted incorrectly? Are questions answered evasively? All these are omens that portend ill for the working conditions and, more importantly, the compensation conditions. If you are offered a nonunion role, ask questions and then trust your instincts. Some nonunion projects do fall into the first category and represent true opportunities for nonunion actors. Beginning actors should familiarize themselves with California labor laws that, at the bare minimum, provide some sense of a safety net. Of course, union actors must abide by SAG Global Rule 1 and accept work only from union signatory producers (California Department of Industrial Relations, *California Labor Code*).

WHAT KINDS OF NONUNION PROJECTS ARE AVAILABLE?

Films

The good. Occasionally a director or actor, for reasons of intellectual or artistic collaboration, may prefer to work in anonymity and outside of the traditional boundaries of the industry. The actual shoot most likely will occur outside the United States, with the film exhibited domestically or going direct to DVD.

The bad. These projects will have a B-movie script and most likely be a youth-oriented, high school/summer camp/forbidden sex/slasher film with uncomfortable location conditions, long action, fewer waits between takes, and nonexistent craft services.

The ugly. These projects will have a half-written script, endless rehearsals, and incessant promises before the director quits and the producer's cell phone number becomes inoperable.

Television

Basic cable airs many nonunion serial and episodic television programs. Their production companies, though reputable, prefer to function outside of union jurisdiction to produce cheaper products for an insatiable market. They do not employ actors but provide "independent contractors" a stipend, not a salary, that is considerably less than union scale and has no provisions for overtime or workman's compensation. Still, national airtime is national airtime. A principal role entitles an actor to bragging rights and announcements to casting directors and can eventually provide key acting clips for a reel.

A great many television pilots begin as short, low budget prototypes, filmed on spec as sales presentations. Actors participate in hopes of participating on the ground floor of the next great sitcom. Sometimes this pays off by being reshot as a network pilot, though not always with the same actors.

Commercials

Nonunion commercial filming prospers in Los Angeles and represents a frustration for union actors. Commercials filmed under SAG jurisdiction not only provide for minimum wages but for residual or buyout payments as well. Nonunion projects generally offer either a one-time stipend payment or a spec promise by some film school graduate. Unfortunately, commercial sponsors easily exploit loopholes in the unions' jurisdiction and in FCC regulations.

Reality Programs

Known as "unscripted projects," reality programs generally fall into three categories:

1. Feel-good makeover shows
2. Contests of some (or little) skill
3. A "real world" group of people forced to live with each other.

These programs don't employ actors. They select contestants or participants. The real reality is that actors comprise an enormous contestant pool for these programs. most of which find their "contestants" through breakdowns to casting services. The selection process even mirrors theatrical casting, but at its end, an actor is offered a contestant or participant contract, rather than a theatrical performance contract, which stipulates "prizes," cash or otherwise, but not wages or terms of employment.

Whether participation is a curse or boon to a career, an actor who appears in a reality program must prepare to perform without a safety net. These programs mostly operate outside the jurisdiction of AFTRA, and producers have little incentive to work through talent agents and managers. For instance:

- An actor may be asked to submit to humiliating and potentially dangerous scenarios and may have to pledge not to sue if plans go awry and cause bodily harm or death.

- An actor must submit to a background check as a condition of participation. Experiences on several notable network programs, such as *Big Brother*, have necessitated careful screening for potential embarrassments and to guarantee the safety of the other participants.
- An actor must fill out a rather long and detailed multipage application form. Producers may contact friends, family, and employers as a condition of participation and may obtain the actor's personal and financial records within the lax legal boundaries prescribed by law.
- The producers may require exclusivity rights, and require the signing of a very scary nondisclosure agreement that threatens financial ruin if violated.

Music Videos

Also mostly operating outside the jurisdiction of the unions, music video production companies pay actors small stipends or an hourly wage, if at all. Expect long, disorganized film shoots with craft services that range from catered gourmet food to pizzas and a few warm sodas. An actor has little incentive to participate except to gain experience and another clip for the reel.

Stage

Nonunion theatre in Los Angeles too often resembles community theatre, complete with dueling egos and artistic vacuity. Equity-Waiver theatre offers a more stable and satisfactory environment for showcasing and doesn't issue contracts, so the actor always has the option of exiting gracefully. Also, Equity-Waiver productions generally pay a small per performance stipend (gas money), while nonunion productions generally expect volunteer efforts.

11
Bookkeeping
The Cost of Doing Business

IRS Deduction Checklist

Contracts
- Talent agent commissions
- Legal fees

Travel	**For**
■ Auto mileage	Auditions
■ Parking fees	Callbacks
■ Tolls	Second job
■ Taxi, train, airfare, bus fare	Rehearsals or meetings
■ Car rental	
■ Lodging	
■ Meals	Per diem

Communication	**For**
■ Cell phone service	Business calls only
■ Telephone service	Basic service
■ Internet access	Monthly service fee
■ E-mail account	Monthly service fee
■ Internet café	Remote access
■ Fax transmissions	Per transmission
■ Paging service	Monthly service fee

Office Supplies
- Paper and ink cartridges
- Postage
- Envelopes and mailers

- Post-it Notes
- Mailing labels or cards
- Film, blank CDs, tapes

Equipment Purchases
- Computer and peripherals
- Software
- Telephone or cell phone
- Answering machine
- Camcorder or digital camera

Marketing Materials
- Photo fees, processing, and printing
- Resume photocopying
- Tape or DVD processing, editing and copying
- Web site creation and hosting
- Business cards

Professional Services
- Union initiation fees and dues
- Electronic casting service fees
- Mailing services
- Makeup and hair care
- Professional organizations
- Audition accompanist

Continuing Education
- Acting, voice, and dance classes
- Workshops
- Theatre and movie tickets
- Dialect, fencing, stage combat coaching

Professional Supplies
- Wardrobe/rehearsal clothes
- Props
- Trade publications
- Business gifts
- Books and research materials

When Bill Clinton nominated actress Jane Alexander to chair the National Endowment for the Arts (NEA) in 1993, she faced a monumental task in preparation for her confirmation hearings. The government required her to assemble the names and addresses of all her employers as an actress. "This was daunting, to say the least," she stated, "because of the numerous engagements I'd had as an actress; some had taken only an hour or two . . . and none, not even performing in a hit play, had lasted longer than a year. When the list reached more than three hundred, I began to give up" (Alexander, *Command Performance*, 19–20).

Actors rarely experience long-term employment and as such may work for a dozen or more employers during the course of a tax year. The added burden for an actor lies not in the 45,000 pages of the tax code but in bookkeeping and knowing the tax liabilities inherent in this profession.

DO ACTORS HAVE ANY SPECIAL TAX LIABILITIES?

Once again the important division lies in union status. Union projects hire actors as employees. Thus, their income takes the form of a salary. Union projects may pay directly to the actor or through the union, but in both cases taxes are withheld and Social Security and Medicare deductions are matched. Still other projects, principally national commercial projects, route through a central advertising booking agency that withholds taxes and then transfers the funds to the actor's commercial talent agent, who deducts his or her commission before issuing a check to the actor. Either way, the actor as an employee signs, receives W-2s at the end of the year from each employer, and files a tax return reporting this income along with any other nonacting income, just as in any other profession.

Nonunion projects do not hire actors as employees but as independent contractors. The IRS considers these actors to be self-employed. Nonunion projects often pay with cash, for which the actor signs a receipt. Others will have the actor sign a voucher for a lump sum check (no deductions). At the end of the year, the actor receives a 1099 form that declares the income. Many companies don't bother if the stipend was under $400, but they are required to if they paid an actor $600 or more. The actor at that time becomes liable not only for the unpaid deductions but also for the matching Social Security and Medicare payments the employer would have paid the IRS. A 15.3 percent self-employment tax reflects this liability.

An actor's fee may represent anything else a producer provides. On location, when catering is not an option, meals may be handled by distributing per diem funds—a set amount of cash, usually $50 per day—with which to purchase food. The producer may add this amount to the actor's earned income. Travel costs, depending on how the contract is written, may provide "reimbursement" for transportation, or may provide "compensation." The former represents the producer's cost of doing business, and the latter represents the actor's. If you are compensated, as opposed to reimbursed, the amount may be added to your reportable earned income. The IRS will expect you to pay taxes on anything of value provided to you during the course of the project.

Proper filing and bookkeeping, as with any business, provides the answer to this problem. Meal and grocery receipts, airline ticket invoices, and taxi vouchers must be retained. Tollbooth fares, private auto mileage, hotel costs, room service, valet services, and gratuities should also be documented. A location shoot can be expensive, so whether you pay or the production company pays, you should keep comprehensive records lest you foot the bill in the end.

DOES THE IRS OFFER ANY SPECIAL TAX INCENTIVES TO AN ACTOR?

Congress designated the category of qualified performing artist in the 1980s with a special tax status. Restrictions apply, of course. An actor must

- have worked for two or more employers during the year as an actor;
- have received at least $200 in wages from each employer;
- have job-related expenses of more than 10 percent of this income; and
- have an adjusted gross income of $16,000 or less.

Actors who meet these criteria may deduct employee business expenses as an adjustment to income rather than as a miscellaneous itemized deduction. The main difference lies in the fact that miscellaneous itemized deductions are subject to a 2 percent limit. You figure your deduction on Schedule A by subtracting 2 percent of the adjusted gross income from the total amount of these expenses. A qualified performing artist is not subject to this limitation (IRS, *Publication 529: Performing Artists*).

WHAT DEDUCTIONS MAY ACTORS TAKE ON THEIR INCOME TAXES?

With professional status comes income, and with income come taxes. But with taxes also come deductions, a small detail all too often overlooked by beginning actors who, more used to paying for the privilege, have developed a hobbyist's mentality. How many costume pieces, makeup items, or props have been paid for out of pocket in an actor's formative community theatre years? An actor beginning a career in Hollywood incurs considerable start-up costs, as well as ongoing overhead and future capital expenditures, most of which are tax deductible.

Actors must demonstrate the discipline to maintain normal business records. During my sabbatical year I booked twenty-four roles. That meant twenty-four different employers, twenty-four different contracts, and theoretically twenty-four different W-2s or 1099s (if no taxes were deducted). Many of those production companies were structured as short-lived, limited partnerships or some other variation on a theme that probably meant they were now defunct or operating under the IRS radar. Still, I counted fifteen different employers that year. The tax preparation was laborious and tedious. Some studios often provide paperwork on location, but this is easily lost and hard to read. Conscientious actors must keep a log of their work each year and retain all paperwork even if it seems insignificant. Sometimes a call sheet retrieved will reveal the name or telephone number needed to secure a W-2 that never came in the mail. I desperately tied together the pieces of my professional life from the assemblage of e-mails, contracts, vouchers, and receipts that documented my year's work. I received a $1,700 refund the following April.

Once again, actors must think of themselves as running a small business. What are the start-up costs? What is the overhead? What are the marketing and advertising costs? Like any other employees, actors may deduct any legitimate unreimbursed employee expenses during the tax year. Even the acting profession has its three-martini lunches. Minimizing one's tax burden means careful bookkeeping and understanding tax deductions.

Commissions and Fees

All commissions, whether to a talent agent or a personal manager, represent a deductible expense. But if SAG franchised, talent agents take their commissions directly from actors' gross union wages before they issue the checks, so their commissions are not deductible for the actors. Talent agents generally don't engage in nonunion projects, so any commissions paid to them by actors remain voluntary. But any commission paid directly to a talent agent or manager by an actor out of his or her net income represents a legitimate deductible expense.

Contract Labor Fees (Services)

From photography to piano tuning, and from accountants to voice-over coaches, any service that helps actors prepare for their craft falls under the heading of professional service. Unfortunately, the IRS does not consider expenses such as gym memberships, physical therapy, and hair styling as legitimate professional expenses, though as actors we know they are indeed. But whether it's the union that protects the work environment, the manager that makes the contacts, the dialect coach, the accompanist, the photographer, the acting coach, or the candlestick maker, their service quickly becomes indispensable. And while many of the chapters in this book have included warnings about a multitude of services that prey upon unwary young actors, a professional does need professional services.

Once found, you must establish a professional relationship with them. A service provider may already have established itself as a corporation or a DBA (doing business as) and will provide an invoice for your records. But others may not, and a personal check to a private party does not suffice to prove payment for services rendered. How does one prove a check represents a fee for a service without documentation of the service? The IRS provides two forms to facilitate this documentation: the W-9 and the 1099. The W-9 first establishes the professional relationship wherein the actor "hires" the service provider, and the 1099 simply documents the amount paid at the end of each year.

Legal Expenses

A talent agent will negotiate most union contracts. But occasionally the contractual complexity exceeds the agent's expertise. Many top talent agents in Hollywood also exhibit legal credentials in entertainment law, but in order to avoid a conflict of interest, all agents should refer actors to a third-party consultant such as an attorney specializing in entertainment law. Most standard contracts conclude in a pretty straightforward manner, but some, such as those for reality programs, stray into nonunion territory where punitive clauses and restrictions apply. Contracts may also make caveats about pregnancy, weight, insurance, or any number of other restrictions. Lawyers in these situations, though expensive, pay for themselves. Don't hesitate to involve professional advice if you feel the room starting to spin.

Professional Registries

Electronic casting services have evolved into a mandatory business expense just as hard copy publications such as the Players Directory had in the past. Any service that legitimately registers and displays actors' marketing materials to elements of the entertainment industry serves an important business function and can be deducted, as can Internet services that provide sides, location maps, labels, or other professional services to actors.

Professional Services

From business managers to dog walkers, actors increasingly rely upon other professional services as their status and pay advance. Business managers pay their bills, publicists get them in the news, personal trainers keep them fit, a personal handler keeps them sober. Lost in that self-indulgent milieu is the bookkeeper, the unassuming accountant that maintains the receipts of an actor's life. Forget the dog walker. Find yourself a good accountant, a loyal accountant, who is not connected contractually or peripherally with any of your business dealings. Such professionals take great pride in the conscientious guardianship of their clients' interests, whether they are making minimum scale or celebrity wages.

Travel

Local Travel

Travel to and from auditions, callbacks, meetings, and rehearsals reflects the cost of obtaining employment and may be deducted at 48.5 cents per mile. But the IRS requires the actor to keep a logbook, some kind of ongoing documentation for each project, such as date, location, and mileage to and from. Don't just estimate. Show the actual odometer readings. And keep all audition materials, such as audition notices, e-mail, and even sides for documentation. You can also deduct parking fees and tolls, but once again, only with a receipt.

Travel to and from work falls into a separate category. No one gets a tax deduction for going to work, actors included. But for many actors, professional acting work represents a second income, a second job, something for which the IRS provides a mileage deduction. You can't count the mileage to your first employment for the day, but from there, to the second and home again does count as deductible mileage.

The deductibility of the fares for public transportation is more complicated. The IRS doesn't allow the deduction of a monthly or yearly bus pass, rightly assuming that one uses a bus pass for more than transportation to and from work. Only the fare for a particular audition, callback, fitting, or filming may be considered. And, of course, all travelers know how much bus drivers love to stop and write out receipts! If you have the cash, take a taxi. Taxi drivers rarely complain about writing receipts.

Out of Town Travel

Any union signatory production company will pay an actor's travel costs, but nonunion production companies may require the actor to pay his or her own way. If they are not reimbursed, the actor can deduct these costs, but only to and from the hotel.

Communication

When Congress deregulated the phone companies, communication was supposed to become simpler and cheaper. It has become just the opposite. The days of actors calling in to an answering service three times a day have long passed. Now most actors carry cell phones and have Internet access. BlackBerries have also grown in popularity. Agents must be able to reach an actor, often at a moment's notice. While most casting directors give twenty-four hour notices of auditions, an agent must confirm it, sides must be provided, and when work is booked, information about wardrobe fittings, rehearsals, meetings, and location needs to be transmitted. An actor out of touch quickly becomes an actor out of work. Industry brokers have little sympathy for those with communication issues, especially ones involving toll calls, pay phones, or missed calls.

Any communication in the daily course of business may be deducted, such as fax transmissions, monthly Internet access or e-mail account costs, or paging services. The IRS allows virtually any cost of keeping in touch, as long as the taxpayer produces a paper trail. So keep all documentation. A scrap of a fax confirmation may offer a telephone number, a business name, a date, and proof of a business related transaction.

These fees represent a deductible expense, but not entirely. What completes the issue is their percentage of use. Though ostensibly for work, their personal use is not restricted. That portion is not deductible. Most accountants suggest a 75–80 percentage for deduction, assuming that 20–25 percent of one's use is personal.

In the Box

One day I stopped by my talent agent's office to drop off photos. She was engaged in a frantic search for an actor who had just been booked for a possible recurring role on a soap opera—a plum role for him and a steady commission for her. But soap operas tape on a tight schedule, and the booking was contingent on the actor making a wardrobe fitting that afternoon for the next day's taping. She had called his cell phone, his home phone, left messages everywhere, and had even called his evening work number. No luck. At 4 p.m. she called the casting director to turn down the booking. As it turns out, the actor was at home, sleeping off a late night bender. When he awoke and returned the message at 6 p.m., he learned a hard lesson: you snooze, you lose.

The IRS may allow a deduction for basic Internet and phone service, but not for its bells and whistles, such as ring tones and iTunes. If possible, keep professional calls to your cell phone and your personal calls to your home phone. Billing statements provide a paper trail for any exceptions, such as personal long distance calls, text messaging, and ring tones. One hesitates to invoke the A word, but one must always ask the question, "Can I justify this in an audit?" If you can't, you can be certain the IRS won't allow it.

Office Supplies

Just as with any other small business, the cost of doing business as an actor includes office supplies. Printer paper and ink, postage, envelopes, Post-it Notes, mailing labels, and every other desktop item needed to maintain the daily production line of submissions to casting directors, prospective talent agents, or managers all count. Those $2 receipts add up. But as any good business manager knows, buying in bulk saves money, but promotional gimmicks not so much. While I am not an advocate of rewards programs, they do work for office supply chains. Discounts kick in not just when you are buying in bulk, but progressively as well. Postage, shipping, and photocopying may be deducted.

Equipment Purchases

Computers have become a necessity for actors. The IRS allows for the business deduction of computers and most peripherals such as printers, scanners, and speakers, as well as a host of other electronic gadgets such as PDAs. Some software can be deducted if one can prove its use for business. Once again, keep all receipts just in case, but remember, the total cost may not be deductible unless the item was used exclusively for business.

The IRS also recognizes the deductibility of other digital technology, such as digital cameras and camcorders. An actor needs documentation of every role with either still photos or video. Learning new songs requires a tape recorder. Vocal and dialect work require precise playback, requiring digital stereo equipment. Once again, the standard remains the percentage of use for business.

The purchase of any expensive equipment for the successful advance of one's career provides two options: the deduction of the purchase price for the current tax year after computing its percent of use, or the depreciation of its cost over its period of functionality. The IRS provides Form 4562 for this purpose, but consulting an accountant might be a safer approach.

Marketing Materials

Good marketing requires good marketing materials. Actors routinely print hundreds of photos, resumes, postcards, and business cards, and they pay for services such as actor's reel creating, editing, and duplicating, and Web site design, hosting, and maintenance. Even the purchase of tickets for prospective talent agents or casting directors when showcasing rises to the level of the cost of doing business. Actors may also try gimmicks, such as T-shirts promoting a play or an ad in a trade publication. One actress has rented a billboard in Hollywood promoting herself for over a decade. It's never gotten her much work, but it's deductible!

In the Box

I had just completed work as an extra. I had been in the right place at the right time. I had been given a line to speak on camera. I had been filmed, and I could now be Taft-Hartleyed into SAG. I needed only the signed waiver by the production assistant to confirm. But would she bother? I called a local florist and ordered a bouquet to be sent to her office. I received that waiver and the next day joined SAG. I'll never know if the flowers made the difference, but it didn't matter. They were deductible.

Continuing Education

An actor must be a lifelong learner. Every role provides new challenges and opportunities to develop skills. Dialects, stage combat, makeup, character research—each challenge should excite an actor's sensibility unless they've chosen the wrong profession. How one pursues that quest remains an individual decision reflecting an actor's professional goals. Fencing lessons may reflect a classical training direction or may only be needed for an audition six months hence—either way, they're an appropriate choice. Casting workshops provide opportunities and access. Acting lessons hone technique, while researching plays and films broadens one's perspective on the industry and the profession. It's not always as important *what* one does to continue one's education, only that one *does* continue one's education. The full tax deductibility of professional development provides an extra incentive. So learn tai chi, take high wire lessons for Cirque du Soleil, or attain proficiency in weapons handling. An actor can justify any skill-building expense.

Professional Supplies

Turning professional means rarely having to pay out of one's pocket for the accoutrements of the profession. But when one does, one may deduct the cost. Trade papers, music, and books are always deductible, but wardrobe purchases must be tied to a specific paid project, except for uniforms or protective clothing for activities such as fencing practice. Makeup and hair care count only during the work period. But so often the purchase of these supplies occurs on the fly, with cash, and with little thought toward maintaining records. An eyebrow pencil, a pair of glasses, a *Backstage West* each week at the convenience store—all those cash transactions so easily forgotten and receipts so easily lost add up over time. The only solution remains organizing one's finances as in any other small business (Actors' Equity Association, "Your Income Tax," 3).

Office Space

Actors renting or leasing a space with a dedicated office room may be able to deduct a percentage of the cost of their rent and utilities. The space cannot contain a bed and must be used exclusively for business. If this is so, then the percentage of that space's square footage to the total square footage may be used to determine the deduction allowable for monthly rent, mortgage interest, utilities, and parking fees.

HOW DO I MAINTAIN THESE RECORDS?

The amount of receipts and records can seem overwhelming, but they are essential to minimizing one's tax burden. The IRS will take exception to many actors' deductions. You must prove otherwise. Unless you develop a strategy for handling receipts and keeping records, you will find yourself working primarily for your talent agent and the IRS.

Begin by stuffing receipts into envelopes or an accordion file for each project and keeping logs of miles traveled, per diems received, supplies purchased, and lessons paid for. More organized actors opt for technological strategies to survive. Many successful actors use BlackBerrys or some other form of PDA to maintain records of work related expenses, especially when on the road or on location. Of course, there is still the problem of documentation. Using your debit or credit card for all business transactions generates an electronic paper trail through the banking institution. Computer programs such as Quicken and Money can organize expenses and provide comprehensive reports at the end of the year. Computerizing your professional business finances should be a no-brainer.

WHAT SHOULD I DO IF I'M AUDITED?

IRS agents have far bigger fish to fry than starving actors, but if you happen to be selected for an audit, the best offense is a good defense. In other words, stretching the truth or pushing the limits only tempts fate. Claiming thousands of dollars in entertainment deductions or trying to count your weekly massage treatments as a professional expense sends up red flags and only invites scrutiny. But if the IRS ever comes calling, don't expect them to understand the needs of an actor. Most IRS auditors wouldn't know a legitimate acting expense from a manicure, which is a legitimate expense in some circumstances. Get my point?

Immediately consult a tax attorney or specialist. First, organize your documents, not by project but by category, unless the IRS is disputing only one particular project. Bring the actual contracts to detail your financial involvement in each project. Don't provide estimates. Have concrete numbers and the paper trail to back it up. Answer the questions, and if you need to gather more information, ask the IRS for an extension. Don't offer information to the auditor.

WHAT FIVE MISTAKES SHOULD I AVOID?

1. **"I'll write it down later."** Sure you will! These famous last words have been the failing of every actor at one moment or another. The truth is you probably won't, and your loss is the IRS's gain.
2. **"It's only a $1.29 receipt."** If only I had a nickel for every time I used that excuse, I could finally have that operation. Better yet, how about $1.29 for every time I didn't utter that excuse!
3. **"I really don't need this piece of paper."** The world is littered with little discarded scraps of paper that collectively could have provided a sizeable refund to any individual but now provide fodder for a landfill or clog a washing machine filter. Save everything and train yourself to place these receipts in a wallet, not in a pocket soon to be forgotten and remembered too late in the washing cycle.
4. **"I needed a new pair of shoes anyway."** That was always the excuse I used when purchasing items for a community theatre production with no budget. It was pathetic then, but it is downright sinful to use as a professional.
5. **"The production company will pay for it."** Beginning actors often live in a dream world, believing that everyone is honest and always tells the truth. "Oh sure, go ahead and pay for it, and we'll reimburse you!" It only takes a deceptive costumer or production assistant to learn that if a production company will pay for it, you shouldn't have to first!

WHAT ITEMS ARE NOT DEDUCTIBLE?

Clothes. These are generally not deductible unless they are specialized articles such as character shoes or tights for dance or uniforms. So the hat you bought for the commercial audition not only didn't get you the job, but it's also not deductible.

Makeup. Anything considered street makeup has long ago been eliminated as a deductible expense. The makeup in question must be theatrical makeup, prosthetics, or fake facial hair.

Health club memberships. We all know that actors must be beautiful and trim, but the IRS views the issue differently. A production company must make the actor's fitness or physical training a condition of employment in order for the IRS to consider it a legitimate employee deduction.

Hair styling. The cost of hair styling for auditions or photography the IRS considers to be at the discretion of the actor. Unless otherwise mandated by the producer, the cost of these services cannot be deducted.

The final word on the subject: *document, document, document!*

Actors Forum

I did two years of community college. And if I could go back in time, I would have left as soon as I could and found a good acting workshop or acting coach, because theatre acting is different than screen acting. You can be the greatest theatre actor in the world, but if you want to be a theatre actor, go to New York. It's always good to know how to act, but there are different ways to act in front of a camera than on a stage. The camera is a little bit subtler. You don't have to project, but it's a little more intimate and you have to really connect with the person you're acting with. There are showcases for different minorities. If you're Asian, East-West Players is a good place to go. I'm sure that Latino and African-American actors have their own showcases, and it does help.

Tang Nguyen

You need to be in a workshop where you can do scenes and auditions and see what you look like on camera. Some people say there's a whole different technique to film. I don't think so. I would say that when you're doing film or television, it's just like doing a scene up close with somebody in a small theatre. I've worked in theatres where the audience was only feet away. You're not yelling across the room. You're doing it two feet away. Your movements are smaller. I don't think it's different acting. It's just more intimate."

Jacque Lynn Colton

If you have any formal training in theatre with a degree, you don't need acting classes in my opinion. You just need to audition and get work. You've done all the training you're going to need. I ask you, where did Cameron Diaz go to school? Where did Brad Pitt go to school? They're two very effective performers. If you really long for more training, then find a class, because that's going to make you happy. But what makes me happy is work. There's an awful kind of semiprofessional quality that is wedded to taking classes. I've been doing it for forty years plus. I've never taken a class in my life. "Give me a job and the rest of the crap will get solved." That's from *A Chorus Line*, the best lyric ever written in any musical.

Gordon Thomson

Actors should absolutely showcase. I found my place at the Laugh Factory. They had an open mike on Tuesdays. I invited all my friends, cold called throughout the industry, and did my five-minute set. I got 119 people there. It's great just to show that you're doing something. Most casting directors don't go to plays. They don't have the time. Why would someone go to a play when they can see something on the Internet? You can have all the training you want, stage or whatever, and it doesn't mean shit! I mean, there's only so much money you can give an acting coach before you need to cut the wings. I could be wrong, but you wouldn't pay a doctor for three and a half years if you weren't getting any healthier, would you? One thing that I learned from my acting coach is that stage acting is completely different from the acting here. In Hollywood you've got a guy with a camera coming up in your face. A lot of theatrical actors come out here after studying for four years and go, "Wow!" It's more intense.

Sajen Corona

12

Continuing Education and Training

We all have passionate beliefs and opinions about the art of acting. My own are new only insofar as they have crystallized for me. I have spent most of my life in the theater and know that the learning process in art is never over. The possibilities for growth are limitless.

Uta Hagen, *Respect for Acting*

Training Resources

BackStage.com
http://www.backstage.com/bso/index.jsp

@LA (acting classes)
http://www.at-la.com/biz/@la-act.htm#act

Thesbian Net—California Acting Schools
http://www.thespiannet.com/acting_schools/california.shtml

The Los Angeles Equestrian Center
http://www.la-equestriancenter.com/faqs.htm
480 Riverside Drive
Burbank, CA 91506
(818) 840-9063

The Internet Movie Database
http://www.imdb.com

Samuel French Theatre & Film
7623 West Sunset Boulevard
Los Angeles, CA
(323) 876-0570

The Samuel French Bookstore
www.samuelfrench.com

The Zami Los Angeles Bookstores – Los Angeles Bookstores
http://losangeles.zami.com/Bookstore/6-A

WHY SHOULD I CONTINUE WITH MY EDUCATION OR TRAINING?

Every profession has its learning curve, and a new actor to Hollywood most certainly suffers under the weight of professional formality, technological sophistication, economic reality, and professional cruelty. For your own sanity, a personal professional development strategy can help you develop supportive skills as required. As your business's only employee, you must decide which pathway to pursue.

If you have *just* completed sixteen or more years of education, the thought of more schooling might seem appalling. So take a break if necessary, but know that in Hollywood it's often more a matter of *what* you know than *who* you know. Sometimes at the end of the day, after all of the auditions, the actor who fits the costume gets the job—or the actor who knows how to surf, speak several languages, holds a black belt in tae kwon do *and* fits the costume. Today's actors find themselves competing in various arenas of their peers, defined by age, ethnicity, gender, and subtler categories, each with certain expectations of skill sets. It's not enough to be pretty or handsome today. Actors must have acquired specialized skills. Television crime dramas require gun handling skills and procedures as well as staged combat skills. Commercial and comedic actors need improvisational skills as well as physical skills such as those used in pratfalls, gymnastics, mime, and role-playing. Breakdowns often specify language skills or sports skills such as rock-climbing, skateboarding, incline skating, and even horseback riding. A working actor must also constantly upgrade his or her skills with technology, such as with squibs, stunts, or voice work. It even helps to sing and dance a little. There is only one way to do all that, namely, the old-fashioned way—school!

WHAT TRAINING OPTIONS DOES AN ACTOR HAVE IN LOS ANGELES?

Actors of all ages, skill levels, and ethnicities arrive in Hollywood equally confident and ready to work. Their limitations lie within. As one of them, carefully survey the professional landscape—the projects, the competition, and the casting process—and determine your own limitations. Where has the bar been raised, and where are you? Every actor competes in a niche market that must live up to certain skill-related expectations. The bar can be set high, and much is expected. And every actor looks relentlessly for whatever will provide that edge over the others competing in the same niche market. Los Angeles offers a dizzying array of possibilities, from academic institutions to acting studios offering classes, workshops, seminars, coaches, informal gatherings of actors and writers, and unlimited research resources.

Academic Institutions

No casting director will be impressed with academic degrees. Their value to an actor lies not in the credentials they confer but in the training the actor received and the relationships that emerged. But for an amateur actor seeking comprehensive training, Los Angeles boasts many extraordinary conservatory-style training programs, and their graduates testify to the advantage that traditional theatrical training provides. Los Angeles offers many reasons to either begin or continue one's college education there. Most programs require an audition, so have two contrasting monologues honed and ready to perform.

Ranked first in the nation by the Princeton Review/Gourman Report, the University of California in Los Angeles (UCLA) School of Theater, Film, and Television (TFT) lives up to the sizable legacy of its alumni by integrating the study of theatre, film, and television within one program. It also has collaborated very successfully with the Geffen Playhouse. (UCLA—School of Theater, Film, and Television, "About the School"). Not to be outdone, TFT's territorial rival, the University of Southern California's (USC) School of Cinematic Arts, utilizes facilities built by the likes of George Lucas and Robert Zemeckis. More economical and less pretentious, but equally respected, Santa Monica College offers an associate conservatory-style degree in traditional theatrical arts (Santa Monica College: Theater Arts, *Performance Training and Opportunities*). Newly located in the old Charlie Chaplin Studios in Hollywood, the highly regarded American Academy of Dramatic Arts is an accredited two-year conservatory for film, television, and stage acting. One might wonder why the New York–based American Musical and Dramatic Academy would open a campus in a city world famous for its moving image arts—that is, until reminded of the many musical influences seen in today's popular TV shows such as *The Drew Carey*

Show, the many commercials that feature singing and dancing, and the current rebirth of the movie musical genre with films such as *Chicago*.

Acting Studios

For actors who have already obtained academic training and now seek to sharpen or mold their acting technique, the legacy of the Group Theatre of the 1930s and '40s still dominates actor training in Los Angeles, with no fewer than three institutions eternalizing its particular flavor of the "Method" school of acting. The Stella Adler Academy of Acting outlines a two-year program of sense-memory based acting concentration; while the Lee Strasberg Theatre Institute's program offers more skill-based electives in film combat, accent reduction, sensory workouts, and jazz and hip-hop dance. Finally, the Sanford Meisner Center, now established in North Hollywood's NoHo Arts District, supports a theatre-intensive pedagogy.

But living and breathing acting teachers flourish in Hollywood as well, all touting recommendations and testimonials from celebrity actors. Some acting coaches, such as Michael Chekov and Eric Morris, do have strong, long-term reputations in Los Angeles, and their institutes offer a comprehensive acting program. But Los Angeles boasts many other acting coaches who own studios bearing their own names and who have various reputations that on occasion border on urban legend. An acting teacher's approach and methodology, not to mention personality, will affect the rehearsal space dynamics. Actors need a degree of safety to experiment, but they also need discipline to succeed. One actor may need the freedom to play without judgment, while another may need the discipline of performance for critique. Most of these acting teachers, though, will allow a potential student to audit a class or two to observe the class inter-action and the teacher's guidance before considering registration. Most teachers will also ask a potential student to audition as a condition of acceptance.

Still other acting studios offer a less individualistic approach in group classes, such as the Acting Corps' Actors' Boot Camp, or the Actor's Playpen. These studios emphasize conditioning as well as process with a variety of classes that combine physical workouts, reflexive action, and even spiritual practices such as meditation and yoga. One particular acting studio, TVI Los Angeles, has been gaining industry attention for its hiring of casting directors and associates of many well-known casting agencies to teach classes. Students pay for the instruction and helpful direction, but undeniably also for access to industry decision-makers.

Other acting studios specialize in career enhancement. Actors academically trained in theatre acting might have difficulty making a transition to the more subtle style of film acting and should consider classes in on-camera technique or cold reading. Both improve audition skills. Comedic actors should consider classes in improvisation. Legendary improvisational groups such as the Groundlings and the Second City, offer ongoing classes or summer boot camps. Casting directors often specify their graduates in breakdowns. Some actors consider focusing on a particular corner of the industry by studying voice-over, stand-up comedy, or commercial acting. And out of new technologies have evolved new acting applications, such as the performance capture animation technology demonstrated by actor Andy Serkin in *The Lord of the Rings* trilogy.

As tastes and trends change, the market for certain physical skills fluctuates and emerges. A generation ago Westerns dominated television programming and an actor needed to know how to ride a horse. After *The Pirates of the Caribbean* premiered in 2003, hundreds of actors scurried to locate fencing studios and classes. Tomorrow martial arts may revive, television variety shows reappear or, God forbid, movies about cheerleading competitions be reborn, for which classes in dance or gymnastics may prove helpful. Los Angeles has both in abundance. For stage combat training, check out the Academy of Theatrical Combat and Swordplay Fencing Studios, both in Burbank. Quieter arts are taught nearby at the Mime Theatre Studio in North Hollywood. And at the Griffith Park Equestrian Center one can even learn to ride a horse.

Workshops

Various theatre groups, casting agencies, film and television unions, and arts-related foundations offer workshops on all relevant topics. Casting workshops specifically have grown in popularity for obvious reasons. Actors pay a fee for the opportunity to meet, obtain advice from, and perform before a guest casting director, who collects headshots, assigns sides, observes and critiques each of a handful of acting scenes after a short rehearsal break, answers questions, and offers auditioning and career advice. Occasionally the advice and feedback is minimal and is given by an associate, not the casting director. But these casting workshops have recently captured the scrutiny of SAG, who has declared them a violation of SAG Rule 11, which prohibits auditioning for a fee, and has prohibited its members from participating in them (SAG, "Tips and Tools") Actors still do, of course, but potentially jeopardize their union status.

Other actors seek out writers workshops, where a natural symbiosis forms between actors, writers, and directors in a collaborative environment. Scripts are often rough, but actors find the space to experiment and to work for the sake of the work. Friendships form, collaborations are forged, and an occasional project is honored. Often talented scriptwriters or directors emerge and recommend familiar actors for roles in future projects. At the very least, an actor will find a multitude of showcase opportunities. First Stage meets at the Hollywood United Methodist Church, and the Los Angeles Writers Center meets in North Hollywood, but new groups form wherever writers and actors meet and socialize.

Finally, "how to" workshops—on getting an audition, an agent, or work—may be required. These can help acquaint an actor with the industry standards if they are taught by true industry professionals. Unfortunately, unscrupulous businesses sometimes offer similar but useless classes as part of a management package. Always find out the credentials of the presenter.

Coaches

Actors may also turn to experts for one-on-one coaching. For instance, in order to prepare for an upcoming role or audition, an actor may choose to consult a dialect coach. Coaches can also help actors familiarize themselves quickly with a particular sport, sharpen certain dance or martial arts skills, or remove an impediment through accent reduction or nonnative English-speaking lessons. Some actors may choose weekly vocal coaching or musical instrument lessons. Whatever the skills, coaching provides a learning alternative essential to any actor's strategic plan.

Pay to play?

Live theatre in Los Angeles ranges from big splashy proscenium shows to tiny storefront performances. Many of these small storefront theatres survive through membership fees paid by the actors to provide the theatre group a financial security blanket. In return, the actors receive the opportunity to experiment and showcase their talents. The practice sits on firm legal ground as long as the theatre company exists as a nonprofit corporation. Membership in such a theatre company may be a prerequisite to being cast in one of its plays—thus the term "pay to play." Membership has its benefits, but their value depends on the value of the product. Research the theatre company carefully, not only for artistic integrity but for longevity and ethics. Too often someone gets rich from actors paying to perform. Perhaps the learning experience might justify the cost, perhaps not. Still, anything more than a short-term membership in such a theatre group can become a security blanket that hinders, not enhances, a career.

WHAT SCAMS DO I NEED TO AVOID?

Hollywood runs on money, power, and sex. The most common scam in Hollywood remains the "management company scenario" in which a "talent scout" or "agency associate" offers to manage an actor's career—for a fee. Legitimate talent agents and talent managers receive only a commission on an actor's earnings, no fees. Any seasoned actor knows enough to avoid these scams. But naive actors arrive on a daily basis, and scam artists still manage to invent variations on the theme. Whether these scams are found on the Internet, ads in the trades, or pull-off tabs on a phone pole, the hook generally involves the promise of fame and fortune. "Major studios are searching for new faces like yours!" or "Agency seeking fresh faces for film casting." Most of the time these involve fees for pictures, headshots, a portfolio, and a whole package of promotional materials that the actor never sees but pays for. More worldly scammers now promise "classes" in modeling, acting, or "how to" skills. Despite the dubious value of these classes, unsuspecting actors believe they will be working with industry insiders—the same scam only dressed up.

WHAT OTHER KINDS OF RESEARCH RESOURCES WILL I FIND IN LOS ANGELES?

A new actor to Los Angeles will have much to learn but also a plenitude of resources to consult.

Internet. Much of the research for this book was conducted on the Internet on specialized Web sites just as easily accessible to anyone who knows where to look. Every arts-related institution, studio, coach, or performance group in Los Angeles has its own Web site. Governmental Web sites provide municipal information. Industry trade magazines offer online editions. SAG and AFTRA can provide comprehensive workplace information and advice. Actors can utilize rental services, classified ads, Craigslist, the IMDB database. Check out everything. You can truly find out anything if you know how to use the tools at your disposal.

Trade magazines. Most actors will recognize the venerable names of the *Hollywood Reporter* and *Variety*, but the trade publication most important to them is the new kid on the block, *BackstageWest*. This weekly publication contains casting notices, trade advertisements. and acting-oriented articles. The casting notices tend to be mostly nonunion, but this periodical still provides an important resource even for union actors. Its seasonal actor-training spotlight editions offer a comprehensive list of actor-training options, supported by a host of advertisements.

This recommendation is not to say that the other trade publications are without merit. *Daily Variety* and the *Hollywood Reporter* provide detailed business information on the entertainment industry: mergers, financing, studio deals, story development, casting news, production information, and hirings and firings. Actors, to be blunt, lie pretty low in the Hollywood food chain, so only by keeping oneself knowledgeable about the industry does one keep from being eaten.

Bookstores. Like any large city, Los Angeles has its collection of venerable bookstores, from new to used to specialty. The Samuel French Bookstore in

West Hollywood and Studio City provides the most comprehensive collection of scripts, books, and periodicals on almost any subject of the entertainment industry. Larry Edmunds Cinema and Theatre in Hollywood provides a more central outlet for much of the same. Studio executives browse alongside actors and writers at Book Soup on the Sunset Strip. Those seeking spiritual wisdom seek out the Bohdi Tree in West Hollywood, where also gay-themed A Different Light Bookstore holds court on Santa Monica Boulevard. The Sisterhood Bookstore in Westwood provides the feminine perspective, and Storyopolis in Beverly Hills the child's.

Libraries. The Los Angeles Public Library maintains an extensive collection of materials for download or checkout through its central facility downtown and an intraloan program with dozens of satellite collections scattered throughout the city. The Beverly Hills Public Library and the Burbank Public Library both offer a well-stocked and accessible reference center. All provide short-term Internet access, copy machines, and typewriters in a pinch.

Network. Talk to friends. Arrange to audit a class. Watch, join in, or ask fellow actors about their experiences. Check Internet blogs, forums, and resource pages for postings from other actors sharing their issues or experiences associated with a particular coach or studio.

Epilogue

If these pages have not dimmed your optimism or frightened your sensibilities, then congratulations. You march to the beat of a different drummer. You truly have the fire in the belly, and nothing will deter you from grasping Los Angeles by the bullhorns and yanking it down to your feet. But it may take longer than you thought, and you may find it more difficult than you imagined. The roller-coaster and the seesaw of hopes, dreams, opportunities, and disappointments, combined with the usual financial pressures, can eventually take its toll. That's where something Ed Asner told me becomes relevant: "You have to stay on the merry-go-round if you want your shot at the gold ring." I got off the merry-go-round, so I'll never know. But if Hollywood does become more than you can take and the inevitable doubts arise, remember those words and then make your decision, never looking back.

Appendix A
Maps

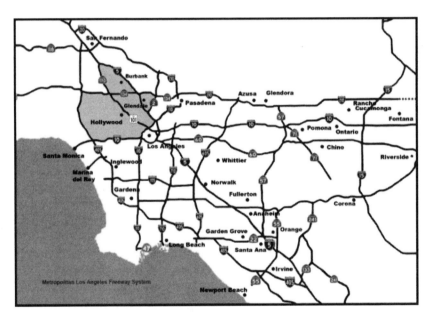

Figure 1. Entertainment Industry Parallelogram

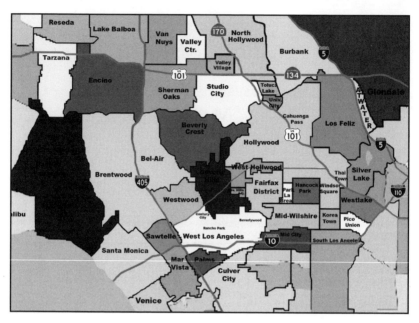

Figure 2. Los Angeles Neighborhoods

Figure 3. Satellite View of Los Angeles

Appendix B
Los Angeles County Neighborhood Statistics

Table 1 - Comparative Statistics

Community	Total pop.	% Caucasian	% Hispanic	% African-Am	% Asian	Median household income	% under 18	% over 65	% below poverty level	% w/ college degree	% w/o HS degree
LA County	9,935,475	29.90%	46.50%	9.80%	12.90%	$41,486.00	27.50%	9.90%	17.70%	24.90%	30.01%
LA City	3,694,820	29.75%	46.53%	11.24%	9.99%	$36,687.00	26.56%	9.56%	22.10%	25.50%	33.40%
Atwater Village	8,042	27.56%	47.90%	2.15%	19.09%	$42,118.00	22.01%	11.46%	12.09%	20.94%	29.99%
Bel Air	7,928	82.95%	4.65%	1.93%	6.84%	$159,008.00	18.76%	20.89%	4.89%	16.69%	4.27%
Beverly Crest	12,331	88.24%	3.79%	1.37%	4.22%	$127,136.00	18.46%	17.18%	21.89%	15.88%	4.36%
Beverly Hills	33,784	85.10%	4.60%	1.80%	7.10%	$70,945.00	20.00%	17.60%	9.10%	54.50%	9.20%
Brentwood	41,791	79.88%	6.20%	1.53%	8.88%	$103,268.00	12.16%	15.52%	12.48%	15.01%	4.86%
Burbank	100,316	59.40%	24.90%	1.90%	9.00%	$47,467.00	22.30%	12.90%	10.50%	29.00%	16.90%
Culver City	38,816	59.20%	23.70%	12.00%	12.00%	$51,792.00	20.90%	13.90%	8.60%	41.20%	12.80%
Glendale	194,973	63.60%	19.70%	1.30%	16.10%	$41,805.00	22.40%	13.90%	15.50%	32.10%	21.00%
Hollywood	167,664	42.82%	39.43%	4.48%	8.98%	$33,409.00	19.70%	9.96%	26.21%	17.30%	30.03%
Los Feliz	40,573	60.54%	16.48%	3.77%	13.61%	$52,104.00	13.59%	13.60%	11.32%	18.78%	12.75%
Koreatown	40,746	4.14%	65.74%	3.86%	25.35%	$21,271.00	27.33%	5.85%	35.89%	12.46%	51.23%
Mid-City West	46,643	74.78%	6.20%	4.74%	10.49%	$50,803.00	12.13%	17.79%	13.60%	18.13%	9.30%
Mid-Wilshire	84,569	25.08%	29.61%	14.56%	28.18%	$41,019.00	21.49%	10.15%	19.71%	19.51%	21.41%
North Hollywood	154,912	29.31%	55.25%	4.79%	6.89%	$34,916.00	28.55%	7.72%	21.31%	18.71%	39.31%
Pacific Palisades	23,940	88.90%	3.66%	6.90%	4.44%	$131,614.00	23.33%	17.26%	3.69%	16.64%	2.34%
Playa del Rey	14,400	72.40%	9.78%	5.53%	8.37%	$74,486.00	11.77%	11.37%	6.47%	21.38%	2.90%
Santa Monica	84,084	78.30%	13.40%	3.80%	7.30%	$50,714.00	14.60%	14.40%	10.40%	54.80%	9.00%
Sherman Oaks	28,601	78.57%	8.52%	3.75%	5.40%	$71,108.00	14.20%	12.81%	6.20%	22.85%	6.66%
Silver Lake	44,351	21.24%	57.35%	2.74%	16.58%	$32,855.00	23.58%	8.45%	23.18%	17.70%	35.78%

Community	Total pop.	% Caucasian	% Hispanic	% African-Am	% Asian	Median household income	% under 18	% over 65	% below poverty level	% w/ college degree	% w/o HS degree
Studio City	39,023	78.17%	9.03%	4.08%	5.44%	$60,014.00	14.48%	12.91%	6.68%	26.85%	4.81%
Toluca Lake	3,528	80.10%	8.93%	4.37%	4.05%	$55,721.00	11.62%	14.65%	2.72%	28.02%	4.45%
Valley Village	16,015	66.51%	18.46%	6.12%	4.93%	$40,128.00	17.52%	13.37%	12.51%	25.70%	13.37%
Venice	37,758	64.06%	21.96%	6.15%	4.15%	$53,074.00	12.60%	8.24%	14.36%	20.27%	13.14%
West Hollywood	35,716	86.40%	8.80%	3.10%	3.80%	$38,914.00	5.70%	17.00%	11.50%	46.80%	8.90%
W. Los Angeles	87,120	56.44%	17.20%	14.09%	7.96%	$55,581.00	19.50%	14.49%	12.86%	20.90%	13.12%
Westwood	47,844	65.23%	7.13%	2.10%	23.06%	$60,752.00	7.23%	12.30%	22.95%	14.86%	5.20%
Wilshire Center	73,534	7.15%	58.06%	4.81%	28.34%	$23,035.00	26.27%	6.10%	30.78%	14.24%	43.28%

Source: U.S. Census Bureau - 2000 Census Statistics

Los Angeles County Neighborhood Statistics
Table 2 - Ranking of Median Household Income

Community	Total pop.	% Caucasian	% Hispanic	% African-Am	% Asian	Median household income	% under 18	% over 65	% below poverty level	% w/ college degree	% w/o HS degree
Bel Air	7,928	82.95%	4.65%	1.93%	6.84%	$159,008.00	18.76%	20.89%	4.89%	16.69%	4.27%
Pacific Palisades	23,940	88.90%	3.66%	6.90%	4.44%	$131,614.00	23.33%	17.26%	3.69%	16.64%	2.34%
Beverly Crest	12,331	88.24%	3.79%	1.37%	4.22%	$127,136.00	18.46%	17.18%	21.89%	15.88%	4.36%
Brentwood	41,791	79.88%	6.20%	1.53%	8.88%	$103,268.00	12.16%	15.52%	12.48%	15.01%	4.86%
Playa del Rey	14,400	72.40%	9.78%	5.53%	8.37%	$74,486.00	11.77%	11.37%	6.47%	21.38%	2.90%
Sherman Oaks	28,601	78.57%	8.52%	3.75%	5.40%	$71,108.00	14.20%	12.81%	6.20%	22.85%	6.66%
Beverly Hills	33,784	85.10%	4.60%	1.80%	7.10%	$70,945.00	20.00%	17.60%	9.10%	54.50%	9.20%
Westwood	47,844	65.23%	7.13%	2.10%	23.06%	$60,752.00	7.23%	12.30%	22.95%	14.86%	5.20%
Studio City	39,023	78.17%	9.03%	4.08%	5.44%	$60,014.00	14.48%	12.91%	6.68%	26.85%	4.81%
Toluca Lake	3,528	80.10%	8.93%	4.37%	4.05%	$55,721.00	11.62%	14.65%	2.72%	28.02%	4.45%
W. Los Angeles	87,120	56.44%	17.20%	14.09%	7.96%	$55,581.00	19.50%	14.49%	12.86%	20.90%	13.12%
Venice	37,758	64.06%	21.96%	6.15%	4.15%	$53,074.00	12.60%	8.24%	14.36%	20.27%	13.14%
Los Feliz	40,573	60.54%	16.48%	3.77%	13.61%	$52,104.00	13.59%	13.60%	11.32%	18.78%	12.75%
Culver City	38,816	59.20%	23.70%	12.00%	12.00%	$51,792.00	20.90%	13.90%	8.60%	41.20%	12.80%
Mid-City West	46,643	74.78%	6.20%	4.74%	10.49%	$50,803.00	12.13%	17.79%	13.60%	18.13%	9.30%
Santa Monica	84,084	78.30%	13.40%	3.80%	7.30%	$50,714.00	14.60%	14.40%	10.40%	54.80%	9.00%
Burbank	100,316	59.40%	24.90%	1.90%	9.00%	$47,467.00	22.30%	12.90%	10.50%	29.00%	16.90%
Atwater Village	8,042	27.56%	47.90%	2.15%	19.09%	$42,118.00	22.01%	11.46%	12.09%	20.94%	29.99%
Glendale	194,973	63.60%	19.70%	1.30%	16.10%	$41,805.00	22.40%	13.90%	15.50%	32.10%	21.00%
LA County	9,935,475	29.90%	46.50%	9.80%	12.90%	$41,486.00	27.50%	9.90%	17.70%	24.90%	30.01%
Mid-Wilshire	84,569	25.08%	29.61%	14.56%	28.18%	$41,019.00	21.49%	10.15%	19.71%	19.51%	21.41%

Community	Total pop.	% Caucasian	% Hispanic	% African-Am	% Asian	Median household income	% under 18	% over 65	% below poverty level	% w/ college degree	% w/o HS degree
Valley Village	16,015	66.51%	18.46%	6.12%	4.93%	$40,128.00	17.52%	13.37%	12.51%	25.70%	13.37%
West Hollywood	35,716	86.40%	8.80%	3.10%	3.80%	$38,914.00	5.70%	17.00%	11.50%	46.80%	8.90%
LA City	3,694,820	29.75%	46.53%	11.24%	9.99%	$36,687.00	26.56%	9.56%	22.10%	25.50%	33.40%
North Hollywood	154,912	29.31%	55.25%	4.79%	6.89%	$34,916.00	28.55%	7.72%	21.31%	18.71%	39.31%
Hollywood	167,664	42.82%	39.43%	4.48%	8.98%	$33,409.00	19.70%	9.96%	26.21%	17.30%	30.03%
Silver Lake	44,351	21.24%	57.35%	2.74%	16.58%	$32,855.00	23.58%	8.45%	23.18%	17.70%	35.78%
Wilshire Center	73,534	7.15%	58.06%	4.81%	28.34%	$23,035.00	26.27%	6.10%	30.78%	14.24%	43.28%
Koreatown	40,746	4.14%	65.74%	3.86%	25.35%	$21,271.00	27.33%	5.85%	35.89%	12.46%	51.23%

Source: U.S. Census Bureau - 2000 Census Statistics

Comparative Statistics for Los Angeles County Neighborhoods
Table 3 - Ranking of Percentage of Population under 18 Years of Age

Community	Total pop.	% Caucasian	% Hispanic	% African-Am	% Asian	Median household income	% under 18	% over 65	% below poverty level	% w/ college degree	% w/o HS degree
North Hollywood	154,912	29.31%	55.25%	4.79%	6.89%	$34,916.00	28.55%	7.72%	21.31%	18.71%	39.31%
LA County	9,935,475	29.90%	46.50%	9.80%	12.90%	$41,486.00	27.50%	9.90%	17.70%	24.90%	30.01%
Koreatown	40,746	4.14%	65.74%	3.86%	25.35%	$21,271.00	27.33%	5.85%	35.89%	12.46%	51.23%
LA City	3,694,820	29.75%	46.53%	11.24%	9.99%	$36,687.00	26.56%	9.56%	22.10%	25.50%	33.40%
Wilshire Center	73,534	7.15%	58.06%	4.81%	28.34%	$23,035.00	26.27%	6.10%	30.78%	14.24%	43.28%
Silver Lake	44,351	21.24%	57.35%	2.74%	16.58%	$32,855.00	23.58%	8.45%	23.18%	17.70%	35.78%
Pacific Palisades	23,940	88.90%	3.66%	6.90%	4.44%	$131,614.00	23.33%	17.26%	3.69%	16.64%	2.34%
Glendale	194,973	63.60%	19.70%	1.30%	16.10%	$41,805.00	22.40%	13.90%	15.50%	32.10%	21.00%
Burbank	100,316	59.40%	24.90%	1.90%	9.00%	$47,467.00	22.30%	12.90%	10.50%	29.00%	16.90%
Atwater Village	8,042	27.56%	47.90%	2.15%	19.09%	$42,118.00	22.01%	11.46%	12.09%	20.94%	29.99%
Mid-Wilshire	84,569	25.08%	29.61%	14.56%	28.18%	$41,019.00	21.49%	10.15%	19.71%	19.51%	21.41%
Culver City	38,816	59.20%	23.70%	12.00%	12.00%	$51,792.00	20.90%	13.90%	8.60%	41.20%	12.80%
Beverly Hills	33,784	85.10%	4.60%	1.80%	7.10%	$70,945.00	20.00%	17.60%	9.10%	54.50%	9.20%
Hollywood	167,664	42.82%	39.43%	4.48%	8.98%	$33,409.00	19.70%	9.96%	26.21%	17.30%	30.03%
W. Los Angeles	87,120	56.44%	17.20%	14.09%	7.96%	$55,581.00	19.50%	14.49%	12.86%	20.90%	13.12%
Bel Air	7,928	82.95%	4.65%	1.93%	6.84%	$159,008.00	18.76%	20.89%	4.89%	16.69%	4.27%
Beverly Crest	12,331	88.24%	3.79%	1.37%	4.22%	$127,136.00	18.46%	17.18%	21.89%	15.88%	4.36%
Valley Village	16,015	66.51%	18.46%	6.12%	4.93%	$40,128.00	17.52%	13.37%	12.51%	25.70%	13.37%
Santa Monica	84,084	78.30%	13.40%	3.80%	7.30%	$50,714.00	14.60%	14.40%	10.40%	54.80%	9.00%
Studio City	39,023	78.17%	9.03%	4.08%	5.44%	$60,014.00	14.48%	12.91%	6.68%	26.85%	4.81%
Sherman Oaks	28,601	78.57%	8.52%	3.75%	5.40%	$71,108.00	14.20%	12.81%	6.20%	22.85%	6.66%

Community	Total pop.	% Caucasian	% Hispanic	% African-Am	% Asian	Median household income	% under 18	% over 65	% below poverty level	% w/ college degree	% w/o HS degree
Los Feliz	40,573	60.54%	16.48%	3.77%	13.61%	$52,104.00	13.59%	13.60%	11.32%	18.78%	12.75%
Venice	37,758	64.06%	21.96%	6.15%	4.15%	$53,074.00	12.60%	8.24%	14.36%	20.27%	13.14%
Brentwood	41,791	79.88%	6.20%	1.53%	8.88%	$103,268.00	12.16%	15.52%	12.48%	15.01%	4.86%
Mid-City West	46,643	74.78%	6.20%	4.74%	10.49%	$50,803.00	12.13%	17.79%	13.60%	18.13%	9.30%
Playa del Rey	14,400	72.40%	9.78%	5.53%	8.37%	$74,486.00	11.77%	11.37%	6.47%	21.38%	2.90%
Toluca Lake	3,528	80.10%	8.93%	4.37%	4.05%	$55,721.00	11.62%	14.65%	2.72%	28.02%	4.45%
Westwood	47,844	65.23%	7.13%	2.10%	23.06%	$60,752.00	7.23%	12.30%	22.95%	14.86%	5.20%
West Hollywood	35,716	86.40%	8.80%	3.10%	3.80%	$38,914.00	5.70%	17.00%	11.50%	46.80%	8.90%

Source: U.S. Census Bureau - 2000 Census Statistics

Los Angeles County Neighborhood Statistics
Table 4 - Ranking of Percentage of Population over 65 Years of Age

Community	Total pop.	% Caucasian	% Hispanic	% African-Am	% Asian	Median household income	% under 18	% over 65	% below poverty level	% w/ college degree	% w/o HS degree
Bel Air	7,928	82.95%	4.65%	1.93%	6.84%	$159,008.00	18.76%	20.89%	4.89%	16.69%	4.27%
Mid-City West	46,643	74.78%	6.20%	4.74%	10.49%	$50,803.00	12.13%	17.79%	13.60%	18.13%	9.30%
Beverly Hills	33,784	85.10%	4.60%	1.80%	7.10%	$70,945.00	20.00%	17.60%	9.10%	54.50%	9.20%
Pacific Palisades	23,940	88.90%	3.66%	6.90%	4.44%	$131,614.00	23.33%	17.26%	3.69%	16.64%	2.34%
Beverly Crest	12,331	88.24%	3.79%	1.37%	4.22%	$127,136.00	18.46%	17.18%	21.89%	15.88%	4.36%
West Hollywood	35,716	86.40%	8.80%	3.10%	3.80%	$38,914.00	5.70%	17.00%	11.50%	46.80%	8.90%
Brentwood	41,791	79.88%	6.20%	1.53%	8.88%	$103,268.00	12.16%	15.52%	12.48%	15.01%	4.86%
Toluca Lake	3,528	80.10%	8.93%	4.37%	4.05%	$55,721.00	11.62%	14.65%	2.72%	28.02%	4.45%
W. Los Angeles	87,120	56.44%	17.20%	14.09%	7.96%	$55,581.00	19.50%	14.49%	12.86%	20.90%	13.12%
Santa Monica	84,084	78.30%	13.40%	3.80%	7.30%	$50,714.00	14.60%	14.40%	10.40%	54.80%	9.00%
Culver City	38,816	59.20%	23.70%	12.00%	12.00%	$51,792.00	20.90%	13.90%	8.60%	41.20%	12.80%
Glendale	194,973	63.60%	19.70%	1.30%	16.10%	$41,805.00	22.40%	13.90%	15.50%	32.10%	21.00%
Los Feliz	40,573	60.54%	16.48%	3.77%	13.61%	$52,104.00	13.59%	13.60%	11.32%	18.78%	12.75%
Valley Village	16,015	66.51%	18.46%	6.12%	4.93%	$40,128.00	17.52%	13.37%	12.51%	25.70%	13.37%
Studio City	39,023	78.17%	9.03%	4.08%	5.44%	$60,014.00	14.48%	12.91%	6.68%	26.85%	4.81%
Burbank	100,316	59.40%	24.90%	1.90%	9.00%	$47,467.00	22.30%	12.90%	10.50%	29.00%	16.90%
Sherman Oaks	28,601	78.57%	8.52%	3.75%	5.40%	$71,108.00	14.20%	12.81%	6.20%	22.85%	6.66%
Westwood	47,844	65.23%	7.13%	2.10%	23.06%	$60,752.00	7.23%	12.30%	22.95%	14.86%	5.20%
Atwater Village	8,042	27.56%	47.90%	2.15%	19.09%	$42,118.00	22.01%	11.46%	12.09%	20.94%	29.99%
Playa del Rey	14,400	72.40%	9.78%	5.53%	8.37%	$74,486.00	11.77%	11.37%	6.47%	21.38%	2.90%
Mid-Wilshire	84,569	25.08%	29.61%	14.56%	28.18%	$41,019.00	21.49%	10.15%	19.71%	19.51%	21.41%

Community	Total pop.	% Caucasian	% Hispanic	% African-Am	% Asian	Median household income	% under 18	% over 65	% below poverty level	% w/ college degree	% w/o HS degree
Hollywood	167,664	42.82%	39.43%	4.48%	8.98%	$33,409.00	19.70%	9.96%	26.21%	17.30%	30.03%
LA County	9,935,475	29.90%	46.50%	9.80%	12.90%	$41,486.00	27.50%	9.90%	17.70%	24.90%	30.01%
LA City	3,694,820	29.75%	46.53%	11.24%	9.99%	$36,687.00	26.56%	9.56%	22.10%	25.50%	33.40%
Silver Lake	44,351	21.24%	57.35%	2.74%	16.58%	$32,855.00	23.58%	8.45%	23.18%	17.70%	35.78%
Venice	37,758	64.06%	21.96%	6.15%	4.15%	$53,074.00	12.60%	8.24%	14.36%	20.27%	13.14%
North Hollywood	154,912	29.31%	55.25%	4.79%	6.89%	$34,916.00	28.55%	7.72%	21.31%	18.71%	39.31%
Wilshire Center	73,534	7.15%	58.06%	4.81%	28.34%	$23,035.00	26.27%	6.10%	30.78%	14.24%	43.28%
Koreatown	40,746	4.14%	65.74%	3.86%	25.35%	$21,271.00	27.33%	5.85%	35.89%	12.46%	51.23%

Source: U.S. Census Bureau - 2000 Census Statistics

Los Angeles County Neighborhood Statistics
Table 5 - Ranking of Percentage of Population below the Poverty Level

Community	Total pop.	% Caucasian	% Hispanic	% African-Am	% Asian	Median household income	% under 18	% over 65	% below poverty level	% w/ college degree	% w/o HS degree
Koreatown	40,746	4.14%	65.74%	3.86%	25.35%	$21,271.00	27.33%	5.85%	35.89%	12.46%	51.23%
Wilshire Center	73,534	7.15%	58.06%	4.81%	28.34%	$23,035.00	26.27%	6.10%	30.78%	14.24%	43.28%
Hollywood	167,664	42.82%	39.43%	4.48%	8.98%	$33,409.00	19.70%	9.96%	26.21%	17.30%	30.03%
Silver Lake	44,351	21.24%	57.35%	2.74%	16.58%	$32,855.00	23.58%	8.45%	23.18%	17.70%	35.78%
Westwood	47,844	65.23%	7.13%	2.10%	23.06%	$60,752.00	7.23%	12.30%	22.95%	14.86%	5.20%
LA City	3,694,820	29.75%	46.53%	11.24%	9.99%	$36,687.00	26.56%	9.56%	22.10%	25.50%	33.40%
Beverly Crest	12,331	88.24%	3.79%	1.37%	4.22%	$127,136.00	18.46%	17.18%	21.89%	15.88%	4.36%
North Hollywood	154,912	29.31%	55.25%	4.79%	6.89%	$34,916.00	28.55%	7.72%	21.31%	18.71%	39.31%
Mid-Wilshire	84,569	25.08%	29.61%	14.56%	28.18%	$41,019.00	21.49%	10.15%	19.71%	19.51%	21.41%
LA County	9,935,475	29.90%	46.50%	9.80%	12.90%	$41,486.00	27.50%	9.90%	17.70%	24.90%	30.01%
Glendale	194,973	63.60%	19.70%	1.30%	16.10%	$41,805.00	22.40%	13.90%	15.50%	32.10%	21.00%
Venice	37,758	64.06%	21.96%	6.15%	4.15%	$53,074.00	12.60%	8.24%	14.36%	20.27%	13.14%
Mid-City West	46,643	74.78%	6.20%	4.74%	10.49%	$50,803.00	12.13%	17.79%	13.60%	18.13%	9.30%
W. Los Angeles	87,120	56.44%	17.20%	14.09%	7.96%	$55,581.00	19.50%	14.49%	12.86%	20.90%	13.12%
Valley Village	16,015	66.51%	18.46%	6.12%	4.93%	$40,128.00	17.52%	13.37%	12.51%	25.70%	13.37%
Brentwood	41,791	79.88%	6.20%	1.53%	8.88%	$103,268.00	12.16%	15.52%	12.48%	15.01%	4.86%
Atwater Village	8,042	27.56%	47.90%	2.15%	19.09%	$42,118.00	22.01%	11.46%	12.09%	20.94%	29.99%
West Hollywood	35,716	86.40%	8.80%	3.10%	3.80%	$38,914.00	5.70%	17.00%	11.50%	46.80%	8.90%
Los Feliz	40,573	60.54%	16.48%	3.77%	13.61%	$52,104.00	13.59%	13.60%	11.32%	18.78%	12.75%
Burbank	100,316	59.40%	24.90%	1.90%	9.00%	$47,467.00	22.30%	12.90%	10.50%	29.00%	16.90%

Community	Total pop.	% Caucasian	% Hispanic	% African-Am	% Asian	Median household income	% under 18	% over 65	% below poverty level	% w/ college degree	% w/o HS degree
Santa Monica	84,084	78.30%	13.40%	3.80%	7.30%	$50,714.00	14.60%	14.40%	10.40%	54.80%	9.00%
Beverly Hills	33,784	85.10%	4.60%	1.80%	7.10%	$70,945.00	20.00%	17.60%	9.10%	54.50%	9.20%
Culver City	38,816	59.20%	23.70%	12.00%	12.00%	$51,792.00	20.90%	13.90%	8.60%	41.20%	12.80%
Studio City	39,023	78.17%	9.03%	4.08%	5.44%	$60,014.00	14.48%	12.91%	6.68%	26.85%	4.81%
Playa del Rey	14,400	72.40%	9.78%	5.53%	8.37%	$74,486.00	11.77%	11.37%	6.47%	21.38%	2.90%
Sherman Oaks	28,601	78.57%	8.52%	3.75%	5.40%	$71,108.00	14.20%	12.81%	6.20%	22.85%	6.66%
Bel Air	7,928	82.95%	4.65%	1.93%	6.84%	$159,008.00	18.76%	20.89%	4.89%	16.69%	4.27%
Pacific Palisades	23,940	88.90%	3.66%	6.90%	4.44%	$131,614.00	23.33%	17.26%	3.69%	16.64%	2.34%
Toluca Lake	3,528	80.10%	8.93%	4.37%	4.05%	$55,721.00	11.62%	14.65%	2.72%	28.02%	4.45%

Source: U.S. Census Bureau - 2000 Census Statistics

Los Angeles County Neighborhood Statistics
Table 6 - Ranking of Percentage of Population with a College Degree

Community	Total pop.	% Caucasian	% Hispanic	% African-Am	% Asian	Median household income	% under 18	% over 65	% below poverty level	% w/ college degree	% w/o HS degree
Santa Monica	84,084	78.30%	13.40%	3.80%	7.30%	$50,714.00	14.60%	14.40%	10.40%	54.80%	9.00%
Beverly Hills	33,784	85.10%	4.60%	1.80%	7.10%	$70,945.00	20.00%	17.60%	9.10%	54.50%	9.20%
West Hollywood	35,716	86.40%	8.80%	3.10%	3.80%	$38,914.00	5.70%	17.00%	11.50%	46.80%	8.90%
Culver City	38,816	59.20%	23.70%	12.00%	12.00%	$51,792.00	20.90%	13.90%	8.60%	41.20%	12.80%
Glendale	194,973	63.60%	19.70%	1.30%	16.10%	$41,805.00	22.40%	13.90%	15.50%	32.10%	21.00%
Burbank	100,316	59.40%	24.90%	1.90%	9.00%	$47,467.00	22.30%	12.90%	10.50%	29.00%	16.90%
Toluca Lake	3,528	80.10%	8.93%	4.37%	4.05%	$55,721.00	11.62%	14.65%	2.72%	28.02%	4.45%
Studio City	39,023	78.17%	9.03%	4.08%	5.44%	$60,014.00	14.48%	12.91%	6.68%	26.85%	4.81%
Valley Village	16,015	66.51%	18.46%	6.12%	4.93%	$40,128.00	17.52%	13.37%	12.51%	25.70%	13.37%
LA City	3,694,820	29.75%	46.53%	11.24%	9.99%	$36,687.00	26.56%	9.56%	22.10%	25.50%	33.40%
LA County	9,935,475	29.90%	46.50%	9.80%	12.90%	$41,486.00	27.50%	9.90%	17.70%	24.90%	30.01%
Sherman Oaks	28,601	78.57%	8.52%	3.75%	5.40%	$71,108.00	14.20%	12.81%	6.20%	22.85%	6.66%
Playa del Rey	14,400	72.40%	9.78%	5.53%	8.37%	$74,486.00	11.77%	11.37%	6.47%	21.38%	2.90%
Atwater Village	8,042	27.56%	47.90%	2.15%	19.09%	$42,118.00	22.01%	11.46%	12.09%	20.94%	29.99%
W. Los Angeles	87,120	56.44%	17.20%	14.09%	7.96%	$55,581.00	19.50%	14.49%	12.86%	20.90%	13.12%
Venice	37,758	64.06%	21.96%	6.15%	4.15%	$53,074.00	12.60%	8.24%	14.36%	20.27%	13.14%
Mid-Wilshire	84,569	25.08%	29.61%	14.56%	28.18%	$41,019.00	21.49%	10.15%	19.71%	19.51%	21.41%
Los Feliz	40,573	60.54%	16.48%	3.77%	13.61%	$52,104.00	13.59%	13.60%	11.32%	18.78%	12.75%
North Hollywood	154,912	29.31%	55.25%	4.79%	6.89%	$34,916.00	28.55%	7.72%	21.31%	18.71%	39.31%
Mid-City West	46,643	74.78%	6.20%	4.74%	10.49%	$50,803.00	12.13%	17.79%	13.60%	18.13%	9.30%
Silver Lake	44,351	21.24%	57.35%	2.74%	16.58%	$32,855.00	23.58%	8.45%	23.18%	17.70%	35.78%

Community	Total pop.	% Caucasian	% Hispanic	% African-Am	% Asian	Median household income	% under 18	% over 65	% below poverty level	% w/ college degree	% w/o HS degree
Hollywood	167,664	42.82%	39.43%	4.48%	8.98%	$33,409.00	19.70%	9.96%	26.21%	17.30%	30.03%
Bel Air	7,928	82.95%	4.65%	1.93%	6.84%	$159,008.00	18.76%	20.89%	4.89%	16.69%	4.27%
Pacific Palisades	23,940	88.90%	3.66%	6.90%	4.44%	$131,614.00	23.33%	17.26%	3.69%	16.64%	2.34%
Beverly Crest	12,331	88.24%	3.79%	1.37%	4.22%	$127,136.00	18.46%	17.18%	21.89%	15.88%	4.36%
Brentwood	41,791	79.88%	6.20%	1.53%	8.88%	$103,268.00	12.16%	15.52%	12.48%	15.01%	4.86%
Westwood	47,844	65.23%	7.13%	2.10%	23.06%	$60,752.00	7.23%	12.30%	22.95%	14.86%	5.20%
Wilshire Center	73,534	7.15%	58.06%	4.81%	28.34%	$23,035.00	26.27%	6.10%	30.78%	14.24%	43.28%
Koreatown	40,746	4.14%	65.74%	3.86%	25.35%	$21,271.00	27.33%	5.85%	35.89%	12.46%	51.23%

Source: U.S. Census Bureau - 2000 Census Statistics

Los Angeles County Neighborhood Statistics
Table 7 - Ranking of Percentage of Population without High School Degree

Community	Total pop.	% Caucasian	% Hispanic	% African-Am	% Asian	Median household income	% under 18	% over 65	% below poverty level	% w/ college degree	% w/o HS degree
Koreatown	40,746	4.14%	65.74%	3.86%	25.35%	$21,271.00	27.33%	5.85%	35.89%	12.46%	51.23%
Wilshire Center	73,534	7.15%	58.06%	4.81%	28.34%	$23,035.00	26.27%	6.10%	30.78%	14.24%	43.28%
North Hollywood	154,912	29.31%	55.25%	4.79%	6.89%	$34,916.00	28.55%	7.72%	21.31%	18.71%	39.31%
Silver Lake	44,351	21.24%	57.35%	2.74%	16.58%	$32,855.00	23.58%	8.45%	23.18%	17.70%	35.78%
LA City	3,694,820	29.75%	46.53%	11.24%	9.99%	$36,687.00	26.56%	9.56%	22.10%	25.50%	33.40%
Hollywood	167,664	42.82%	39.43%	4.48%	8.98%	$33,409.00	19.70%	9.96%	26.21%	17.30%	30.03%
LA County	9,935,475	29.90%	46.50%	9.80%	12.90%	$41,486.00	27.50%	9.90%	17.70%	24.90%	30.01%
Atwater Village	8,042	27.56%	47.90%	2.15%	19.09%	$42,118.00	22.01%	11.46%	12.09%	20.94%	29.99%
Mid-Wilshire	84,569	25.08%	29.61%	14.56%	28.18%	$41,019.00	21.49%	10.15%	19.71%	19.51%	21.41%
Glendale	194,973	63.60%	19.70%	1.30%	16.10%	$41,805.00	22.40%	13.90%	15.50%	32.10%	21.00%
Burbank	100,316	59.40%	24.90%	1.90%	9.00%	$47,467.00	22.30%	12.90%	10.50%	29.00%	16.90%
Valley Village	16,015	66.51%	18.46%	6.12%	4.93%	$40,128.00	17.52%	13.37%	12.51%	25.70%	13.37%
Venice	37,758	64.06%	21.96%	6.15%	4.15%	$53,074.00	12.60%	8.24%	14.36%	20.27%	13.14%
W. Los Angeles	87,120	56.44%	17.20%	14.09%	7.96%	$55,581.00	19.50%	14.49%	12.86%	20.90%	13.12%
Culver City	38,816	59.20%	23.70%	12.00%	12.00%	$51,792.00	20.90%	13.90%	8.60%	41.20%	12.80%
Los Feliz	40,573	60.54%	16.48%	3.77%	13.61%	$52,104.00	13.59%	13.60%	11.32%	18.78%	12.75%
Mid-City West	46,643	74.78%	6.20%	4.74%	10.49%	$50,803.00	12.13%	17.79%	13.60%	18.13%	9.30%
Beverly Hills	33,784	85.10%	4.60%	1.80%	7.10%	$70,945.00	20.00%	17.60%	9.10%	54.50%	9.20%
Santa Monica	84,084	78.30%	13.40%	3.80%	7.30%	$50,714.00	14.60%	14.40%	10.40%	54.80%	9.00%
West Hollywood	35,716	86.40%	8.80%	3.10%	3.80%	$38,914.00	5.70%	17.00%	11.50%	46.80%	8.90%
Sherman Oaks	28,601	78.57%	8.52%	3.75%	5.40%	$71,108.00	14.20%	12.81%	6.20%	22.85%	6.66%

Community	Total pop.	% Caucasian	% Hispanic	% African-Am	% Asian	Median household income	% under 18	% over 65	% below poverty level	% w/ college degree	% w/o HS degree
Westwood	47,844	65.23%	7.13%	2.10%	23.06%	$60,752.00	7.23%	12.30%	22.95%	14.86%	5.20%
Brentwood	41,791	79.88%	6.20%	1.53%	8.88%	$103,268.00	12.16%	15.52%	12.48%	15.01%	4.86%
Studio City	39,023	78.17%	9.03%	4.08%	5.44%	$60,014.00	14.48%	12.91%	6.68%	26.85%	4.81%
Toluca Lake	3,528	80.10%	8.93%	4.37%	4.05%	$55,721.00	11.62%	14.65%	2.72%	28.02%	4.45%
Beverly Crest	12,331	88.24%	3.79%	1.37%	4.22%	$127,136.00	18.46%	17.18%	21.89%	15.88%	4.36%
Bel Air	7,928	82.95%	4.65%	1.93%	6.84%	$159,008.00	18.76%	20.89%	4.89%	16.69%	4.27%
Playa del Rey	14,400	72.40%	9.78%	5.53%	8.37%	$74,486.00	11.77%	11.37%	6.47%	21.38%	2.90%
Pacific Palisades	23,940	88.90%	3.66%	6.90%	4.44%	$131,614.00	23.33%	17.26%	3.69%	16.64%	2.34%

Source: U.S. Census Bureau - 2000 Census Statistics

Appendix C:

Forms

EXHIBIT F
SAG TELEVISION COMMERCIALS
AGENCY CONTRACT

THIS AGREEMENT, made and entered into at _____ ,

by and between _____ , a talent agent, hereinafter called the "Agent",
(please print or type)

and _____ , _____ ,
(please print or type) (social security number)

hereinafter called the "Actor".

WITNESSETH

(1) The Actor engages the Agent as his agent for television commercials under Screen Actors Guild jurisdiction, and the Agent accepts such engagement. This contract is limited to television commercials and to contracts of the Actor as an actor in television commercials, and any reference herein to contracts or employment whereby Actor renders his services refers to contracts or employment in television commercials unless otherwise specifically stated.

(2) The term of this contract shall be for a period of _____ , commencing

_____ , 19_____ .

(3)(a) Except as expressly provided herein, the Actor agrees to pay to the Agent as commissions a sum equal to _____ percent of all moneys or other consideration received by the Actor, directly or indirectly, under contracts of employment (or in connection with his employment under said employment contracts) entered into during the term specified in Paragraph (2) or in existence when this agency contract is entered into except to such extent as the Actor may be obligated to pay commissions on such existing employment contract to another agent. Commissions shall be payable when and as such moneys or other consideration are received by the Actor, or by anyone else for or on the Actor's behalf.

(b) Commissions on commercials shall be subject to the following:

Where an Actor consents to the use of a commercial for a period beyond the maximum period of use provided in the applicable Screen Actors Guild Commercials Contract, the Agent shall not be entitled to receive commissions on reuse fees paid to the Actor for such additional period of use, except under the following circumstances:

(i) If not more than 120 days prior to the expiration of such maximum period of use, the Actor specifically authorizes the Agent, in writing, to attempt to secure overscale reuse fees or a guarantee acceptable to the Actor for reuse of the commercial during the renewal period, the Agent, shall be entitled to commissions with respect to the use of the commercial during such renewal period, as follows:

a) If overscale compensation is obtained for the Actor, to the extent only that such commmmissions do not reduce the Actor's compensation below minimum scale; or

b) If a guarantee is obtained for the Actor, commission shall be payable on the amount of the guarantee.

The above-referred-to authorization from the Actor to the Agent shall in no event be construed as authorizing the Agent to give any notice that the Actor intends to terminate the advertising agency's right of renewed use of the commercial.

(ii) Where the Actor's original employment contract for a commercial provides for overscale compensation or a guarantee for use of the commercial during a renewal period, the Agent shall be entitled to commissions for such renewal period to the extent provided in subparagraphs (i) a) and b) above.

This Section shall be applicable to all commercials heretofore or hereafter produced with respect to which the Agent is entitled to commissions.

(c) No agency commission shall be payable on any of the following:

(i) Separate amounts paid to Actor not as compensation but for travel or living expenses incurred by Actor;

(ii) Separate amounts paid to Actor not as compensation but as reimbursement for necessary expenditures actually incurred by Actor in connection with Actor's employment, such as for damage to or loss of wardrobe, special hairdress, etc.;

(iii) Amounts paid to Actor as penalties for violations by Producer of any of the provisions of the SAG collective bargaining contract, such as meal period violations, rest period violations, penalties or interest on delinquent payments.

(iv) Sums payable to Actors for foreign telecasting on free television of television commercials under the provisions of the applicable collective bargaining agreement; however, if an individual Actor's contract provides for compensation in excess of the minimum under the applicable collective bargaining agreement in effect at the time of employment, commissions shall be payable on such sums.

(d) Any moneys or other consideration received by the Actor, or by anyone for or on his behalf, in connection with any termination of any contract of the Actor by virtue of which the Agent would otherwise be entitled to receive commission, or in connection with the settlement of any such contract, or any litigation arising out of any such contract, shall also be moneys in connection with which the Agent is entitled to the aforesaid percentage; provided, however, that in such event the Actor shall be entitled to deduct attorney's fees, expenses and court costs before computing the amount upon which the Agent is entitled to his percentage. The Actor shall also be entitled to deduct reasonable legal expenses in connection with the collection of moneys or other consideration due the Actor arising out of an employment contract in television commercials before computing the amount upon which the Agent is entitled to his percentage.

(e) The aforesaid percentage shall be payable by the Actor to the Agent during the term of this contract and thereafter only where specifically provided herein and in the Regulations.

(f) The Agent shall be entitled to the aforesaid percentage after the expiration of the term specified in Paragraph (2) for so long a period thereafter as the Actor continues to receive moneys or other consideration under or upon employment contracts entered into by the Actor during the term specified in Paragraph (2) hereof, including moneys or other consideration received by the Actor under the extended term of any such employment contract, resulting from the exercise of an option or options under such an employment contract, extending the term of such employment contact, whether such options be exercised prior to or after the expiration of the term specified in Paragraph (2), subject, however, to the applicable limitations of the Regulations.

(g) If during the period the Agent is entitled to commissions a contract of employment of the Actor be terminated before the expiration of the term thereof, as said term has been extended by the exercise of options therein contained, by joint action of the Actor and employer, or by the action of either of them, other than on account of Act of God, illness, or the like, and the Actor enters into a new contract of employment with said employer within a period of sixty (60) days, such new contract shall be deemed to be in substitution of the contract terminated as aforesaid, subject, however, to the applicable limitations of the Regulations. No contract entered into after said sixty (60) day period shall be deemed to be in substitution of the contract terminated as aforesaid. Contracts of substitution have the same effect as contracts for which they were substituted; provided, however, any increase or additional salary, bonus or other compensation payable to the actor thereunder over and above the amounts payable under the contract of employment which was terminated shall be deemed an adjustment and, unless the Agent shall have a valid agency contract in effect at the time of such adjustment, the Agent shall not be entitled to any commissions on any such additional or increased amounts. In no event may a contract of substitution with an employer extend the period of time during which the Agent is entitled to commission beyond the period that the Agent would have been entitled to commission had no substitution taken place. A change in form of an employer for the purpose of evading this provision or a change in the corporate form of an employer resulting from reorganization or the like shall not preclude the application of these provisions.

(h) So long as the Agent receives commissions from the Actor, the Agent shall be obligated to service the Actor and perform the obligations of this agency contract with respect to the services of the Actor on which such commissions are based, unless the Agent is relieved therefrom under express provisions of the Regulations.

(i) The Agent has no right to receive money unless the Actor receives the same, or unless the same is received for or on his behalf, and then only in the above percentage when and as received. Money paid pursuant to legal process to the Actor's creditors, or by virtue of assignment or direction of the Actor, and deductions from the Actor's compensation made pursuant to law in the nature of a collection or tax at the source, such as Social Security, Old Age Pension taxes, State Disability taxes or income taxes shall be treated as compensation received for or on the Actor's behalf.

(j) Should the Agent, during the term specified in Paragraph (2), negotiate a contract of employment for the Actor and secure the for Actor a bona fide offer of employment, which offer is communicated by the Agent to the Actor in reasonable detail and in writing or by other corroborative action, which offer the Actor declines, and if, within sixty (60) days after the date upon which the Agent gives such information to the Actor, the Actor accepts said offer of employment on substantially the same terms, then the Actor shall be required to pay commissions to the Agent upon such contract of employment. If an agent employed under a prior agency contract is entitled to collect commissions under the foregoing circumstances, the Agent with whom this contract is executed waives his commission to the extent that the prior agent is entitled to collect the same.

(4)(a) The Agent may represent other persons who render services in television commercials, or in other branches of the entertainment industry.

(b) Unless and until prohibited by the Actor, the Agent may make known the fact that he is the sole and exclusive representative of the Actor in television commercials. However, it is expressly understood that even though the Agent has not breached the contract the Actor may at any time with or without discharging the Agent, and regardless of whether he has legal grounds for discharge of the Agent, by written notice to the Agent prohibit him from rendering further services for the Actor or from holding himself out as the Actor's Agent, and such action shall not give Agent any rights or remedies against Actor, the Agent's rights under this paragraph continuing only as long as Actor consents thereto but this does not apply to the Agent's right to commissions. In the event of any such written notice to the Agent the right of termination set forth in Paragraph (6) of this agency contract is suspended and extended by the period of time that the Agent is prohibited from rendering services for the Actor.

(5) It is expressly understood and agreed that the Agent's right to commissions on minimum reuse payments for television commercials is conditioned on faithful performance by Agent of the duties and services listed herein.

Agent shall:

(a) Seek and arrange interviews, negotiate terms and conditions of employment, and examine proposed employment contracts to check conformity with deal negotiated;

(b) Advise Actor concerning any provisions of the employment contract pertaining to exclusivity, releases, warranties or other special clauses;

(c) Maintain records and keep Actor advised of any exclusivity commitments, use best efforts to clear conflicting exclusivity commitments and engagements and obtain releases for Actor where necessary, negotiate for releases of exclusivity commitments and other restrictions where commercials have been withdrawn from use;

(d) Maintain adequate records showing dates of employment, dates of first usage, class of usage, cycles of usage, and payments made for employment and usage;

(e) Where necessary, send reminder to employer of payments due for employment and usage and promptly report to SAG any cases of repeated late payments or other violations;

(f) Where employer seeks to acquire other rights or services in addition to the performance of the Actor in a commercial, Agent shall bargain separately for such rights and services;

(g) Maintain records regarding maximum periods of use and reuse, advise Actor of expiration dates of periods of use, give written notices to advertising agencies of Actor's election not to grant right of renewed use;

(h) Make periodic inquiries to determine if commercials have been withdrawn from use;

(i) With respect to compensation for television commercials collected by the Agent and paid over to the Actor: the Agent shall accompany each such check with a voucher which shall contain the name of the employer or advertising agency, name of product, nature of payment (whether session fee, holding fee, use payment, wardrobe fee, overtime, travel time, travel expense, etc.), cycle dates and date of payment. If the voucher supplied by the advertising agency contains all of the information set forth above, the Agent may deliver such voucher, or a copy thereof, in lieu of a separate voucher. If the advertising agency or production company fails to provide the Agent with a voucher after demand therefore by the Agent, the Agent shall notify SAG to this effect but shall not be responsible for failure of the advertising agency or production company to deliver such voucher.

(j) Notify the Actor and SAG whenever a late penalty is due an Actor

(k) The Agent shall notify the Actor not less than 120 days prior to the expiration of the maximum period of use of the forthcoming expiration of said period.

(6) If, during the period of 91 days immediately proceeding the giving of notice of termination, the Actor fails to receive compensation in the sum of $3,500 or more for services and reuse fees for commercials in which the Actor was employed during the term of this contract (including a prior contract which this contract renews), then either the Actor or the Agent may terminate the engagement of the Agent hereunder by written notice to the other party; provided, however, that if this contract is not a renewal contract, then such notice may not

...

Whether or not the Agent is the Actor's agent at the time this contract is executed, it is understood that in executing this contract each party has independent access to the Regulations and has relied exclusively upon his own knowledge thereof.

IN WITNESS WHEREOF, the parties hereto have executed this agreement the _____

day of _____ , 19_____ .

_____
Actor

_____
Agent

By _____
(Parties please sign in ink)

This talent agent is licensed by the Labor Commissioner of the State of California.

This talent agent is franchised by the Screen Actors Guild, Inc.

The form of this contract has been approved by the State Labor Commissioner of the State of California on March 2, 1988.

This form of contract has been approved by the Screen Actors Guild, Inc.

(The foregoing references to California may be deleted or appropriate substitutions made in other states.)

Screen Actors Guild

Taft-Hartley Statement

INSTRUCTIONS: It is the producer's responsibility to complete this report in its entirety or it will be returned for completion.
Please be certain resume lists all training and/or experience in the entertainment industry. Attach photo and resume of principal talent.
Submit this report to: Taft Hartley Dept. SAG, 5757 Wilshire Blvd. Los Angeles, CA 90036-3600 Fax: 323-549-6886

EMPLOYEE INFORMATION

Name _____ SSN _____

Address _____ City _____ ST ____ Zip _____

Date of Birth (If minor) _____ Phone (____) _____

EMPLOYER INFORMATION

Name _____

Address _____

City _____ ST _____ Zip _____ Phone (____) _____

Check One: Ad Agency _____ Studio _____ Production Co _____ Other: _____

EMPLOYMENT INFORMATION

Contract Type: TV/Theatrical ____ Commercial ____ Industrial/Interactive ____
Engagement Contract: Daily ____ 3-Day ____ Weekly ____
Performer Category: Actor ____ Singer ____ Stunt ____ Other ____

Work Date(s): _____ Salary: _____

Production Title: _____ ID #: _____

Shooting Location (City and State): _____
Reason: For Hire (Please be specific):

Employer is aware of the General Provision, Section 14 of the Screen Actors Guild Codified Basic Agreement for Independent
Producers, as amended, that applies to Theatrical and Television production; Schedule B of the Commercials Contract and Section 13
of the Codified Industrial and Educational Contract wherein Preference of Employment shall be given to qualified professional actors
(except as otherwise stated). Employers will pay to the guild, as liquidated damages, the sums indicated for each breach by the
employer of any provisions of those sections.

Signature _____ Title _____ Date _____

Print Name _____ Phone (____) _____

ADVERTISING AGENCY _____ PRODUCER _____

COMMERCIAL TITLE(S) AND

CODE NO.(S) _____ PRODUCT _____

DATES WORKED	WORK TIME FROM/TO	MEALS FROM/TO	TRAVEL TO LOCATION FROM/TO	TRAVEL FROM LOCATION FROM/TO	FITTINGS, MAKEUP, TEST, IF ON DAY PRIOR TO SHOOTING FROM/TO

Performer's Signature or Initials: _____ .

EXHIBIT A-2
STANDARD SCREEN ACTORS GUILD EMPLOYMENT CONTRACT FOR PERFORMERS ENGAGED AS EXTRAS IN TELEVISION COMMERCIALS

Date _____ ,20 _____

Producer, _____ , engages Extra Performer, _____

and Extra Performer agrees to perform services for Producer in television commercials as follows:

Commercial title(s) and code No.(s) _____ No. of commercials _____

Such commercial(s) are to be produced by _____ _____
                                                    (Advertising Agency)   (Address)

On behalf of _____ _____
                        (Advertiser)   (Product(s))

Date and time of engagement: _____ Place of engagement: _____
                                                                                            (City and State)

Category and Type	Adjustments
☐ Commercial Extra Performer ☐ 13 Weeks Use	☐ Wet, Snow, Smoke or Dust ($40.00)
☐ Hand Model ☐ Unlimited Use	☐ Hazard Adjustment $ _____
☐ Stand-In ☐ Produced for Cable Only	☐ Make-up, Skull Cap, Hairgoods ($31.40)
☐ Photo Double	☐ Night Premium _____
☐ Other (Describe)	☐ Other _____

Allowances(Check if applicable)

☐ Flight Insurance ($11.30) Payable   ☐ Vehicle: Type_____   Mileage_____
                                                            Tolls _____   Parking_____
☐ Wardrobe to be furnished:
   ☐ By Producer   ☐ By Extra Performer
   If furnished by Extra Performer   @ $17.20_____   @ $28.65_____   Total Wardrobe Fee
   No. of costumes requested by producer   (Non Evening Wear)   (Evening Wear) $ _____
Props:
☐ Books ($2.50 each)   ☐ Luggage ($5.50 each piece)   ☐ Tennis Racquet ($5.50)
☐ Binoculars or   (includes bookbags & briefcases)   (only if not already being paid as
   Opera Glasses ($5.50)   ☐ Pet ($23.00)   part of a tennis wardrobe
☐ Camera ($5.50)   ☐ Skis ($12.00)   allowance)
☐ Golf clubs and bag ($12.00)   (includes poles and boots)   ☐ Other
☐ Large portable radio ($5.50)   Fee $_____
                                                                   ☐ Other
                                                                      Fee $_____

Extra Performer authorizes Producer to make payment to Extra Performer as follows:

   ☐ To Extra Performer at _____
                                                    (Address)
   ☐ To Extra Performer c/o _____at _____
                                                              (Address)
Special Provisions:

This contract is subject to all of the terms and conditions which pertain to Extra Performers in the applicable Commercials Contract. Employer of Record for income tax and unemployment insurance purposes is:

_____   _____
       (Name)   (Address)

Producer: Extra
By:_____   Performer: _____
          (Signature)   (Signature)

Extra Performer hereby certifies that he/she is 21 years of age or over. (if under 21 years of age, this contract must be signed below by a parent or guardian.)
I, the undersigned hereby state that I am the _____of the above named Extra Performer and do hereby consent and give my permission to this agreement.   (Mother, Father, Guardian)

                                  _____
                                  (Signature of Parent or Guardian)

The Artist Cannot Waive Any Portion of the Union Contract Without Prior Consent of Screen Actors Guild, Inc.

SCREEN ACTORS GUILD
STANDARD EMPLOYMENT CONTRACT
INDUSTRIAL/EDUCATIONAL FILM or VIDEOTAPE PROGRAMS

This Agreement made this ⎿_____⏌ day of ⎿_____⏌, 19 _____

between ⎿_____⏌, Producer, and ⎿_____⏌, Performer.

1. SERVICES - Producer engages Performer and Performer agrees to perform services in a program tentatively entitled ⎿_____⏌ to portray the role of ⎿_____⏌ to be produced on behalf of ⎿_____⏌ (client).

2. CATEGORY - indicate the intitial, primary use of the program.

☐ Category I (industrial/Educational)
☐ Category II (Point of Purchase, includes Category I)

3. NUMBER OF CLIENTS - Indicate number of clients for which program will be used.

☐ Single Client
☐ Multiple Clients

4. TERM - Performer's employment shall be for the continuous period commencing ⎿_____⏌, 19____ and continuing until completion of photography and recordation of said role. EXCEPTION (for Day Performers only) - Performer may be dismissed and recalled once without payment for intervening period providing such period exceeds 5 calendar days and Performer is informed of firm recall date at time of engagement. If applicable to this contract, Performer's firm recall date is ⎿_____⏌, 19____.

5. COMPENSATION - Producer employs Performer as: ____ On-Camera ____ Off-Camera ____ On-Camera Narrator/Spokesperson

☐ Day Performer   ☐ Singer, Solo/Duo   ☐ General Extra Player
☐ 3-Day Performer   ☐ Singer, Group   ☐ Special Ability Extra Player
☐ Weekly Performer   ☐ Singer, Step Out   ☐ Silent Bit Extra Player

at the salary of on-camera $ ⎿_____⏌ per ☐ DAY ☐ 3-DAYS ☐ WEEK
off-camera $ ⎿_____⏌ for first hour, $ ⎿_____⏌ for each additional half-hour

Producer must mail payment not later than twelve (12) days (exclusive of Saturdays, Sundays, and holidays) after the day(s) of employment.

6. OVERTIME - All overtime rates MUST be computed on Performer's full contractual rate, up to permitted ceilings (NO CREDITING). Straight time rate is 1/8th of Day Performer's Rate, 1/24 of 3-Day Performer's Rate, 1/40th of Weekly Performer's Rate. Time-and-one-half rate - payable per hour (1.5 x straight time rate) **Doubletime rate** - payable per hour (2 x straight time rate) See section 50 of the Basic Contract for details of Weekly and 3-Day Performer for time and one-half and doubletime rates per hour.

7. WEEKLY CONVERSION RATE - See Section 49 of the Basic Contract for details (Day Performers or 3-Day Performers Only). The Performer's weekly conversion rate is $ ⎿_____⏌ per week.

8. PAYMENT ADDRESS - Performer's payment shall be sent to or c/o ⎿_____⏌

9. ADDITIONAL COMPENSATION FOR SUPPLEMENTAL USE - Producer may acquire the following **supplemental use rights** by the payment of the indicated amounts. (Check appropriate items below.) See Section 30 of Basic Contract for details of payment.

		Within 90 Days (Total Applic. Salary)	Beyond 90 Days (Total Applic. Salary)
☐	A. Basic Cable Television, 3 years	15%*	65%*
☐	B. Non-Network Television, Unlimited Runs	75%	125%
☐	C. Theatrical Exhibition, Unlimited Runs	100%	150%
☐	D. Foreign Television, Unlimited Runs outside U.S. & Canada	25%	75%
☐	E. Integration and/or Customization	100%	150%
☐	F. Sale and/or Rental To Industry	15%	25%
☐	G. "Package" rights to A, B, C, D, E & F above	200%	Not Available
☐	H. Category I I (point-of-purchase use of Category I program only)	50%	100%
☐	I. Program for Government Service only.	40%	Not Available
	Non-network television, theatrical and foreign television rights.		* % of total **actual** salary

J. Network Television (available only by prior negotiation with and approval of Screen Actors Guild)
☐ PERFORMER does not consent to the use of his/her services made hereunder for Network Television.

K. Pay Cable Television (available only by prior negotiation with and approval of Screen Actors Guild)
☐ PERFORMER does not consent to the use of his/her services made hereunder for Pay Cable Television.

10. SALE AND/OR RENTAL OF PROGRAMS TO THE GENERAL PUBLIC -Producer may acquire said rights only by prior negotiation with and approval of Screen Actors Guild.
☐ PERFORMER does not consent to the use of his/her services made hereunder for sale and/or rental of programs to the general public.

11. WARDROBE - If PRINCIPAL PERFORMER furnishes own wardrobe, the following fees shall apply for each two-day period or portion thereof: Ordinary Wardrobe $ ⎿_____⏌ ($18.00 minimum); Evening or Formal Wardrobe $ ⎿_____⏌ ($28.00 minimum) For **Extra Players'** wardrobe fees, please see Basic Contract.

12. SPECIAL PROVISIONS - ⎿_____⏌

13. GENERAL - All terms and conditions of the current Producer-Screen Actors Guild Industrial and Educational Contract (Basic Contract) shall be applicable to such employment.

Producer ⎿_____⏌   Performer ⎿_____⏌
            signature   signature - (if minor, parent s or guardian's signature)
by ⎿_____⏌   Soc. Sec. ⎿_____⏌
        Name and Title

An Actor's Film and Television Glossary

above the line costs	Portion of a project budget allocated to a creative team of writers, actors, director, and designers.
A-list	Top tier of actors who are paid the highest salaries.
ambient light	Natural or available light for a scene.
anachronism	Element out of the intended time and place of a scene.
ancillary rights	Agreement over percentage of profits from film tie-in products such as CDs, T-shirts, or action figures.
anime	Distinct style of animation derived from Japanese comic books.
anthropomorphism	The attribution of human qualities to animals or objects.
archetype	Specific genre or classification of character, place, or thing, such as the town sheriff, the drunk, the saloon owner, and the whore with the golden heart in Westerns.
arc shot	Film shot in which the camera moves by circling around the subject.
art director	Member of the film's art department responsible for the overall look of the set and prop construction and dressing.
artifacts	Damage to a film, such as specks, scratches, and defects printed from the film negative.
audio bridge	Music or dialogue that connects two scenes by continuing from one to the other uninterrupted.
B-film	Refers to low budget, independent films with unknown actors, gratuitous violence and sex, cheap special effects, and an uninspired script.

backlighting	Lighting from behind the subject that puts the figures in the foreground either in darkness or silhouette.
back end	Refers to the profit participation after production and distribution costs are recovered.
back lot	Sector of a studio complex in which various outdoor sets have been built and maintained for continued film use.
back story	The history of a character before the beginning of the film's story line.
barney	A blanket placed over a camera to dampen its operational noise.
basic cable	Contractual term referring to cable stations that exist between the public airwaves, ABC, NBC, CBS, etc., and premium or pay-per-view channels such as HBO.
below the line costs	Portion of the budget set aside for technical and production costs.
best boy	Gaffer's assistant or apprentice.
bit part	Small acting role usually with one scene and only a few lines.
blue-screen	Special effects technique in which an actor works in front of a monochromatic blue or green background, allowing computer generated or previously filmed footage to be added later.
body double	Actor that temporarily replaces the principal performer for scenes in which specific body parts are filmed without facial close-ups.
Bollywood	Center of India's film industry. A combination of "Bombay" and "Hollywood."
bookends	Framing devices in which complementary scenes are used to begin and end a film.
boom	Telescoping extension pole upon which a microphone or camera may be suspended above or outside of a scene during filming.
breakdown	Character descriptions for a project.
bridging shot	Transitional shot between scenes.
buddy film	Film genre in which mismatched or contrasting characters act as foils to each other.
buyout	Contractual term referring to the offer to an actor of a one-time payment instead of a long-term residual.

buzz track	Natural or atmospheric soundtrack, added to a film to provide additional realism.
call sheet	Schedule provided to actors and crew detailing the shoot schedule and who is required to report at what times.
cameo	Special screen appearance of a famous actor or prominent person in a walk-on role with minimal lines and screen time.
can	Film canister that holds the film for transport. A completed film is referred to as "in the can," and rerecorded footage is referred to as "canned footage."
cap	The maximum payment allotted.
casting couch	Illegal practice of trading sexual favors for a role in a film project.
CGI	Initials for "Computer Generated Imagery," the technology that adds digital 3D graphics to create special effects on film.
chopsocky	Slang term for martial arts films.
Cinemascope	Trademark name for 20th Century Fox's widescreen process.
cinema verité	Style of documentary that employs minimalist techniques of filming and editing to provide a more realistic or "truthful" result.
clapboard	Originally, a small, hinged chalkboard that displayed film information such as scene, title, date, and take number, and was slated or clapped in front of the camera before each new shot. Now production companies use a digital version of the same.
Class A	Commercial contract specifying sponsorship of a particular network program or series that runs concurrently in more than twenty-one cities for a thirteen-week cycle.
clean contract	Contract in which no paragraph has been struck out and all affirmative boxes have been initialed by the actor.
coda	Epilogue or ending scene to a film that provides a conclusion or closure to the story line.
coming-of-age	Genre of film portraying the teen or childhood rites of passage such as loss of innocence.
continuity	Process of documenting and recreating an exact scene for shooting on multiple days or multiple takes and angles.
contract player	Any actor who is under contract with a production company.

Coogan's Law	Landmark 1930's legislation that protects a child actor's earnings in a court-administered trust fund; named after child actor Jackie Coogan.
coverage	Term referring to all the shots needed by a director to complete a particular scene or location of a film.
craft services	Catering services for location filming.
cross-cutting	Editing technique that alternates or interweaves two different story lines.
crossover appeal	Ability to appeal to two or more different demographic groups.
cue cards	Cards on which dialogue has been printed to help the actor or announcer.
cutaway shot	Brief scene inserted to interrupt the main action, such as a view of a newspaper headline.
dailies	Raw footage from the previous day, screened to preview film progress.
dark horse	Industry vernacular for a film unlikely to succeed, such as a low-budget independent film.
day player	Actor contracted for one day's work, usually for a small supporting role.
deal memo	Letter written to confirm the negotiated points of a pending contract.
deferred payment	Agreement to work without payment until the time the project recovers additional production costs and turns a profit.
director's cut	Director's final edited version of a film before editing by studios and producers.
discovery shot	Sequence in which the camera suddenly discloses a person or object.
dissolve	Transitional editing technique that blends one scene into the next.
dolly	Platform or track on which a camera moves either in or out of the scene or alongside the subject.
double	Person who stands in for a principal actor for stunts, nude scenes, or photographically.
downgrade	Notification that an actor's status has been reduced as a result of editing.

drop and pick up	Contractual clause that allows an actor to be dropped for up to ten days and then brought back to complete filming with no pay for the intervening days.
dubbing	Act of recording a soundtrack of music, dialogue, or sound effects to match already filmed sequences.
dutch tilt	Camera shot made by leaning the camera to one side to film on a diagonal angle.
ensemble	Large cast of actors in which all roles are equal and there are no true leading roles.
episodic	Television program composed of weekly installments loosely related by plot and character.
establishing shot	Long, wide-angle shot providing an overview of the scene to identify the locale and characters involved.
exhibitor	Movie theatre owner.
experimental film	Film, usually low budget, that challenges conventional filmmaking techniques.
exploitation film	Film designed to appeal to sensationalistic appetites of sex or violence in order to ensure commercial profitability.
extras	Actors hired for nonspeaking, nonspecific roles for crowd scenes or background. Often referred to as *background* or *atmosphere*.
favored nations	Contractual term in which all actors receive equal treatment with regard to pay, billing, and other designated provisions.
featurette	Short subject film, twenty to forty-five minutes in length.
film noire	Dark, sober films characterized by low lighting and black and white cinematography, depicting an underworld of crime and corruption.
final cut	Final official edited version of the film.
first refusal	A casting director's request for the actor to call before accepting another booking.
fish eye lens	Wide-angled lens with a short focal point that exaggerates and distorts an image as if through a glass ball.
flash frame	Barely perceptible clear frame inserted into a scene to give the perception of a flash of white.
Foley artist	Named after radio sound effects master Jack Foley, Foley artists create and synchronize the sound effects added to the film during the editing process, such as footsteps, slamming doors, and fight scenes.

force majeure	Contract clause that sets or suspends certain financial obligations as the result of any catastrophic event that interrupts the progress of the film.
foreground	Action closest to the camera, as opposed to background. Stage equivalent is downstage.
freeze-frame	Optical printing technique that gives the illusion of the scene freezing into a still photograph.
gaffer	Chief or lead lighting technician on a film crew.
generation	Reference to the number of times a videotape has been reproduced from the master tape.
greenlight	Industry vernacular denoting production approval.
grindhouse film	Film genre characterized by more sex, nudity, and violence than actual plot, ranging from B-movie action-adventure films to slasher films and soft porn.
grip	Film crew member responsible for setup and teardown of the film equipment, set pieces, and supplies.
guerrilla film	Low budget film created outside the rule of permits, unions, and corporations.
head-on shot	Camera setup in which the action either moves directly into the camera or the camera moves directly into the action.
high-angle shot	Camera setup in which the subject is filmed directly from above.
hi-def	Slang for high definition television, which increases the lines of resolution on a television screen, substantially increasing the level of detail.
hitting a mark	Actor's term that refers to executing the movement to an exact predetermined position during camera takes.
hold	A conditional booking with a cancellation fee in effect.
hold over	Contractual term that refers to an actor required to work more additional days than originally contracted.
holding fee	Retainer paid to an actor in exchange for exclusivity rights for a fixed cycle.
horse opera	Originally referred to the singing cowboy films of the 1950s but more generally refers to all Westerns.
hype	Slang for hyperbole or exaggeration. The manufactured buzz generated through marketing and advertising programs.
in the can	Studio lingo indicating that the day's shooting or entire film has been completed.

infomercial	Classification of taped programming that primarily promotes the attributes of a particular product.
jump cut	Abrupt transitional editing device in which the action is advanced in time to create discontinuity.
juvenile role	Role meant for an underage actor who, if hired, requires additional supervision and restraints.
key light	Primary light of the scene.
kick-off	First day of principal photography for a project.
Klieg light	Carbon-arc lamp that produces an intense light; used principally for large-scale filming and movie premieres.
lavalier	Tiny wireless body microphone clipped to an actor.
leadman	Member of the art department often in charge of the set dressers.
legs	Refers to a film with strong growing commercial appeal that will carry it forward for months.
letterboxing	Process of reformatting a film to portray its entire width on a television screen, creating black bands above and below the film image.
lip sync	Synchronization of mouth movement on film with a vocal track.
location	Anywhere other than the studio or studio backlot in which filming is conducted in order to lend a sense of realism to the scene.
logline	Short summary of a screenplay provided on the first page.
looping	The process of rerecording dialogue by the actors in the recording studio as part of the postproduction process.
magic hour	Time just before sunset or after sunrise that provides low-level soft and colorful light.
majors	Term used to refer to the major studios of Hollywood.
mark	(1) Designation on the ground indicating an actor's final destination during filming. (2) The sound created by clapping the slate board used to synchronize the soundtrack.
master shot	A long take that shows the main action of a scene in its entirety.
matte shot	Optical process used to combine different film shots together side by side.
miniatures	Models photographed to give them a full scale illusion.

mockumentary	Farcical documentary that may look like the real thing but in actuality mocks the subject matter.
money shot	Scene that provides the audience with the payoff or climax.
monitor	Small television screen used to oversee filming as it happens.
Moppet	A child actor.
morph	Process of transforming one digital image into another using animation techniques.
multiple tracking	A rerecording by the artist(s) of an existing recording.
MPAA	Abbreviation for the Motion Picture Association of America, which represents the interests of the studios and is responsible for the rating of commercially released films.
new media	Reference to the evolving and emerging media forms and platforms being developed for podcasts, Webcasts, cell phones, and technology still under development.
nontraditional casting	Casting strategy referring to inclusive and diverse use of people of color and persons with disabilities in roles not specifically requiring them.
NTSC	Abbreviation for the National Television System Committee. Refers to a film format standard for North America and Japan.
off-Hollywood	Independent films made outside of the Hollywood studio system.
omnie	Speech sounds used as general background noise, such as party chatter.
omniscient point of view	Narrative perspective in which the camera reveals every character's thoughts and actions.
on-spec	Working without pay on the gamble that the project will lead to something else more profitable.
optical	Any visual device that must be added during postproduction.
outtakes	Film takes that have been edited out of a film's final cut.
outgrade	Notification to an actor that his or her image or soundtrack has been completely edited from the final version of the commercial; required within sixty days after the completion date.
overcrank	Filming technique in which the camera speed is increased so that when played back it will give the impression of slow motion.

overlap	To carry over dialogue, music, or sounds from one scene to the next.
over- the-shoulder	Camera angle in which the camera films the action from behind the head of another character.
PAL	(Phase Alternation Line) Film format standard adopted by Europe.
pan	Abbreviation for "panorama," meaning to move the camera from one side to the other.
payoff	Dramatic scene that provides an explanation or climax to the film's main plot line.
payola	An illegal system of under-the-table payoffs.
pitch	Sales proposal for a film project to obtain financial backing.
postproduction	Final stage in film production, in which the film is edited and opticals, sound effects, dubbing, and title sequences are added.
potboiler	Reference to detective or crime thrillers.
preproduction	Initial stage of film production, in which the planning of storyboards, budgets, location scouting, design, and the shooting schedule takes place.
prequel	Film sequel that tells the backstory of a character before the time of the original film.
principal performer	Lead role.
principal photography	Reference to primary filming of lead characters and main action sequences.
product placement	Advertising strategy in which major brand name items are intentionally placed in a scene for recognition.
production value	Refers to the level of perfection or quality expected by the director or producer.
PSA	Public service announcement
Q rating	Advertising research rating that gauges an actor's household recognition factor.
reaction shot	Cutaway shot of a character's reaction to another character's statement or action.
real time	Actual time in which an event occurs.
rear projection	Antiquated technique in which actors are filmed in front of a screen on which a background is projected.

redlighted	Opposite of *greenlighted*, referring to a project that has not been approved for production.
reissue	Rerelease of a film project by a studio.
residuals	Contractual term that refers to the payment of a royalty to each creative member of a project each time the project is shown or sold.
revival house	Movie theatre dedicated to the exhibition of classic films.
rider	An amendment to a contract.
rough cut	First edited version of the project.
rushes	Previous day's rough takes, often called *dailies*.
safety	Additional take filmed as a backup.
scale	Minimum pay as set by one of the four actors unions.
scale plus 10	Minimum pay plus an additional 10 percent to pay the talent agent's commission.
schlock film	Inferior, low budget, exploitation film.
screener	Promotional DVD version sent to voters of a film award.
second banana	Sidekick, foil, or straight man to a lead comedian.
second-unit photography	Smaller, subordinate film crew that films crowd scenes, locations, and other secondary film shots.
sepia tone	Brown and grey tones added to a black and white image to enhance the dramatic effect.
serial	Television show with a multi-episode story line, such as a soap opera.
setup	Placement of the camera, scenery, and characters for a particular shot.
sfx	Shorthand for "sound effects."
shooting script	Film script version in which scenes are numbered and camera directions inserted.
sides	Script excerpts used for auditioning actors.
signatory	Production company that has signed a union production contract.
slate	Digital board held in front of the camera to identify the production, scene, shot, and take. A clapper is activated to mark the scene for sound synchronization. As a verb, an actor's filmed audition introduction, stating his or her name and role being read.
sleeper	Project that unexpectedly attains great success.

soft focus	Camera technique in which gauze or Vaseline covers the film lens to blur the image, create romantic effects, or rejuvenate an actor's face.
spaghetti Western	Low budget Western made in Italy or Spain.
spoiler	Specific information about a film's ending that if known will impair the dramatic effect of the film for the audience.
squib	Small explosive charge taped underneath an actor's clothing that when activated gives the impression of a bullet strike.
stand-in	Actor who is physically similar to a principal actor and who takes the principal's place during camera setup and focusing.
star vehicle	Film customized to show off a particular celebrity's talents.
static shot	Camera setup in which the camera never moves.
steadicam	Special hydraulic, gyroscopic handheld camera that allows the operator to move with the action without the need of a track.
stills	Photographs taken during filming, later used for publicity, advertising, or documentation and continuity.
stock footage	Common or previously filmed footage, such as of tourist attractions, archived for future use.
stop motion	Animation technique where 3D objects, filmed one frame at a time, are repositioned minutely each time, thus giving the illusion of motion.
story reader	Individual hired by studios and production companies to read, analyze, and evaluate submitted scripts.
storyboard	Sequential scene-by-scene drawing of the project, somewhat resembling a cartoon.
subjective point of view	Narrative technique in which the camera provides a limited perspective, thus confusing the viewer.
syndication	Distribution deal providing television programming to independent commercial stations for airing.
sweetening	The addition of a new additional recording over the original recording.
take	Filmed sequence, often repeated until the director is satisfied.
talent	General reference to the actors in a film.
telefilm	Made-for-television film.
tie-in	Commercial project or products associated with a film.
topline	Top billing above the title of the film.

tracking shot	Camera setup in which the camera moves with the action along a preset track or a road, utilizing a truck.
trades	Daily and weekly periodicals that report the entertainment industry news.
trailer	Short teaser or publicity preview of a film.
treatment	Summary of a proposed project detailing the story line and characters; designed to be a sales presentation.
triple threat	Refers to an actor who can sing, dance, and act equally well.
underground film	Low budget, noncommercial film, independently produced outside of the mainstream film industry.
voice-over (VO)	Off-camera recorded voice or narration.
walk-on	Brief but featured on-camera performance without dialogue.
walk-through	First rehearsal day on a film set in which all technical elements are added.
wild spot	Commercial usage assigned on a per city or region basis rather than by program or network.
wrap	Completion of filming for the day.
yawner	Dull film that puts its audience to sleep.
zoom	To quickly change lens perspective from wide angle to telephoto.

Works Cited

BOOKS

Alexander, Jane. *Command Performance: An Actress in the Theater of Politics*. New York: PublicAffairs, 2000.

Caine, Michael. *What's It All About: An Autobiography*. New York: Ballantine, 1992.

Davis, Bette, with M. Merskowitz. *This 'n ' That*. New York: G. P. Putnam's Sons, 1987.

Holden, Anthony. *Behind the Oscar: The Secret History of the Academy Awards*. New York: Penguin, 1993.

Litwak, Mark. *Contracts for the Film and Television Industry*. 2nd ed. Beverly Hills, CA: Silman-James Press, 1998.

Mamet, David. *True and False: Heresy and Common Sense for the Actor*. New York: Vintage, 1997.

Selznick, David O. *Memo from David O. Selznick*. Edited by Rudy Behlmer. New York: Modern Library, 2000.

Thoreau, Henry David. *Walden and Other Writings*. Edited by Joseph Wood Krutch. New York: Bantam, 1981

Williams, Tennessee. *Camino Real*. (author's foreword), *New York Times*, March 15, 1953.

MAGAZINES

Actors' Equity Association. "Your Income Tax." *Equity News*, vol. 91:2. March 6, 2006.

City of West Hollywood. *Highlights of West Hollywood*. Fall 2006.

Screen Actors Guild. *Screen Actor Magazine*.

"Commercials Used on the Internet." Spring 2007.

"General Services Agreements." Spring 2007.
"The Guild's New Commercial Appeal." Fall 2006.
"Rules of Engagement. How Do I Know I Am Booked?" Fall 2006.
"Q & A." Fall 2006.
"What Actors Should Remember on the Set." Winter 2006.

WEB SITES

Academy of Motion Picture Arts and Sciences. "History and Structure." http://www.oscars.org/academy/history.html (accessed on February 12, 2007).

Actors' Equity Association. "About Equity: Historical Overview." http://www.actorsequity.org/AboutEquity/historicaloverview.asp (accessed on April 20, 2007).

———. "Constitution." http://www.actorsequity.org/AboutEquity/constitution.asp (accessed on April 20, 2007).

Actors Ink. "Ask the Voice Cat." http://www.nowcasting.com/actorsink (accessed on May 5, 2006).

American Academy of Dramatic Arts. "The Academy." http://www.aada.org/html/academy/index.html (accessed on January 27, 2007).

American Federation of Television & Radio Artists (AFTRA). "How to Join." http://www.aftra.com/benefits/join.htm (accessed on January 29, 2007).

American Musical and Dramatic Academy. "Programs." http://www.amda.edu/pages.cfm?page=programs (accessed on January 21, 2007).

Association of Talent Agents. "Excerpts from the California Labor Code." 2007. http://www.agentassociation.com/frontdoor/news_detail.cfm?id=%20429 (accessed on March 30, 2007).

———. "Talent Agent Act: Don't Procure Employment without a License" http://www.agentassociation.com/frontdoor/news_detail.drm?id=306 (accessed on March 30, 2007).

California Department of Consumer Affairs (CDCA). "California Tenants: A Guide to Residential Tenants' and Landlords' Rights and Responsibilities." Updated 2006. Boards, Bureaus, and Committees. http://www.dca.ca.gov/aboutdca/about_dca/entities.shtml (accessed on November 19, 2006).

California Department of Labor Relations. "California Labor Code." http:www.leginfo.ca.gov/cgi-bin.calawquery?codesection=lab&codebody= (accessed on April 22, 2007).

California Renters Resources. "Oh My Apartment." http://ohmyapt.apartmentratings.com/california-tenants-law.html (accessed on November 27, 2006).

Casting Society of America (CSA). "Who We Aren't." http://www.castingsociety.com/about/whowearent (accessed on January 1, 2007).

City of Burbank. "Demographic Profile." 2006. http://www.burbankca.org/ redevelopment/demoprof.html (accessed on December 16, 2006).

―――. "History of Burbank." http://www.ci.burbank.ca.us/citymanager/ history.htm (accessed on September 26, 2006).

City of Glendale. "Census Information." http://www.ci.glendale.ca.us/planning/ census.asp (accessed on October 18, 2006).

City of Santa Monica. "About Santa Monica." http://www.smgov.net/residents/ aboutsm.htm (accessed on December 15, 2006).

County of Los Angeles, Department of Consumer Affairs (accessed on November 26, 2006).
"Credit Checks." http://consumeraffairs.co.la.ca.us/tsCreditChecks.html.
"Holding Deposits." http://consumer-affairs.co.la.ca.us/tsHoldingDepo. html.
"Information for Tenants and Landlords." http://consumer-affairs.co.la.ca. us/mnRenters.htm.
"Late Fees." http://consumer-affairs.co.la.ca.us/tsLateFees.html.
"Rental Agreements and Leases." http://consumeraffairs.co.la.ca.us/ tsRentalAgree.htm.
"Rent Control." http://consumer-affairs.co.la.ca.us/tsRentControl.html.
"Security Deposits." http://consumer-affairs.co.la.ca.us/tsSecurityDeposits. html.

Federal Trade Commission: Facts for Consumers. "If You've Got the Look, Look Out! Avoiding Modeling Scams." http://www.ftc.gov/bcp/conline/ pubs/services/model.htm (accessed on April 30, 2007).

Internal Revenue Service. *Publication 529: Performing Artists.* http://www.irs.gov/ publications/p529/ar02.html#d0e344 (accessed on April 22, 2007).

Jaynes, Gregory. *In Search of the Angeles.* http://www.time.com/time/magazine/ article/0,9171,926712-2,00.html (accessed on March 31, 2007).

Los Angeles Almanac
"City of Los Angeles Communities Median Home Value." http://laalmanac. com/LA/la58.htm (accessed on October 16, 2007).
"City of Los Angeles Demographics—2000 Census." http://www.laalmanac. com/LA/la09.htm (accessed on October 16, 2007).
"City of Los Angeles Population by Age and by Community—2000 Census." http://www.laalmanac.com/LA/la01a.htm (accessed on December 3, 2006).
"City of Los Angeles Population by Community and Race—2000 Census." http://www.laalmanac.com/population/po24la.htm (accessed on October 16, 2006).
"Educational Attainment by Community." http://www.laalmanac.com/LA/ la05a.htm (accessed on December 3, 2006).

"Poverty Statistics for City of Los Angeles Communities." http://
laalmanac.com/LA/la11c.htm (accessed on October 16, 2006).

"Temperature Normals and Records." http://www.laalmanac.com/weather/
we01.htm (accessed on November, 10, 2006).

"Total Seasonal Rainfall." http://www.laalmanac.com/weather/we13.htm
(accessed on October 10, 2007).

LA Stories. "Stories about Life in Los Angeles." http://www.lastories.com
(accessed on March 31, 2007).

Lawrence, David. "Los Angeles Acting Blog." http://laacting.blogspot.com
(accessed on January 25, 2007).

Los Angeles Apartments and Rentals Survey. "Find Articles." http.//findarticles.
com/p/articles/mi_pwwi/is_200608/ai_n16692522 (accessed on March 12,
2007).

Los Angeles Better Business Bureau. "Modeling and Acting Scams."
http://www.labbb.org/BBBWeb/Forms/General/
GeneralStaticPage.aspx?Page=to pic116&sm (accessed on April 1, 2007).

Los Angeles County Metropolitan Transportation Authority (LACMTA).
"Bus Ridership Estimates." 2007. http://www.mta.net/news_info/
ridership_avg.htm (accessed on November 3, 2006).

———. "Facts at a Glance." http://www.metro.net/press/pressroom (accessed
on November 3, 2006).

Los Angeles Department of Health Services (LADHS). "The Spirit of
LAC+USC Healthcare Network." http://www.ladhs.org (accessed on April
14, 2007).

Los Angeles Fire Department (LAFD). "LAFD News." http://lafd.blogspot.com
(accessed on November 7, 2006).

Manners, Scott. "Notable Quotes." http://www.calliopetalent.com/all-quotes/
insider (accessed on March 18, 2006).

McCabe, DBA, Mary Beth. "San Diego Hispanic Television Station Boom!"
Sun Marketing, Advertising & Media. http://www.sunmarketing.net/
pages/hispanic-research.html (accessed on January 8, 2007).

McCanles, Penny. "Scam Avoidance 101 and What to Do If It's Too Late."
http://www.actorpoint.com/features/biz/actingscams.html (accessed on
March 30, 2007).

McRee, Tina. "The Center for the Health Professions: University of California,
San Francisco, 2003. http://www.futurehealth.ucsf.edu/home.html (accessed on November 17, 2006).

Montopoli, Brian. "CBS to YouTube: Who Loves You Baby?" July 17, 2006.
http://www.cbsnews.com/blogs/2006/07/17/publiceye/entry1809404.shtml
(accessed on February 21, 2007).

Pelisek, Christie. "Tenant's Rights." http://laweekly.com/general/features/
tenants-rights/704 (accessed on November 27, 2007).

"Reading by 9." Los Angeles Times Media Center. http://latimes.com/services/ newspaper/mediacenter/releases/la-mediacenter-factsheet-rb9,0,4895831.story?coll=la-mediacenter-factsheets (accessed on November 7, 2006).

Santa Monica College: Theatre Arts. http://smc.edu/theatre/ (accessed on January 27, 2007).

Screen Actors Guild. http://www.sag.org.

"2004 SAG Data Report" (accessed on January 29, 2007).

"Agent Information: An Important Message about Dealing with Your Agent" (accessed on January 29, 2007).

"Commercials Contract Digest" (accessed on January 29, 2007).

"An Important Message about Dealing with Your Agent" (accessed on March 30, 2007).

"Frequently Asked Questions" (accessed on February 22, 2007).

"Tips and Tools: Beware of Audition Scams" (accessed on January 29, 2007).

"Inside SAG: Constitution and By-laws" (accessed on April 21, 2007).

Sonderup, Laura. "Hispanic Marketing: A Critical Market Segment." *Advertising & Marketing Review.* http://www.ad-mkt-review.com/public_html/ docs/fs075.html (accessed on January 8, 2007).

Studio City Chamber of Commerce. "About Studio City." http://www. studiocitychamber.com/aboutstudiocity.php (accessed on October 16, 2006).

Talent Managers Association. "Most Frequently Asked Questions." http:// www.talentmanagers.org/faq.php (accessed on April 1, 2007).

Troster, Gavin. "Agent Information." http://www.sag.org/sagWebApp/Content/ Public/beware.htm (accessed on January 9, 2007).

UCLA—School of Theater, Film, and Television. "About the School." http:// www.tft.ucla.edu/about.cfm (accessed on January 21, 2007).

Universal City/North Hollywood Chamber of Commerce. "NoHo Arts District." http://www.noho.org/visit/noho_arts_history.htm (accessed on December 3, 2006).

University of Southern California—School of Cinematic Arts. "Facilities and Equipment." http://cinema.usc.edu (accessed on January 21, 2007).

U.S. Census Bureau. "Los Angeles City—People QuickFacts." 2000. http:// quickfacts.census.gov/qfd/states/06/0644000.html (accessed on December 16, 2006).

———. "Los Angeles County—People QuickFacts." 2004. http://quickfacts. census.gov/qfd/states/06/06037.html (accessed on December 3, 2006).

———. "Small Area Income and Poverty Statistics." 2004. http:// www.census.gov/cgi-bin/saipe/saipe.cgi (accessed on December 3, 2006).

U.S. Census Bureau: American Factfinder. "2005 American Community Survey Data Profile Highlights." http://factfinder.census.gov/servlet/AC-SSAFFFacts?_submenuId=factsheet_1&_s se=on (accessed on December 3, 2006).

U.S. Federal Trade Commission. "Federal Trade Commission v. American Bartending Institute." 2004. http://www.ftc.gov/os/caselist/abi/050801-compabi.pdf (accessed on December 3, 2006).

LEGAL AGREEMENTS

Alliance of Motion Picture and Television Producers. "Screen Actors Guild Television Agreement." 2001.

Screen Actors Guild (SAG). "Background Actors Contract Summary." 2005.

———. "Codified Agency Regulations Rule 16 (g)." 1990.

———. "Codified Basic Agreement for Independent Producers." 1995.

———. "Contract Summary: Theatrical Motion Pictures and Television Contract." 2005.

———. "Commercials Contract Digest." 2003.

———. "Film Contracts Digest." SAGIndie. 2005.

———. "Industrial/Educational Films and Videotapes Digest." 1996–1999.

———. "Memorandum of Agreement with Independent Film Producers." Revised 2005.

Screen Actors Guild and Alliance of Motion Picture and Television Producers. "Television Agreement." 2001.

Screen Actors Guild and ANA-AAAA Joint Policy Committee on Broadcast Talent Relations. "Commercials Contract." 2003.

GOVERNMENTAL DOCUMENTS

California Department of Industrial Relations. "California Entertainment Commission Report." December 2, 1985.

City of Los Angeles. *Landlord-Tenant Handbook.* Housing Department: Customer Service and Information. Revised November 2006.

Katz, Stephen. *The Migration of Feature Film Production from the U.S. to Canada: Year 2001 Production Report.* The Center for Entertainment Industry Data and Research (CEIDR). 2002.